Professional Web APIs: Google®, eBay®, Amazon.com®, MapPoint®, FedEx®

Denise Gosnell

WILEY

Wiley Publishing, Inc.

Professional Web APIs: Google®, eBay®, Amazon.com®, MapPoint®, FedEx®

About the Author

Denise Gosnell is a software attorney with Woodard, Emhardt, Moriarty, McNett & Henry LLP (www.uspatent.com), a worldwide intellectualproperty law firm based in Indianapolis, Indiana. Denise has a unique background in both technology and law, and presently uses her deep technical and legal expertise to counsel hightech clients on intellectual property and technical matters.

Denise has over ten years of experience creating software applications, ranging from standalone and clientserver to enterprisewide applications. Denise has worked for leading software companies, such as Microsoft and EDS, and has earned a worldwide reputation for her technology expertise. She received a Bachelor of Arts degree in Computer Science – Business (summa cum laude) from Anderson University, and a Doctor of Jurisprudence degree from Indiana University School of Law in Indianapolis.

Denise has coauthored six other software development books to date: *Beginning Access 2003 VBA* (Wiley Publishing, Inc.), *Visual Basic .NET and SQL Server 2000: Building An Effective Data Layer* (Wrox Press), *Beginning Visual Basic.NET Databases* (Wrox Press), *Professional .NET Framework* (Wrox Press), *Professional SQL Server 2000* (Wrox Press), and *MSDE Bible* (IDG Books). Denise was a featured technology speaker at the Microsoft European Professional Developer's Conference in December 2001 and has on numerous occasions assisted Microsoft's Training and Certification group in creating new exams for their MCSD and MCSE certifications. She herself holds the MCSD certification.

Denise can be reached at dgosnell@uspatent.com or denisegosnell@yahoo.com.

Credits

Vice President and Executive Group Publisher:
Richard Swadley

Vice President and Publisher:
Joseph B. Wikert

Executive Editor:
Chris Webb

Editorial Manager:
Mary Beth Wakefield

Development Editor:
Sharon Nash

Senior Production Editor:
Angela Smith

Technical Editor:
Daniel Solin

Text Design & Composition:
Wiley Composition Services

Acknowledgments

Until I became an author, I had no idea that so many people other than the author have to spend countless hours to make a book a reality. It would be impossible for me to thank everyone who made this book possible, but I would like to acknowledge the fine staff at Wiley for their dedication to this project and all he other projects that they work on each day.

I would like to offer a special thanks to Chris Webb, my Executive Editor, for all of his input initially on the direction this book should take and for his continued assistance throughout the editorial process. I also owe a special thanks to Sharon Nash, my Development Editor, for her editorial input that added the finishing touches to my work. A special thanks is also due to Daniel Solin for his technical review of the book and his great feedback.

I would like to thank my husband, Jake, and my friends and family, for their continued support of my authoring efforts. I spend many moments of my spare time working on new books, and without your patience and understanding, this would not be possible.

Thanks to Carl and Leona Stapel of Oshkosh, Wisconsin, for showing me and my husband the world through our many travels with you. I have gained a much broader perspective in our travels, and that has made me a better person and author.

And last, but not least, I thank God for giving me the talent, energy, and positive attitude that allow me to pursue my dreams.

Contents

Contents

Contents

Contents

Introduction

Web APIs are a set of application programming interfaces that can be called over standard Internet protocols. Web APIs and Web services are finally getting real attention in the mainstream. Various types of Web APIs are now available from leading technology companies such as Google, Amazon, eBay, Microsoft, and others. Federal Express, UPS, and many other leading companies have recently released or are working on Web APIs as well. Most of these companies offer a free account for limited use of their Web APIs, but some charge a fee for certain levels of usage.

If you like the idea of generating applications that capitalize on the services of some of these wellknown companies, or if you just want to learn from what these leading companies are doing to aid you in implementing your own Web APIs, then this is the book for you.

Who This Book Is For

The ideal reader has had prior experience with Microsoft .NET development, such as WinForms and WebForms applications because most or all code examples will be written with .NET. However, the book also provides general explanations that will be useful for people who are familiar with other languages. Thus, prior .NET development experience is not required, but people with prior .NET development experience will find the code examples more familiar and easier to follow.

What This Book Covers

This book provides a handson guide to using some of the most popular Web APIs in software applications. It provides the nutsandbolts details on how several APIs work, and then offers numerous examples of how to use the APIs in real world situations.

While reading this book, you will learn:

- ❑ Basic concepts of Web APIs
- ❑ How Web APIs can be used for professional application development
- ❑ How to call Web APIs using SOAP over HTTP
- ❑ How to call Web APIs using HTTPGET (REST)
- ❑ How to call Web APIs using HTTPPOST
- ❑ How to use the Google API
- ❑ How to use the MapPoint API

❑   How to use the Amazon API

❑   How to use the eBay API and SDK

❑   How to use the PayPal API

❑   How to locate additional APIs

❑   Some thirdparty extensions of existing APIs

❑   How to create your own API

❑   How to call Web APIs from Microsoft Office applications

❑   How to call Web APIs from mobile devices

❑   How to use multiple APIs together in realworld case studies

How This Book Is Structured

When designing the direction for this book, one issue I struggled with was whether to spend multiple chapters on a single Web API or whether to cover each API solely in its own chapter. I came up with a solution that provides a very good balance.

The first part of the book is a cookbook of sorts that illustrates how to use various Web APIs. Chapter 1 introduces some general Web API concepts. Chapter 2 covers Google, Chapter 3 covers Microsoft MapPoint, Chapter 4 covers Amazon.com, Chapter 5 covers eBay, and Chapter 6 covers PayPal. Chapter 7 includes some additional APIs, including FedEx, UPS, InterFax, and Bloglines. Each APIspecific chapter is structured in the same fashion and provides the following:

1.   An introduction to the general features that vendor offers (not specific to the Web API)

2.   Details about how the API works and how to obtain an account to work with it

3.   A stepbystep example to illustrate using the Web API (from .NET and in general)

4.   Five creative examples to illustrate how to further use the API

5.   Additional ideas on how the API can be used to give you other options to explore on your own

6.   Examples to show how other people have used the API

The latter part of the book includes nonAPIspecific chapters to really illustrate the creative ways you can work with Web APIs. Chapter 8 discusses calling the Web APIs from Mobile Devices. Chapter 9 discusses how to call the Web APIs from Microsoft Office. Chapter 10 then explores how to create Web APIs from scratch and how to capitalize on that offering. Chapters 11 and 12 are case studies that combine multiple Web APIs in an integrated solution.

For example, in Chapter 11, you will build a Customer Relations Management application that allows users to track information about customers and potential customers, including such information as name, address and phone number. The Google API and MapPoint API are used to further extend the capabilities of the application. For example, the application uses the Google API to retrieve and display the first five sites that mention the particular contact when you open a contact record. An example of this is shown in Figure 11-18.

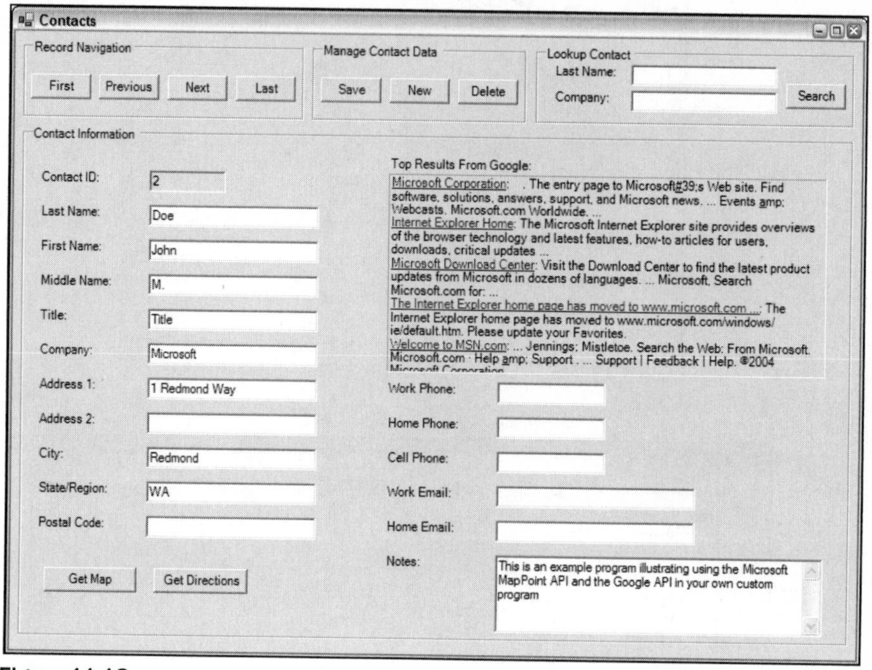

Figure 11-18

The idea behind this Google box is to allow you to see current information about your contacts or their companies before giving them a call. The MapPoint API is then used to enable you to retrieve a map or driving directions to the contact's specified address, as shown in Figures 11-19 and 11-21.

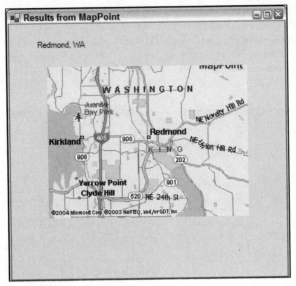

Figure 11-19

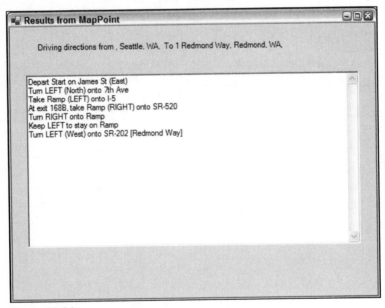

Figure 11-21

In Chapter 12, you build an Executive Dashboard Application, which is a browserbased application that combines results from multiple APIs. The application can be used to retrieve product information and reviews from Amazon.com, Google, and eBay for display on a single Web page.

After entering a search criteria and selecting a search option, you see the Amazon.com page first that most closely matched the criteria. An example of this is illustrated in Figure 12-11.

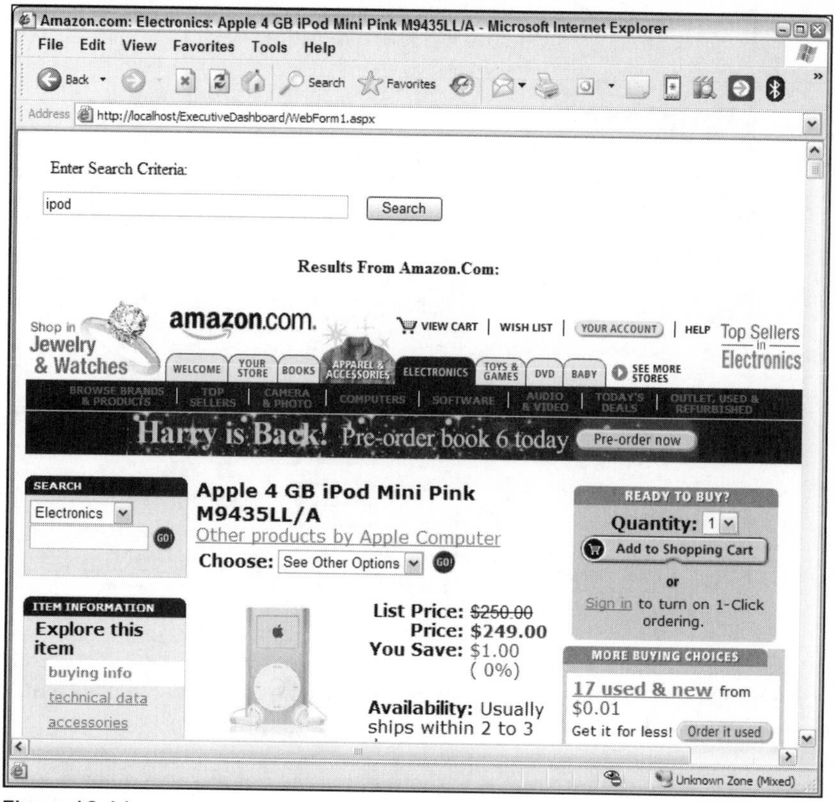

Figure 12-11

Upon scrolling down in the browser, you also see a product review page from Epinions.com that most closely matches the criteria. The page was retrieved by running a Google search that was limited to the Epinions.com site. An example of this is shown in Figure 12-12.

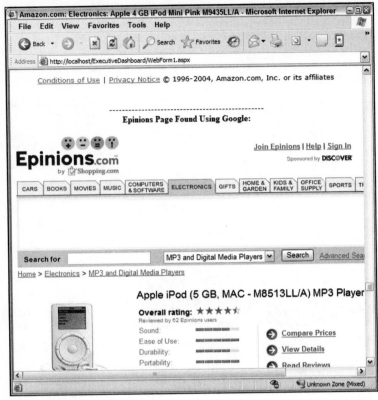

Figure 12-12

Finally, as shown in Figure 12-13, when you scroll down to the bottom of the page, you see listings from eBay that contain the search criteria.

The chapters are structured with standalone examples that do not require you to follow the chapters in order. This structure enables you to go straight to a chapter that interests you or to skip around among chapters as desired. Certainly, some chapters will not make as much sense unless you have read the prior chapters or are already familiar with the topics covered therein.

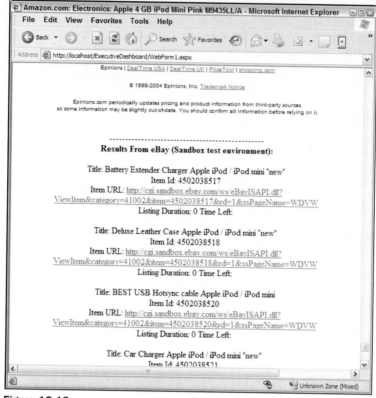

Figure 12-13

What You Need to Use This Book

In order to use this book, you need to obtain the toolkit for each API, as well as any developer keys. An Internet connection is needed to connect to the Web APIs. Visual Studio .NET or the .NET Framework (which is free) is also required if you want to run the code examples yourself. If you use the .NET Framework and a text editor (such as Notepad), then the user interface screens for designing the application won't be present.

> *Open source tools are also available for download. These provide a graphical user interface for writing applications using the .NET Framework. An example of one such tool is Sharp Develop, which can be found at:* `http://www.icsharpcode.net/`.

For Chapter 9, the Office Web Services toolkit is required if you want to run the examples using VBA in Microsoft Office to call a Web API. Office 2003 and the Visual Studio Tools for the Microsoft Office System are also required for examples illustrating how to use Office 2003 apps to call .NET apps. For Chapter 10, the .NET Compact framework is needed in order for the examples in the Mobile Devices chapter to work. For Chapter 11, Microsoft Access is needed for the database.

Conventions

To help you get the most from the text and keep track of what's happening, I've used a number of conventions throughout the book.

Examples that you can download and try out for yourself generally appear in a box like this:

> **Boxes like this one hold important, nottobe forgotten information that is directly relevant to the surrounding text.**

Tips, hints, tricks, and asides to the current discussion are offset and placed in italics like this.

As for styles in the text:

- ❏ I *highlight* important words when I introduce them
- ❏ I show keyboard strokes like this: Ctrl+A
- ❏ I show filenames, URLs and code within the text like so: `persistence.properties`
- ❏ I present code in two different ways:

```
In code examples we highlight new and important code with a gray background.
```

```
The gray highlighting is not used for code that's less important in the present context or has been shown before.
```

Source Code

As you work through the examples in this book, you may choose either to type in all the code manually or to use the source code files that accompany the book. All the source code used in this book is available for download at `http://www.wrox.com`. Although the examples in the book are illustrated in Visual Basic .NET, source code is available for download for both Visual Basic .NET and C#.

After you reach the site, simply locate the book's title (either by using the Search box or by using one of the title lists) and click the Download Code link on the book's detail page to obtain all the source code for the book.

Because many books have similar titles, you may find it easiest to search by ISBN; for this book the ISBN is 0-7645-8445-6.

After you download the code, just decompress it with your favorite compression tool. Alternately, you can go to the main Wrox code download page at http://www.wrox.com/dynamic/books/download.aspx to see the code available for this book and all other Wrox books.

Errata

We make every effort to ensure that there are no errors in the text or in the code. However, no one is perfect, and mistakes do occur. If you find an error in one of our books, like a spelling mistake or faulty piece of code, we would be very grateful for your feedback. By sending in errata you may save another reader hours of frustration and at the same time you will be helping us provide even higher quality information.

To find the errata page for this book, go to http://www.wrox.com and locate the title using the Search box or one of the title lists. Then, on the book details page, click the Book Errata link. On this page you can view all errata that has been submitted for this book and posted by Wrox editors. A complete book list including links to each book's errata is also available at www.wrox.com/miscpages/booklist.shtml.

If you don't spot your error on the Book Errata page, go to www.wrox.com/contact/techsupport.shtml and complete the form there to send us the error you have found. We'll check the information and, if appropriate, post a message to the book's errata page and fix the problem in subsequent editions of the book.

p2p.wrox.com

For author and peer discussion, join the P2P forums at p2p.wrox.com. The forums are a Webbased system for you to post messages relating to Wrox books and related technologies and interact with other readers and technology users. The forums offer a subscription feature to e-mail you topics of interest of your choosing when new posts are made to the forums. Wrox authors, editors, other industry experts, and your fellow readers are present on these forums.

At http://p2p.wrox.com you will find a number of different forums that will help you not only as you read this book, but also as you develop your own applications. To join the forums, just follow these steps:

1. Go to p2p.wrox.com and click the Register link.
2. Read the terms of use and click Agree.
3. Complete the required information to join as well as any optional information you wish to provide and click Submit.

4. You will receive an e-mail with information describing how to verify your account and complete the joining process.

You can read messages in the forums without joining P2P but in order to post your own messages, you must join.

After you join, you can post new messages and respond to messages other users post. You can read messages at any time on the Web. If you would like to have new messages from a particular forum e-mailed to you, click the Subscribe to this Forum icon by the forum name in the forum listing.

For more information about how to use the Wrox P2P, be sure to read the P2P FAQs for answers to questions about how the forum software works, as well as answers to many common questions specific to P2P and Wrox books. To read the FAQs, click the FAQ link on any P2P page.

Professional Web APIs: Google®, eBay®, Amazon.com®, MapPoint®, FedEx®

Anatomy of a Web API

In this chapter, you will learn the basic concepts of Web APIs that I use throughout the rest of the book. Web APIs are application programming interfaces that can be called over standard Internet protocols. Many companies are using Web APIs to expose functionality in their existing systems in a platform-neutral manner. Other companies are building applications from the ground up as Web APIs. Web APIs generally allow remote computers on different platforms to talk to each other using methods that were previously very difficult. This chapter will specifically cover the following:

❑   What a Web API is and how it differs from a Web service

❑   The current status of Web APIs in the industry

❑   Calling a Web API using REST (HTTP-GET)

❑   Calling a Web API using HTTP-POST

❑   Calling a Web API using HTTP and SOAP

Web APIs versus Web Services

Web APIs are application programming interfaces that are available over the Internet. They are also sometimes referred to as Web services. It is helpful to think of a Web API as a series of Web services, each of which has one or more procedures that can be called using the Internet. An example of a Web API includes the Google API, which makes various search functions available over the Internet for use in third-party applications. Although Web APIs and Web services are separate concepts, it is common and acceptable to refer to the two concepts interchangeably because they are so closely related.

In the most generic sense, a Web service is merely a function or procedure that can be called over the Internet. This generic definition includes Web services that can be called only from specific platforms, such as Windows, and only after installation of certain software on the client. However, in the context of this book, the term *Web service* refers to services that are platform-neutral and so can be called from any platform capable of communicating using standard Internet protocols. These platform-neutral Web services are sometimes referred to as *XML Web services* because XML is typically the data transfer format used for them. XML is a text-based syntax that can be understood by various platforms, as I discuss in a later section. Despite common misconceptions, XML Web services can be called from applications that are not browser-based, such as traditional Windows applications. As long as the application can communicate using Internet protocols, non-Web–based applications can make use of the same functionality.

Despite the great value of Web services, their adoption industry-wide has been slow in coming. The great news is that, as of this writing, Web APIs and Web services have finally been adopted by big players in the industry. Industry leaders such as Google, Amazon, and eBay have embraced the Web services concept and have created Web APIs that enable you to implement their core features in your own applications. This recent movement toward Web APIs is my primary reason for writing this book. In it, you will, of course, explore several leading Web APIs to learn how you can use them in your applications.

As you will see in the following chapters, most of these leading Web APIs require you to obtain a developer token that must be included in each request. Vendors require a developer token in order to control how much you use (and thus not abuse) the service and/or how much they should charge you. Most Web APIs have a free limited-use license or trial period, and some of them require payment for the service.

Web APIs as XML Web Services

As I mentioned previously, Web APIs are typically a related collection of Web services. Most of the Web services available today are based on XML and can, therefore, be called from various platforms. The focus of this book is primarily on XML Web services. Therefore, a brief explanation on XML is appropriate before you learn the basics of calling XML Web services in your programs.

What Is XML?

XML stands for *eXtensible Markup Language*, which is a text-based markup language. XML is similar to HTML in many ways, such as how it describes data by using tags. A very simple example of an XML document is shown here.

```
<?xml version="1.0" encoding="UTF-8"?>
<contact>
<name ContactType="Business">
  <first>John</first>
  <last>Doe</last>
</name>
 <name ContactType="Personal">
  <first>Jane</first>
  <last>Doe</last>
 </name>
</contact>
```

As you can see from the previous code example, this is a contact record with two contacts, John Doe and Jane Doe. For each contact, a contact type and a first and last name are specified. This XML document can be sent to a mainframe, a Windows computer, a UNIX computer, and a Linux computer. All these computers can read it because it is a text file.

Invoking an XML Web Service

A very important aspect of communicating with a Web service is how you can physically execute a specified function. XML Web services are based on standard Internet protocols and allow you to invoke Web services through communication mechanisms such as *HTTP-GET, HTTP-POST, or SOAP over HTTP*, as I describe in more detail in the following sections. Some Web APIs covered in this book, such as Amazon's Web API, support both the HTTP-GET and SOAP options, although others support only one method. Web service providers can enable all three methods, but they typically disable one or more that they decide are not appropriate or desirable for various reasons. The fact that vendors support different methods is the subject of much debate. You should, however, understand how to use each method so you can work with the various Web APIs that are available. The methods are introduced here, but I will cover them in greater detail in the chapters that follow.

Invoking a Web Service Using REST (HTTP-GET)

REST stands for *Representational State Transfer*. It refers to invoking a Web service using parameters included in a URL. REST uses HTTP-GET to retrieve data and is not typically used for data updates. After a request is processed, REST returns an XML document.

Let's look at an example of calling an Amazon Web service using REST. Suppose you have the following URL:

```
http://aws-
beta.amazon.com/onca/xml?Service=AWSProductData&SubscriptionId=YOUR_ID_GOES_HERE&Op
eration=ItemSearch&SearchIndex=Books&Keywords=Denise%20Gosnell
```

Notice how the first part of the URL contains the traditional domain information. Next, you see the various parameters being passed. These parameters are being passed to an Amazon API (currently version 4.0 beta). The URL includes a parameter for the service being called (AWSProductData), the subscription ID (your developer token), the operation to perform (a search), the search index to use (books), and the keywords to search on (Denise Gosnell). Parameters are separated by ampersands (&), and spaces are indicated by %20.

As you can see, it is really quite easy to call a Web service using REST, if the Web service supports REST. You can then use your programming language of choice to execute the HTTP-GET command containing the URL and process the XML file that is returned. You will see examples of this in action throughout the book.

It is very easy to test a REST Web service from your Web browser. Pasting the URL listed previously into a Web browser returns results similar to those shown in Figure 1-1.

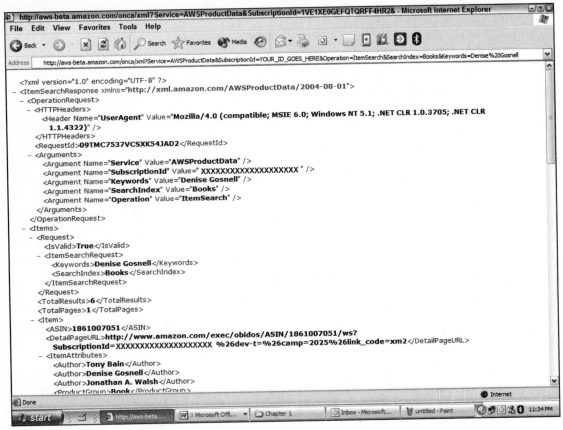

Figure 1-1

The steps for calling a Web service using REST are summarized as follows:

1. Identify the Web service you would like to call and the parameters it accepts.

2. Formulate the URL containing the parameters.

3. Test the URL from a Web browser to ensure it works correctly.

4. Use your programming language of choice to call the HTTP-GET command with the URL.

5. Receive the results in an XML document and parse the document using an XML parsing method of choice.

Despite the advantages of REST, it also has limitations. For example, you do not want to use REST when you need to transmit sensitive data because you do not want to include sensitive data in a text URL. Also, the URL has a size limit, so REST does not work for all Web APIs. Because REST is performing a HTTP-GET (data retrieval only) operation, it cannot be used to post data. It can still be used to update data as long as the values in the URL do not exceed the maximum allowed length. Let's now look at another way of invoking a Web service — using HTTP-POST.

Invoking a Web Service Using HTTP-POST

HTTP-POST is very similar to HTTP-GET, but also introduces additional complexities and advantages. When you call a Web service using HTTP-POST, you actually post an XML document that contains the required information for calling the Web service. HTTP-POST then returns an XML document in response. HTTP-POST can be used for data retrieval as well as updates, and it is better for transmitting sensitive information than REST, which sends the information in clear text in a URL.

The steps for calling a Web service using HTTP-POST are summarized as follows:

1. Identify the Web service you would like to call and the parameters it accepts.
2. Formulate an XML document containing the parameters.
3. Use your programming language of choice to call the HTTP-POST command to POST the XML document to the desired Web service.
4. Receive the results in an XML document and parse the document using an XML parsing method of choice.

The following code segment illustrates an example of using HTTP-POST to interact with a Web API.

```
Dim web As New System.Net.WebClient

Dim strXML As String

strXML = "Your XML Document Here"

'add the xml string to the byte array
Dim d As Byte() = System.Text.Encoding.ASCII.GetBytes(strXML)

'call the api and pass the byte array containing the XML string
Dim res As Byte() = web.UploadData("URLForAPI", "POST", d)

'display the results in a message box
MsgBox(System.Text.Encoding.ASCII.GetString(res))
```

As you will see later in this book, eBay supports the HTTP-POST method as well as SOAP, which is described next.

Invoking a Web Service Using SOAP

Another way to call an XML Web service is using *SOAP*. SOAP stands for *Simple Object Access Protocol* and is an XML-based protocol for exchanging structured and type information over the Internet. SOAP, unlike HTTP-GET and HTTP-POST, supports both simple and complex types. Thus, complex types such as datasets, structs, and classes can be used in SOAP communications. SOAP is the primary message format used by the .NET Framework for communicating with XML Web services.

The following is an example of a SOAP document that calls a function named `getUserInfo` on a Web service located on arcweb.esri.com to retrieve user info for the specified token.

```
<SOAP-ENV:Envelope xmlns:SOAP-ENV="http://schemas.xmlsoap.org/soap/envelope/"
xmlns:SOAP-ENC="http://schemas.xmlsoap.org/soap/encoding/"
xmlns:xsi="http://www.w3.org/2001/XMLSchema-instance"
xmlns:xsd="http://www.w3.org/2001/XMLSchema" SOAP-
ENV:encodingStyle="http://schemas.xmlsoap.org/soap/encoding/">
  <SOAP-ENV:Body>
    <m:getUserInfo xmlns:m="http://arcweb.esri.com/v2">
      <token xsi:type="xsd:string">MyToken</token>
    </m:getUserInfo>
  </SOAP-ENV:Body>
</SOAP-ENV:Envelope>
```

As you can see, SOAP documents are a little more difficult to understand than XML documents. But there is good news. Visual Studio .NET and the .NET Framework can handle the SOAP creation for you simply by adding a reference to your project in Visual Studio .NET or by using a compiler tool if you are using just the .NET Framework. Then, all you have to do is declare and call the Web service from your code just as you call other objects. We'll walk through an example later in this chapter so you can see how this works.

Another important concept to understand when working with Web services using SOAP is *Web Services Description Language (WSDL)*. WSDL is an XML-based language that was started as a joint effort by Microsoft and IBM as a way to document what messages the Web service accepts and generates in order to document what procedures you can call and what type of values they will return.

Following are excerpts of a WSDL file that describes the Amazon Web API (version 4.0 beta), which can currently be found at `http://aws-beta.amazon.com/AWSSchemas/AWSProductData/beta/US.wsdl`.

```
<definitions xmlns="http://schemas.xmlsoap.org/wsdl/"
xmlns:soap="http://schemas.xmlsoap.org/wsdl/soap/"
xmlns:xs="http://www.w3.org/2001/XMLSchema"
xmlns:tns="http://xml.amazon.com/AWSProductData/2004-08-01"
targetNamespace="http://xml.amazon.com/AWSProductData/2004-08-01">
<types>
<xs:schema targetNamespace="http://xml.amazon.com/AWSProductData/2004-08-01"
elementFormDefault="qualified">

...[portions omitted]...

<xs:element name="ItemSearch">
<xs:complexType>
<xs:sequence>
  <xs:element name="SubscriptionId" type="xs:string" minOccurs="0" />
  <xs:element name="AssociateTag" type="xs:string" minOccurs="0" />
  <xs:element name="Validate" type="xs:string" minOccurs="0" />
  <xs:element name="XMLEscaping" type="xs:string" minOccurs="0" />
  <xs:element name="Shared" type="tns:ItemSearchRequest" minOccurs="0" />
  <xs:element name="Request" type="tns:ItemSearchRequest" minOccurs="0"
maxOccurs="unbounded" />
  </xs:sequence>
  </xs:complexType>
  </xs:element>
```

```
  <xs:complexType name="ItemSearchRequest">
  <xs:sequence>
    <xs:element name="Actor" type="xs:string" minOccurs="0" />
    <xs:element name="Artist" type="xs:string" minOccurs="0" />
    <xs:element ref="tns:AudienceRating" minOccurs="0" maxOccurs="unbounded" />
    <xs:element name="Author" type="xs:string" minOccurs="0" />
    <xs:element name="Brand" type="xs:string" minOccurs="0" />
    <xs:element name="BrowseNode" type="xs:string" minOccurs="0" />
    <xs:element name="City" type="xs:string" minOccurs="0" />
    <xs:element name="Composer" type="xs:string" minOccurs="0" />
    <xs:element ref="tns:Condition" minOccurs="0" />
    <xs:element name="Conductor" type="xs:string" minOccurs="0" />
    <xs:element name="Cuisine" type="xs:string" minOccurs="0" />
    <xs:element ref="tns:DeliveryMethod" minOccurs="0" />
    <xs:element name="Director" type="xs:string" minOccurs="0" />
    <xs:element name="ISPUPostalCode" type="xs:string" minOccurs="0" />
    <xs:element name="ItemPage" type="xs:positiveInteger" minOccurs="0" />
    <xs:element name="Keywords" type="xs:string" minOccurs="0" />
    <xs:element name="Manufacturer" type="xs:string" minOccurs="0" />
    <xs:element name="MaximumPrice" type="xs:nonNegativeInteger" minOccurs="0" />
    <xs:element name="MerchantId" type="xs:string" minOccurs="0" />
    <xs:element name="MinimumPrice" type="xs:nonNegativeInteger" minOccurs="0" />
    <xs:element name="MusicLabel" type="xs:string" minOccurs="0" />
    <xs:element name="Neighborhood" type="xs:string" minOccurs="0" />
    <xs:element name="Orchestra" type="xs:string" minOccurs="0" />
    <xs:element name="PostalCode" type="xs:string" minOccurs="0" />
    <xs:element name="Power" type="xs:string" minOccurs="0" />
    <xs:element name="Publisher" type="xs:string" minOccurs="0" />
    <xs:element name="ResponseGroup" type="xs:string" minOccurs="0"
maxOccurs="unbounded" />
    <xs:element name="SearchIndex" type="xs:string" minOccurs="0" />
    <xs:element name="Sort" type="xs:string" minOccurs="0" />
    <xs:element name="State" type="xs:string" minOccurs="0" />
    <xs:element name="TextStream" type="xs:string" minOccurs="0" />
    <xs:element name="Title" type="xs:string" minOccurs="0" />
    </xs:sequence>
    </xs:complexType>

...[portions omitted]...

<service name="AWSProductData">
<port name="AWSProductDataPort" binding="tns:AWSProductDataBinding">
  <soap:address location="http://aws-
beta.amazon.com/onca/soap?Service=AWSProductData" />
  </port>
  </service>
  </definitions>
```

Notice that details about the `ItemSearch` and `ItemSearchRequest` elements are described. These are functions that can be called in the `AWSProductData` Web service of the Amazon API. The elements that you see for these functions are the parameters that the functions can accept.

The general steps for calling a Web service using SOAP from the .NET Framework (without using Visual Studio .NET) include the following:

1. Using a text editor (such as Notepad), create all or part of the .NET program where you want to use the Web service.

2. Create a *Web Service Proxy Class DLL* manually using the *WSDL.EXE* command line tool.

3. Revise the .NET program to import the namespace of the Web Service Proxy Class DLL created in Step 2.

4. Revise the .NET program to include the lines of code that call one or more functions of the Web service.

The general steps for calling a Web service using SOAP from Visual Studio .NET include the following:

1. Create a new project in Visual Studio .NET.

2. Add a Web Reference to point to the Web service you wish to call.

3. Add code in your program to create an instance of the class representing the Web service, and then call the appropriate methods in the Web service.

Walkthrough Example — Calling a Web Service Using SOAP from Visual Studio .NET

Now that you have been introduced to some basic concepts, let's walk through a step-by-step example of using SOAP and WSDL to call a Web service from Visual Studio .NET. In this example, you call the same Amazon Web service with the same search criteria that you saw in the REST examples earlier in this chapter. Because this example uses SOAP and Visual Studio.Net, the steps are quite different to call that same Web service.

Note that you need to obtain your own Amazon Web API Associate ID/Developer ID if you want to run the following example yourself. You can find more details about how to obtain an Amazon Associate ID in Chapter 4.

1. Open Visual Studio .NET.

2. Select File ⇨ New ⇨ Project, and select Windows Application as the type of project.

3. Specify `TestAmazonWebService` or another suitable name for the Name and change the project location if desired. Then click OK.

4. Select Project ⇨ Add Web Reference, as shown in Figure 1-2.

5. A screen like the one shown in Figure 1-3 is then displayed to allow you to specify the Web service to which you want to add a reference.

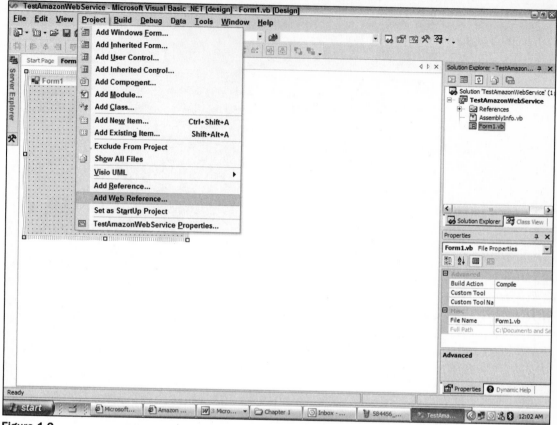

Figure 1-2

6. In the URL field, type or paste the URL where the WSDL file of the API you want to work with is located. Alternatively, you can search for Web services using the links indicated. In this example, specify the location of the Amazon API (version 4.0 or higher), which is currently located at:
    `http://webservices.amazon.com/AWSECommerceService/AWSECommerceService.wsdl`

7. After specifying the URL for the location of the WSDL file, click Go. A list of the methods available for that Web service is then displayed, as shown in Figure 1-4.

8. Change the Web reference name to `Amazon` and click the Add Reference button indicated on Figure 1-4.

9. You will notice that multiple references are added to the project, as shown in Figure 1-5, along with a Web reference called `Amazon`. This name is the Web reference name that was specified on the Add Reference dialog box.

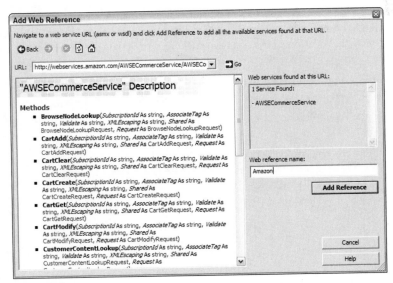

Figure 1-3

Figure 1-4

Figure 1-5

10. Add the following code to the `Form1_Load` event of Form1.

```vb
Private Sub Form1_Load(ByVal sender As System.Object, ByVal e As _
    System.EventArgs) Handles MyBase.Load

    Dim AmazonProductData As New _
        TestAmazonWebService.Amazon.AWSECommerceService
    Dim AmazonSearch As New TestAmazonWebService.Amazon.ItemSearch
    Dim AmazonResponse As New _
        TestAmazonWebService.Amazon.ItemSearchResponse
    Dim AmazonRequest(1) As _
        TestAmazonWebService.Amazon.ItemSearchRequest

    'Developer/Subscription Code
    AmazonSearch.SubscriptionId = "YOUR ID GOES HERE"

    'We are only making one request, not batching multiple requests
    'Thus element 0 of the array is all we need to assign and work with
    AmazonRequest(0) = New _
        TestAmazonWebService.Amazon.ItemSearchRequest
    AmazonRequest(0).SearchIndex = "Books"
    AmazonRequest(0).Keywords = "Denise Gosnell"

    'assign the search object to request object with the assigned parameters
    AmazonSearch.Request = AmazonRequest

    'run the search and populate the response
    AmazonResponse = AmazonProductData.ItemSearch(AmazonSearch)

    Dim item As New TestAmazonWebService.Amazon.Item
    Dim strOutput As String

    strOutput = "Search results for keyword(s): " & AmazonRequest(0).Keywords &
" in " & AmazonRequest(0).SearchIndex & ":" & vbCrLf & vbCrLf
```

```
              'loop through the results
              For Each item In AmazonResponse.Items(0).Item
                  strOutput = strOutput & item.ItemAttributes.Title & vbCrLf & vbCrLf
              Next

              'display the results in a message box
              MsgBox(strOutput)

         End Sub
```

Note that you must specify your own Associate ID for the Associate ID value in the previous code or the example will not run for you.

11. Run the program by pressing F5 or by selecting Debug ⇨ Start. You should see results similar to those shown in Figure 1-6.

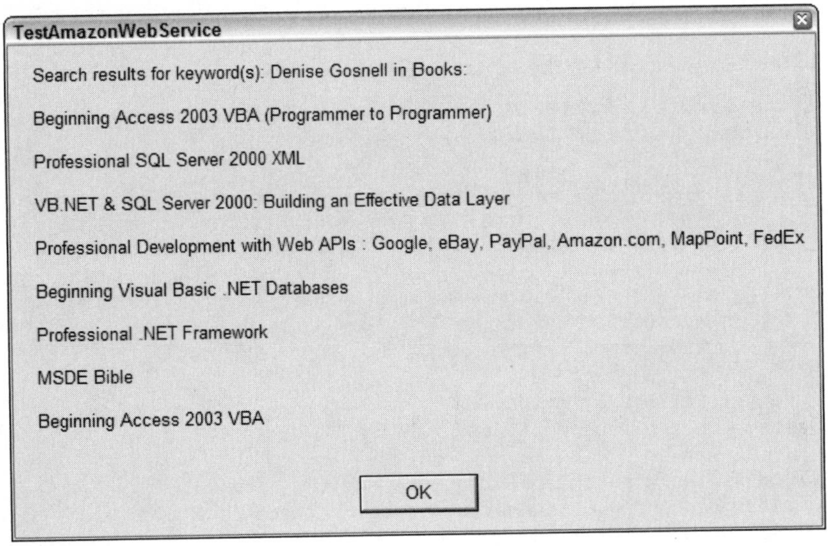

TestAmazonWebService

Search results for keyword(s): Denise Gosnell in Books:

Beginning Access 2003 VBA (Programmer to Programmer)

Professional SQL Server 2000 XML

VB.NET & SQL Server 2000: Building an Effective Data Layer

Professional Development with Web APIs : Google, eBay, PayPal, Amazon.com, MapPoint, FedEx

Beginning Visual Basic .NET Databases

Professional .NET Framework

MSDE Bible

Beginning Access 2003 VBA

OK

Figure 1-6

Also note that if you receive an error message when running the program stating that CustomerReviews1 cannot be reflected, please consult Chapter 4 for specific instructions on how to resolve the error.

Let's briefly review what just happened. You added a Web reference to the Amazon Web service (you pointed to the Amazon WSDL file). Visual Studio .NET used the WSDL file to create the objects that enable you to use the IntelliSense feature as you type and to refer to the Web services in your code just as you do other objects.

You then added code to the Form_Load event of Form1 to call one of the available Amazon Web services and to display a message box illustrating part of the search results. Review the VB code in more detail to see exactly how that works.

First, you declared various Amazon Web service objects that are required in order to execute an item search.

```
    Dim AmazonProductData As New TestAmazonWebService.Amazon.
AWSECommerceService
    Dim AmazonSearch As New TestAmazonWebService.Amazon.ItemSearch
    Dim AmazonResponse As New TestAmazonWebService.Amazon.ItemSearchResponse
    Dim AmazonRequest(1) As TestAmazonWebService.Amazon.ItemSearchRequest
```

You then supplied an Amazon Subscription ID.

```
    'Developer/Subscription Code
    AmazonSearch.SubscriptionId = "YOUR ID GOES HERE"
```

Because only one request is being made to the Web service, as opposed to a batch with multiple requests, element 0 of the array is used and assigned the search parameter values.

```
    'We are only making one request, not batching multiple requests
    'Thus element 0 of the array is all we need to assign and work with
    AmazonRequest(0) = New TestAmazonWebService.Amazon.ItemSearchRequest
    AmazonRequest(0).SearchIndex = "Books"
    AmazonRequest(0).Keywords = "Denise Gosnell"
```

You then assign the search object to the request object so that the search object will have the required parameters.

```
    'assign the search object to the request object with the assigned
parameters
    AmazonSearch.Request = AmazonRequest
```

Next, you called the ItemSearch method and assigned the results to the AmazonResponse variable.

```
    'run the search and populate the response
    AmazonResponse = AmazonProductData.ItemSearch(AmazonSearch)
```

Finally, you looped through the items in the response to build an output string for display to the user.

```
    Dim item As New TestAmazonWebService.Amazon.Item
    Dim strOutput As String

    strOutput = "Search results for keyword(s): " & AmazonRequest(0).Keywords &
" in " & AmazonRequest(0).SearchIndex & ":" & vbCrLf & vbCrLf

    'loop through the results
    For Each item In AmazonResponse.Items(0).Item
        strOutput = strOutput & item.ItemAttributes.Title & vbCrLf & vbCrLf
    Next

    'display the results in a message box
    MsgBox(strOutput)

    End Sub
```

This is just one example of the many ways you can use the Amazon Web service. For more information on the Amazon Web API, consult Chapter 4, which is dedicated exclusively to the Amazon Web API.

Summary

In this chapter, you explored the world of Web APIs and Web services. You learned about the various ways to call a Web service, such as using HTTP-GET, HTTP-POST, and SOAP.

Web services are growing in popularity every day. Now that major players such as Google, Amazon, eBay, and others have released Web APIs, Web services will pick up even more steam. By using the Web service APIs of these leading vendors, you can enhance your own applications tremendously. The remaining chapters are dedicated to illustrating several different Web service APIs in detail and to providing you with some real-world examples of using those APIs alone and in combination from mobile devices, Microsoft Office, and in various other ways.

Let's turn to the next chapter, which focuses on the Google API.

Using the Google API

A lot of attention has surrounded Google and the services it provides, especially with media attention focused on Google as a new publicly held company. Google has made several of its popular features available in an API to developers to use in their own applications. This chapter covers the Google API in great detail and is the first of several API-specific chapters in which I explore a particular API in detail. The following topics will be covered:

- ❑ Introduction to Google as a search engine
- ❑ How to obtain license keys for the Google API
- ❑ The syntax of Google API queries
- ❑ How to call the Google API from Visual Studio .NET
- ❑ How to call the Google API from the .NET Framework
- ❑ Five detailed examples of how to use the Google API
- ❑ Additional ideas for how you might use the Google API
- ❑ Third-party uses of the Google API

Google 101

Before jumping into the Google API, take a moment to review some of the features that Google offers in general. You are no doubt already aware that Google is a search engine that enables you to retrieve a list of Web sites that match search criteria you enter. For example, if you navigate to www.google.com and type some key words, you can get a list of potential Web pages of interest. An example of a search result in Google is shown in Figure 2-1.

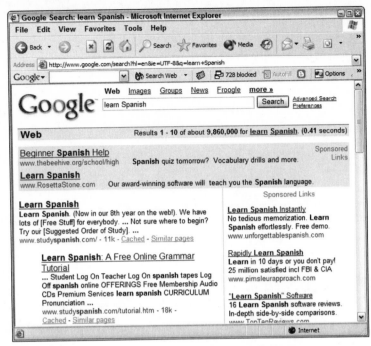

Figure 2-1

In the example of Figure 2-1, the search returns pages that have content related to the search phrase `learn Spanish`. Google's default Boolean type of search is AND, which means that it looks for pages that contain both words. If you want to specify that either word is acceptable, you type the following: `learn OR Spanish`.

In addition to traditional search results based on Google's page-ranking index, Google also displays links to related sponsor pages. Because the Google search engine is free to Internet users, Google makes money by selling advertising.

If you are like most people, you already know how to use Google to do simple searches such as the one shown in Figure 2-1. However, what you may not know is that Google also allows a user to perform more advanced searching by limiting the search results in various ways. Google has various search options that can be used to further limit the searching and it also offers features such as language translation, spell checking, and more.

Let's look briefly at some of these advanced features that you can include as part of your Google search query.

cache:

Using this option, you can retrieve a copy of a specified Web page from the Google cache if, for example, the Web page is no longer available at the original location or it has changed and you want to see an earlier version. Google returns a copy of the page from the last time the page was indexed by Google.

```
cache:www.microsoft.com
```

daterange:

Using this option, your search can be limited to a particular date or date range during which a page was indexed. Note that this search is not based on when a page was created, but when it was indexed by Google. Unfortunately, `daterange:` works with Julian dates instead of the calendar dates, so you must use a Julian date conversion tool to calculate the Julian date.

```
SAT daterange:2453253-2453283
```

filetype:

This option allows you to limit your search results to files of a particular type. Suppose, for example, you want to limit your search results of *learn Spanish* to only those files that are in PDF format. You can use the following search:

```
learn Spanish filetype:pdf
```

Upon executing the previous search on `www.google.com`, you might see results similar to those shown in Figure 2-2.

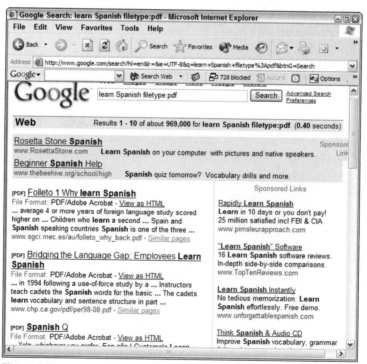

Figure 2-2

Notice that the primary search results now include only links to PDF documents that match the search criteria.

inanchor:

This option allows you to search for items that appear in the descriptive text of a link. The descriptive text of a link is what gets displayed to the user, and it is often different from the underlying URL address to which the link points.

```
inanchor:"traffic"
```

info:

This option allows you to retrieve links to more information about a particular URL. For example, you can obtain links to the list of pages that link to or are related to that URL as well as a link to the URL's cache. After it executes the `info:` command, Google returns a page that allows you to select from multiple link categories to retrieve this additional information.

```
info:www.microsoft.com
```

intext:

This option enables you to limit your search to body text only. In other words, the URLs, titles, and links are ignored. This option is great for running searches that involve words that are common in titles or URLs.

```
intext:"asp"
```

intitle:

This option allows you to limit your search to Web page titles. `Allintitle:` is a variation that finds Web pages where all the words specified make up the title of the Web page.

```
intitle:"George Bush"
allintitle:"election day" vote
```

inurl:

This option allows you to limit your search to the URLs of Web pages. `AllinURL:` is a variation that finds all the words listed in the URL.

```
inURL:aboutus
allinURL:contact us
```

link:

This option returns a list of Web pages that link to the specified URL. You do not need to include the http:// syntax.

```
link:www.intel.com
```

phonebook:

This option allows you to look up a phone number.

```
phonebook:317-634-3456
```

related:

This option allows you to retrieve a list of pages that are related to the one you specified. This might be useful, for example, to find alternative sites to search in the same category.

```
related:www.google.com
```

site:

This option allows you to limit your search to a site or a domain.

```
site:gov grants

site:uspto.gov utility patent
```

Google provides numerous other advanced features, such as spelling, language translation, and more. Now that you have briefly reviewed some features offered by Google, it's time to turn to the Google API.

Introduction to the Google API

You should recall from Chapter 1 that you can call an XML Web service in at least three different ways—using SOAP with HTTP, using HTTP-GET (REST), and using HTTP-POST. The Google API is currently available using SOAP with the HTTP protocol. At the time of this writing, the Google API was in beta. Therefore, the examples in this chapter are written using the beta version.

Signing Up and Obtaining a Key

Before you can use the Google API, you must first obtain a developer registration key. Although obtaining and using the developer key is free, Google currently enforces a limitation of 1,000 queries per developer per day. To sign up to use the Google API and to obtain a developer registration key, go to www.google.com/apis/ as illustrated in Figure 2-3.

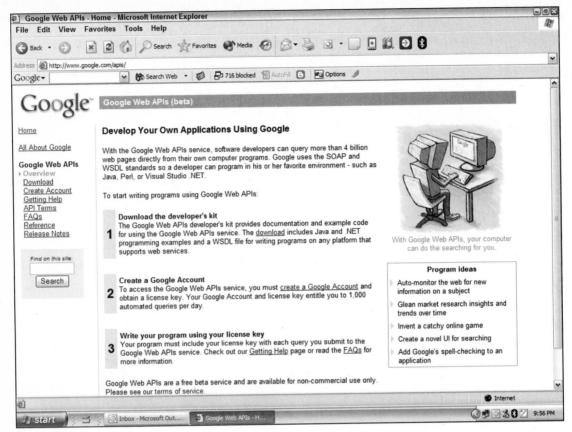

Figure 2-3

You are provided with step-by-step instructions for how to sign up for and use the Google API. First, you are told to download the developer's kit. When you click the link to download the Google API, you are presented with a license agreement (similar to the one shown in Figure 2-4) that you must accept before the file can be downloaded. You select the Agree option and then click the Download Now button to start the download.

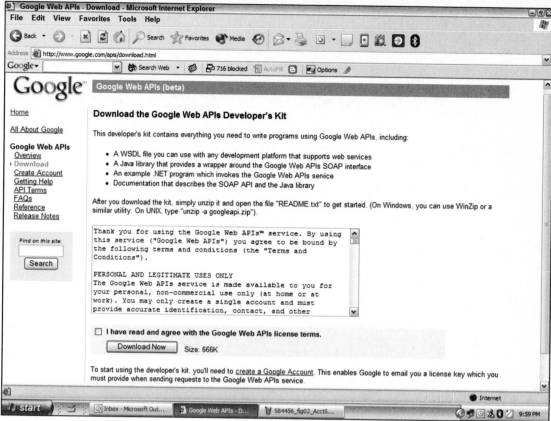

Figure 2-4

The Developer's Kit contains several code examples that illustrate how to call the Google API from various programming languages, including .NET. After downloading the developer's kit to your hard drive, you create a Google account. When you click the link to create a Google account, you see a screen similar to the one shown in Figure 2-5.

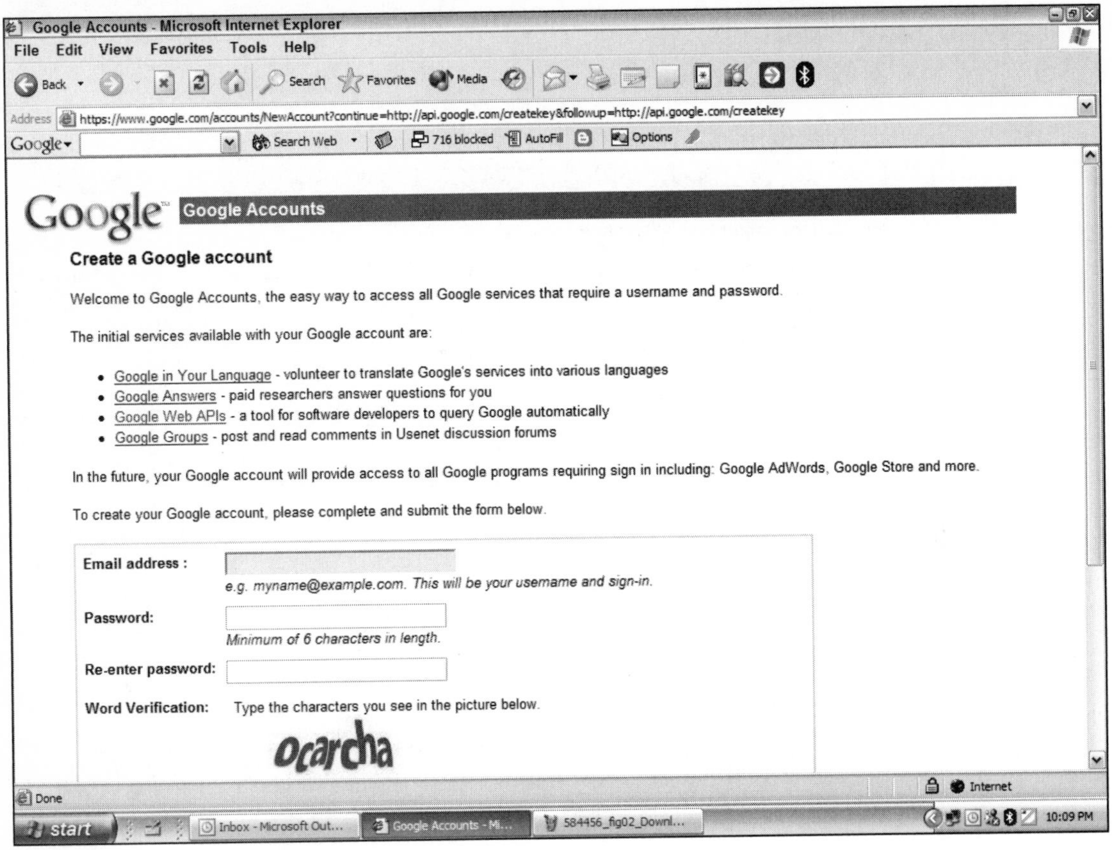

Figure 2-5

To create a Google account, you are prompted to specify an e-mail address, a password, and a password confirmation. You are also prompted to type the word verification. After clicking the button to proceed, you receive a confirmation screen similar to the one shown in Figure 2-6 informing you that your key has been sent by e-mail to the address of your account.

Open the e-mail and copy the developer key to a place where you can easily access it. Later, you will need the developer key for all calls to the Google API.

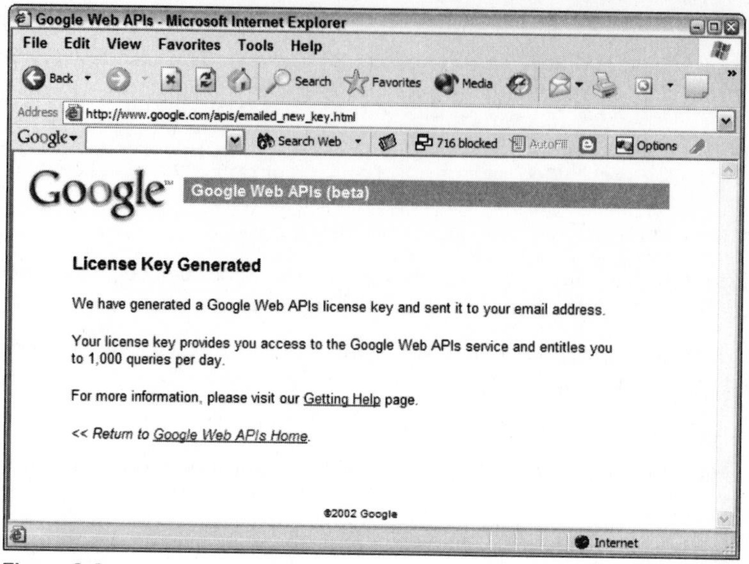

Figure 2-6

Anatomy of a Google API Query

In this section, you explore the structure of a Google API query and learn the basics of how to execute a query and work with the results.

Query Syntax

The Google API supports search requests, retrieving pages from the Google cache, and spelling suggestions. Let's now look at each of these in greater detail.

Search Requests

In addition to simple keyword searches, the Google API supports the following search options:

```
allintext:
allinlinks:
cache:
daterange:
filetype:
info:
intitle:
inURL:
link:
related:
site:
```

Syntax of a Google Search Request

The `doGoogleSearch` method enables you to execute a Google search request. A typical Google API search request using `doGoogleSearch` is structured as follows:

```
SearchResult = Search.doGoogleSearch(Key, q, _
                   Start, MaxResults, Filter, Restrict, SafeSearch, lr, ie, oe)
```

❑   `Key` is the developer key that Google provided for you.

❑   `q` is the search string text of your search command, which can be just a simple search or can include the advanced options reviewed earlier in this chapter.

❑   `Start` is the starting index where you want the results to start. You should use 0 if you want the first set of results.

❑   `MaxResults` is the maximum number of results to return. It can be a value from 1 to 10.

❑   `Filter` is a Boolean value that specifies whether your results go through automatic query filtering.

❑   `Restrict` is a text value that will restrict your search to a specific country or one of Google's topical searches. This field is usually left blank to leave the search unrestricted.

❑   `SafeSearch` is a Boolean value that specifies whether the results will be filtered to remove adult content.

❑   `lr` stands for *language restrict* and allows you to limit your search results to a particular language.

❑   `ie` stands for input encoding and allows you to specify the type of character encoding that your query will use. Google's documentation says that request data should use the UTF-8 format. You can leave this field blank.

❑   `oe` stands for output encoding, which should be UTF-8. You can leave this field blank.

Syntax of a Google Search Response

The most important aspects of the search response are returned in a `resultElements` list that contains elements such as the following:

❑   *<title>* is the HTML title of the page.

❑   *<URL>* is the URL of the search result, including the HTTP://.

❑   *<summary>* is the summary of the site from the Google Directory, if available.

❑   *<snippet>* is a brief portion of the Web page and has the search terms highlighted in bold tags (<b></b> tags).

❑   *<cachedSize>* is the size in kilobytes of the version of the page contained in the Google cache, if available.

Other result values are also included in the search response, but are used less frequently. Please consult the Google API documentation for a complete list.

Cache Requests

Another method supported by the Google API is the `doGetCachedPage` method. This method allows you to retrieve the cached version of a URL from the Google cache. The `doGetCachedPage` method returns a byte array and has the following syntax:

```
bytPage() = Search.doGetCachedPage(Key, URL)
```

❑   `Key` is the developer key you were provided by Google.

❑   `URL` is the URL of the site you wish to retrieve from the Google cache.

Spelling Requests

A third method supported by the Google API is the `doSpellingSuggestion` method. This method allows you to retrieve a spelling suggestion/correction for a particular search phrase. The `doSpellingSuggestion` method returns a string and has the following syntax:

```
strSuggestedSpelling = Search.doSpellingSuggestion(Key, Phrase)
```

❑   `Key` is the developer key you were provided by Google.

❑   `Phrase` is the text phrase for which you would like to receive a spelling suggestion.

The details of how to call each of these three methods are explained later in this chapter. Now that you have the basic idea of the types of queries that can be executed using the Google API, let's look at an example of how to execute a search request.

Executing a Query

In this section, I walk you through examples that illustrate how to execute a Google API query using Visual Studio .NET as well as directly from the .NET Framework.

Executing a Query Using Visual Studio .NET

1.   Open Visual Studio .NET and select File ➪ New ➪ Project.

2.   Select Visual Basic Project as the Project Type, and select Console Application as the Template. For the project name, specify `GoogleSearchConsole` or another suitable name. For the path specify the location where you want the project to be created. Click OK to create the new project.

3.   Add a reference to the Google API by selecting Project ➪ Add Web Reference. For the URL field, specify `http://api.google.com/GoogleSearch.wsdl`. You may recall from Chapter 1 that the WSDL file of a Web service explains the features that are available in the service. Click the GO button so that Visual Studio can locate the Google service. A screen similar to that shown in Figure 2-7 is displayed.

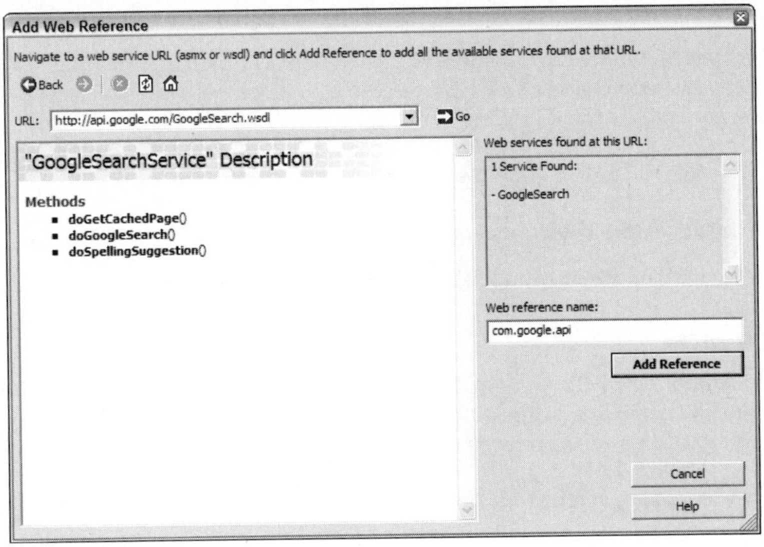

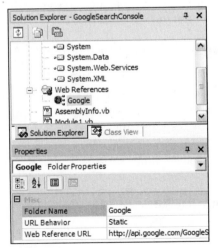

Figure 2-7

4. Click the Add Reference button to add the reference to your project. Visual Studio .NET uses the WSDL file to identify the methods available for execution from your project.

5. In the Solution Explorer of the project, navigate to the Web references node and select the Google Web service that was added. Modify the properties of the Folder Name for the Web service to Google so that you can use a shorter name in your code. The results of this modification are shown in Figure 2-8.

Figure 2-8

6. Add the following `Sub Main` procedure to `Module1` of your project:

```
Sub Main()

    'Create a Google Search object
    Dim Search As New Google.GoogleSearchService

    Dim strLicense As String
    Dim strSearchText As String
    Dim intStart As Integer
    Dim intMaxResults As Integer

    'set the values to pass to the Google web service
    strLicense = "YOUR KEY GOES HERE"
    strSearchText = "web service API"
    intStart = 0
    intMaxResults = 3

    Try
        'execute the doGoogleSearch method (i.e. run the Google Search)
        Dim SearchResult As Google.GoogleSearchResult = _
                Search.doGoogleSearch(strLicense, strSearchText, _
                intStart, intMaxResults, False, "", False, "", "", "")

        'if no results were returned then exit
        If SearchResult.resultElements Is Nothing Then Exit Sub

        'write the results to the console
        Dim result As Google.ResultElement
        For Each result In SearchResult.resultElements
            Console.WriteLine()
            Console.WriteLine(result.title)
            Console.WriteLine(result.URL)
            Console.WriteLine(result.snippet)
            Console.WriteLine()
        Next

        'get input from the user so display will pause until enter pressed
        Console.ReadLine()

    Catch exception As System.Web.Services.Protocols.SoapException
        MsgBox(exception.Message)
    End Try
End Sub
```

7. Input your developer license key on the line of code that says YOUR KEY GOES HERE.

8. Select File ➪ Save All to save all changes to the project.

9. Select Debug ➪ Start (or press F5) to run the project. You should see a console window similar to Figure 2-9 that retrieves information from the Google API based on the criteria specified in your code.

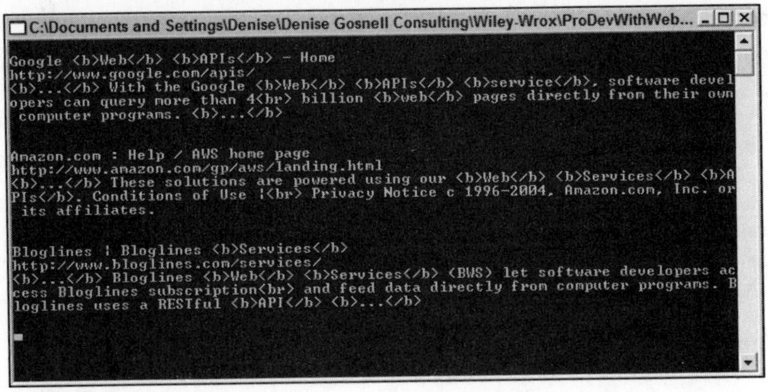

Figure 2-9

10. Click Enter in the console window to end the application.

The essence of this example is included in the Sub Main procedure, so let's walk through it in further detail to see how it works.

First, you created a new Google Search Service.

```
'Create a Google Search object
Dim Search As New Google.GoogleSearchService
```

Next, you declared various variables to hold the parameters to pass to the search query.

```
Dim strLicense As String
Dim strSearchText As String
Dim intStart As Integer
Dim intMaxResults As Integer
```

You then assigned the values to the search variables, such as the developer key, the search string, the starting position for the query, and the maximum number of results to return.

```
'set the values to pass to the Google web service
strLicense = "YOUR KEY GOES HERE"
strSearchText = "web service API"
intStart = 0
intMaxResults = 3
```

You then executed the doGoogleSearch method and passed the search variables defined previously.

```
Try
    'execute the doGoogleSearch method (i.e. run the Google Search)
    Dim SearchResult As Google.GoogleSearchResult = _
            Search.doGoogleSearch(strLicense, strSearchText, _
            intStart, intMaxResults, False, "", False, "", "", "")
```

If no results were returned, you exited the procedure.

```
'if no results were returned then exit
If SearchResult.resultElements Is Nothing Then Exit Sub
```

For each result that was returned, some key information about the result was written to the output window.

```
'write the results to the console
Dim result As Google.ResultElement
For Each result In SearchResult.resultElements
    Console.WriteLine()
    Console.WriteLine(result.title)
    Console.WriteLine(result.URL)
    Console.WriteLine(result.snippet)
    Console.WriteLine()
Next
```

You then specified a readline command so the screen would pause for user input.

```
'get input from the user so display will pause until enter pressed
Console.ReadLine()
```

An error handler is used to catch any errors during this process.

```
Catch exception As System.Web.Services.Protocols.SoapException
    MsgBox(exception.Message)
End Try
End Sub
```

See how simple it is to execute a search using the Google API! Let's look at how to generate this exact same example using just the .NET Framework.

Executing a Query Using the .NET Framework

In this section, you execute the same Google query using the .NET Framework directly without using Visual Studio .NET.

1. Add the following code (using Notepad or another text editor) to a new file called GoogleSearchConsole.vb.

```
Imports System

Module Module1

  Sub Main()

        'Create a Google Search object
        Dim Search As New Google.GoogleSearchService

        Dim strLicense As String
```

```
        Dim strSearchText As String
        Dim intStart As Integer
        Dim intMaxResults As Integer

        'set the values to pass to the Google web service
        'strLicense = "YOUR KEY GOES HERE"
        strSearchText = "web service API"
        intStart = 0
        intMaxResults = 3

        Try
            'execute the doGoogleSearch method (i.e. run the Google Search)
            Dim SearchResult As Google.GoogleSearchResult = _
                    Search.doGoogleSearch(strLicense, strSearchText, _
                    intStart, intMaxResults, False, "", False, "", "", "")

            'if no results were returned then exit
            If SearchResult.resultElements Is Nothing Then Exit Sub

            'write the results to the console
            Dim result As Google.ResultElement
            For Each result In SearchResult.resultElements
                Console.WriteLine()
                Console.WriteLine(result.title)
                Console.WriteLine(result.URL)
                Console.WriteLine(result.snippet)
                Console.WriteLine()
            Next

            'get input from the user so display will pause until enter pressed
            Console.ReadLine()

        Catch exception As System.Web.Services.Protocols.SoapException
            MsgBox(exception.Message)
        End Try
    End Sub

End Module
```

This code is identical to the code you used in the prior example except that it also includes the Imports statement to use the System library. When you use Visual Studio .NET, this information is stored in a separate file and generated for you (usually called AssemblyInfo.vb).

2. Next, you have to link the code to the Google WSDL file (that is, you must perform the equivalent of adding a Web reference and generating the files necessary to communicate with the Web service). Visual Studio .NET does this automatically, but to do so manually, you must open a command window and navigate to the directory where your code is located. This step is easiest to perform if you open the command window using the Visual Studio .NET Command Prompt. Then, execute the following command.

```
wsdl.exe /l:vb http://api.google.com/GoogleSearch.wsdl
```

If you receive an error indicating that the WSDL.exe file could not be located, make sure that Windows knows where to find the WSDL.exe file. One way is to open the Command Window from Start ⇨ Programs ⇨ Visual Studio .NET ⇨ Visual Studio .NET Tools ⇨ Visual Studio .NET Command Prompt so that the proper path settings are included automatically. Another way is to specify the complete path to the WSDL.exe file in the command. One example of where you might find the WSDL.exe file is C:\Program Files\Microsoft Visual Studio .NET 2003\SDK\v1.1\Bin.

3. Alternatively, instead of specifying the long path to the WSDL file on the Google server, you can download a copy of the WSDL file to your working directory and then use a command such as this:

```
wsdl.exe /l:vb GoogleSearch.wsdl
```

4. A new vb file is created in your directory after running the wsdl.exe utility that contains the SOAP proxy client information needed to call the Google Web API.

5. You are now ready to compile the application using the vbc.exe compiler with the following command:

```
vbc /out:GoogleSearchConsole.exe *.vb
```

In some environments, you may also need to specify the complete path to vbc.exe which is included with Visual Studio .NET and the .NET Framework.

6. Run the GoogleSearchConsole.exe program.

There are fewer files to work with when you use the command line tools instead of the Visual Studio .NET graphical user interface, but you have to manually generate the SOAP proxy client and compile the program. The remaining examples in this chapter are implemented using Visual Studio .NET so you can visually inspect the forms and features.

Looping through Results

Google returns only ten results per query. Other results are available to you, but you have to loop and query for the next set of ten. You can expand the prior console application to loop through multiple sets of ten results. Open the GoogleSearchConsole project and replace Sub Main with the code that follows:

```
Sub Main()

    'Create a Google Search object
    Dim Search As New Google.GoogleSearchService

    Dim strLicense As String
    Dim strSearchText As String
    Dim intStart As Integer
    Dim intMaxResults As Integer

    Try

        'set the values to pass to the Google web service
        strLicense = "YOUR KEY GOES HERE"
```

```
              strSearchText = "web service API"
              intStart = 0
              intMaxResults = 10

              'call the search method 3 times to get 30 results
              Dim intCounter As Integer
              intCounter = 1
              For intCounter = 1 To 3

                    'execute the doGoogleSearch method (i.e. run the Google Search)
                    Dim SearchResult As Google.GoogleSearchResult = _
                          Search.doGoogleSearch(strLicense, strSearchText, _
                          intStart, intMaxResults, False, "", False, "", "", "")

                    'if no results were returned then exit
                    If SearchResult.resultElements Is Nothing Then Exit Sub

                    'write the results to the console
                    Dim result As Google.ResultElement
                    For Each result In SearchResult.resultElements
                          Console.WriteLine()
                          Console.WriteLine(result.title)
                          Console.WriteLine(result.URL)
                          Console.WriteLine(result.snippet)
                          Console.WriteLine()
                    Next

                    'increment the counter used for retrieving the next
                    'set of 10 results
                    intStart = intCounter * 10

              Next

                    'get input from the user so display will pause until enter pressed
                    Console.ReadLine()


          Catch exception As System.Web.Services.Protocols.SoapException
                MsgBox(exception.Message)
          End Try
    End Sub
```

The previous intStart variable is what controls which set of results is returned. Because the intMaxResults value is set to 10, each time the intStart variable is incremented by 10, the next ten search results are returned. The previous example performs the same Google search three times so that it can receive the first set of ten results, the second set of ten results, and the third set of ten results.

Five Creative Ways to Use the Google API

In this section, you learn five additional ways to use the Google API.

#1 — Build a Google Search Feature

In this example, you build a Google search feature into your own Web application.

1.   From Visual Studio .NET, select File ➪ New ➪ Project and select ASP.NET Web Application as the template. Specify `http://localhost/GoogleExample1` for the Location and `GoogleExample1` or any other suitable name for the Name.

2.   Use the toolbox to drag and drop a label, a text box, and a button control onto the Form.

3.   Using the Properties Window, change the name of ID property of the text box to `txtSearch` and the ID property of the button to `btnSearch`. Change the name of the Text property of the label to `Search Google` and that of the button to `Search Now`. The Form should now look similar to the one shown in Figure 2-10.

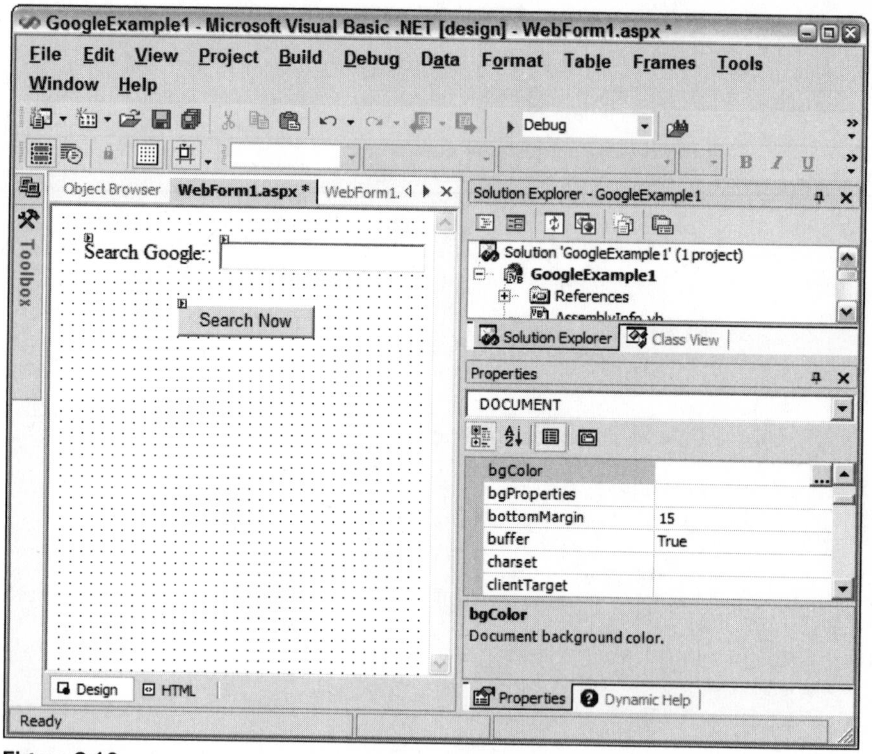

Figure 2-10

4.   Select Project ➪ Add Web Reference. In the URL, specify the location of the Google WSDL file `http://api.google.com/GoogleSearch.wsdl` and click the GO button.

33

5. Change the Web Reference Name to `Google` so that you can use a shorter name in your project.

6. Select the `Add Reference` button to add a reference to your project.

7. Add the following code to `btnSearch_Click` event, inserting your developer key in the appropriate line of code. Note that by double-clicking on the button, you cause VS.NET to automatically generate an empty click event.

```vbnet
Private Sub btnSearch_Click(ByVal sender As System.Object, ByVal e As _
    System.EventArgs) Handles btnSearch.Click

        'Create a Google Search object
        Dim Search As New Google.GoogleSearchService

        Dim strLicense As String
        Dim strSearchText As String
        Dim intStart As Integer
        Dim intMaxResults As Integer

        Try

            'set the values to pass to the Google web service
            strLicense = "YOUR KEY GOES HERE"
            'get the value the user typed in the search text box
            strSearchText = txtSearch.Text
            intStart = 0
            intMaxResults = 10

            'execute the doGoogleSearch method (i.e. run the Google Search)
            Dim SearchResult As Google.GoogleSearchResult = _
                    Search.doGoogleSearch(strLicense, strSearchText, _
                    intStart, intMaxResults, False, "", False, "", "", "")

            'if no results were returned then exit
            If SearchResult.resultElements Is Nothing Then Exit Sub

            'insert some blank lines in the browser
            Response.Write("<BR><BR><BR><BR><BR><BR>")

            'write the results to the browser
            Dim result As Google.ResultElement
            For Each result In SearchResult.resultElements
                'write the results to the browser adding proper HTML tags for
                'carriage return and for hyperlink
                Response.Write(result.title & "<BR>")
                Response.Write("<a href =" & result.URL & ">" & result.URL & _
                    "</a><BR>")
                Response.Write(result.snippet & "<BR><BR>")
            Next


        Catch exception As System.Web.Services.Protocols.SoapException
            MsgBox(exception.Message)
        End Try
    End Sub
```

8. Save and run the program. You should see a screen similar to that shown in Figure 2-11.

Figure 2-11

9. Type in your search command in the text box and click the Search Now button. You should see results similar to those shown in Figure 2-12.

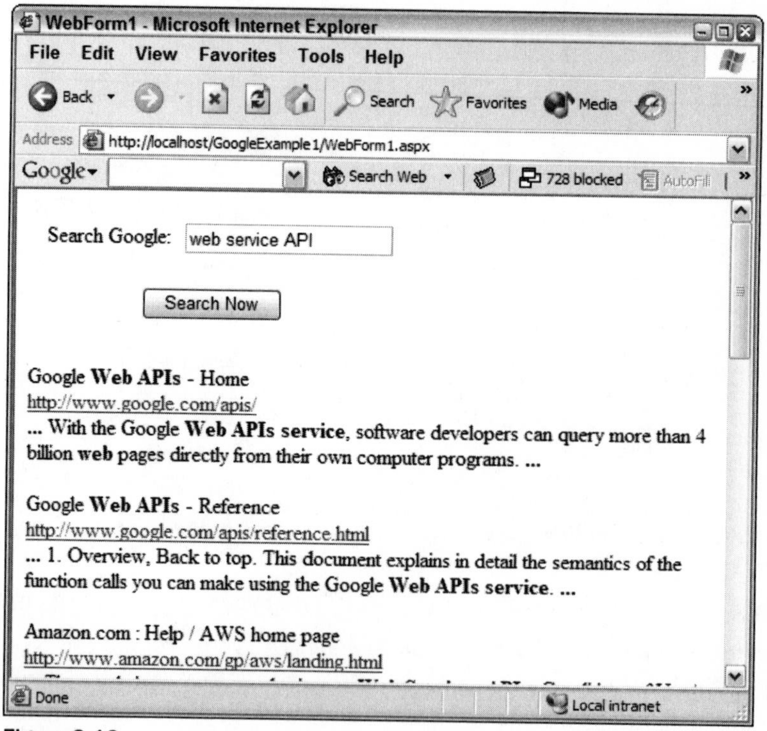

Figure 2-12

#2 — Return Random Pages

In this next example, you retrieve a random Web page, such as one for expansion of knowledge. If you want, you can modify the prior example instead of creating a new ASP.NET project from scratch. This example automatically navigates you to a random page selected from the keywords you specified.

1. From Visual Studio .NET, select File ⇨ New ⇨ Project and select ASP.NET Web Application as the template. Specify `http://localhost/GoogleExample2` for the Location and `GoogleExample2` or another appropriate name for the Name.

2. Use the toolbox to drag and drop a button control onto the form.

3. Using the Properties Window, change the ID property of the button control to `btnRetrieve` and the Text property to `Return Random Page`. The form should now look similar to the one shown in Figure 2-13.

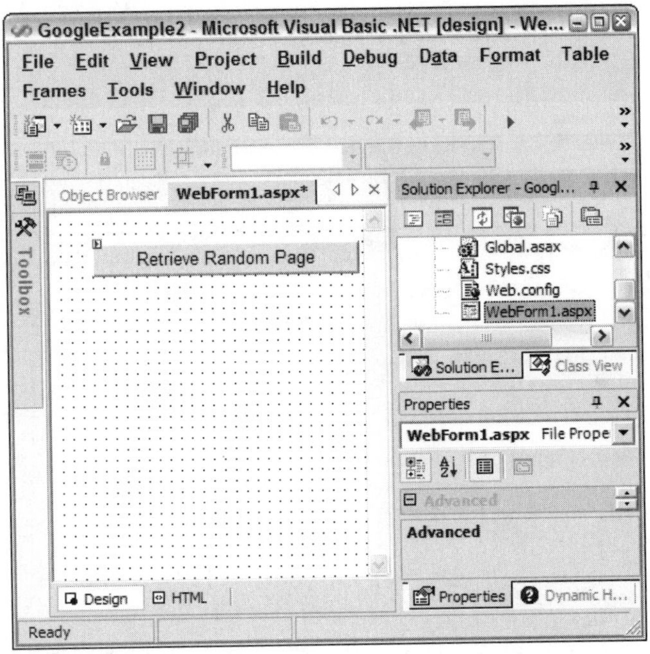

Figure 2-13

4. Select Project ⇨ Add Web Reference. In the URL, specify the location of the Google WSDL file `http://api.google.com/GoogleSearch.wsdl` and click the GO button.

5. Change the Web Reference Name to `Google` so that you can use a shorter name in your project.

6. Select the Add Reference button to add a reference to your project.

7. Add the following code to the `btnRetrieve_Click` event, inserting your developer key in the appropriate line of code:

```
Private Sub btnRetrieve_Click(ByVal sender As System.Object, ByVal e As _
    System.EventArgs) Handles btnRetrieve.Click

        'Create a Google Search object
        Dim Search As New Google.GoogleSearchService

        Dim strLicense As String
        Dim strSearchText As String
        Dim intStart As Integer
        Dim intMaxResults As Integer

        Try

            'set the values to pass to the Google web service
            strLicense = "YOUR KEY GOES HERE"
            'specify a search term
            strSearchText = "world traveling"
            'specify a random number to use for retrieving random page
            intStart = Rnd() * 100 + 1
            intMaxResults = 1

            'execute the doGoogleSearch method (i.e. run the Google Search)
            Dim SearchResult As Google.GoogleSearchResult = _
                    Search.doGoogleSearch(strLicense, strSearchText, _
                    intStart, intMaxResults, False, "", False, "", "", "")

            'if no results were returned then exit
            If SearchResult.resultElements Is Nothing Then Exit Sub

            'redirect to the random page that was returned
            Dim result As Google.ResultElement
            For Each result In SearchResult.resultElements
                Response.Redirect(result.URL)
                Exit For
            Next

            Exit Sub

        Catch exception As System.Web.Services.Protocols.SoapException
            MsgBox(exception.Message)
        End Try
    End Sub
```

8. Save and run the program.

9. Click the Retrieve button and you will then be redirected to a random page. Take a minute to read something on the random page and learn something new.

#3 — Save the Results of a Google Search to a File

In this example, you save the results of a search to a file.

1. Open Visual Studio .NET and select File ➪ New ➪ Project.

2. Select Visual Basic Project as the Project Type, and select Windows Application as the Template. For the project name, specify `GoogleExamples3and4` or another suitable name, and for the path specify the location where you want the project to be created. Click OK to create the new project.

3. Add a reference to the Google API by selecting Project ⇨ Add Web Reference. For the URL field, specify `http://api.google.com/GoogleSearch.wsdl`. Make sure to change the Web reference name to Google before clicking the Add Reference button.

4. Drag and drop three labels, two text boxes, and one button to the form. Arrange the controls and change the Text properties of each control as shown in Figure 2-14.

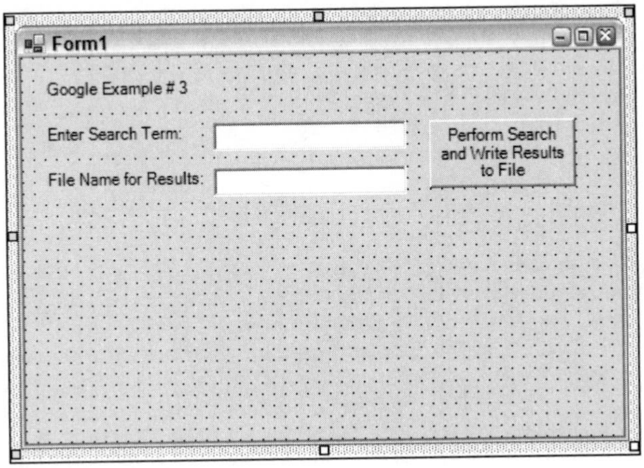

Figure 2-14

5. Change the Name property of the top text box to `txtSearch`, and change the Name property of the bottom one to `txtFileName`. Change the Name property of the button to `btnSearch`.

6. Add the following imports statement to the top of the class module before all other declarations:

```
Imports System.IO
```

7. Add the following code to the class module, inserting your developer key in the appropriate line of code:

```
Private Sub btnSearch_Click(ByVal sender As System.Object, ByVal e As _
        System.EventArgs) Handles btnSearch.Click

        'Create a Google Search object
        Dim Search As New Google.GoogleSearchService

        Dim strLicense As String
        Dim strSearchText As String
        Dim intStart As Integer
        Dim intMaxResults As Integer

        Try
```

```
                    'set the values to pass to the Google web service
                    strLicense = "YOUR KEY GOES HERE"
                    'get the search string from the text box
                    strSearchText = txtSearch.Text
                    intStart = 0
                    intMaxResults = 10

                    'execute the doGoogleSearch method (i.e. run the Google Search)
                    Dim SearchResult As Google.GoogleSearchResult = _
                            Search.doGoogleSearch(strLicense, strSearchText, _
                            intStart, intMaxResults, False, "", False, "", "", "")

                    'if no results were returned then exit
                    If SearchResult.resultElements Is Nothing Then Exit Sub

                    'write the search results to the file specified in
                    'the file name text box.
                    Dim fileStream As FileStream
                    Dim streamWriter As StreamWriter
                    Dim streamReader As StreamReader

                    fileStream = New FileStream(Path:=txtFileName.Text, _
                        mode:=FileMode.Create, access:=FileAccess.Write)

                    'create an instance of a character writer
                    streamWriter = New StreamWriter(stream:=fileStream)

                    'write the results to the open file
                    Dim result As Google.ResultElement
                    For Each result In SearchResult.resultElements
                        streamWriter.WriteLine()
                        streamWriter.WriteLine(result.title)
                        streamWriter.WriteLine(result.URL)
                        streamWriter.WriteLine(result.snippet)
                        streamWriter.WriteLine()
                    Next

                    'update the file
                    streamWriter.Flush()

                    'close the writer object
                    streamWriter.Close()

                    'close the file
                    fileStream.Close()

                Catch exception As System.Web.Services.Protocols.SoapException
                    MsgBox(exception.Message)
                End Try

            End Sub
```

8. Save and run the program.

9. Enter a search string as well as a text file where you want the search results stored. An example of a search is shown in Figure 2-15.

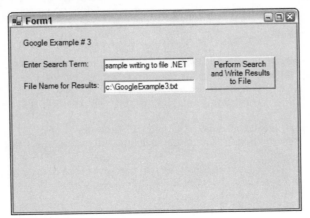

Figure 2-15

10. Click the Perform Search button. After waiting a few seconds, navigate on your hard drive and locate the new text file that was created with the results of the search. An example of text file output is shown in Figure 2-16.

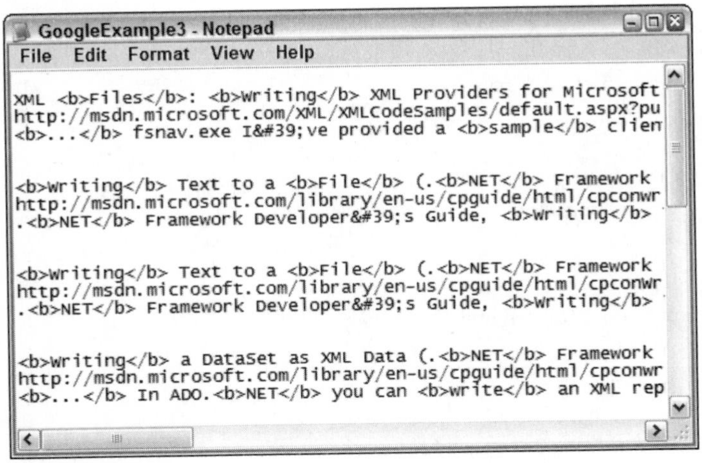

Figure 2-16

#4 — Use Google to Check Spelling

In this example, you use the Google spell checking feature to suggest alternate spellings to the word or phrase specified. You can expand upon the project you created in the prior example.

1. Use the toolbox to add two labels, one text box, and one button to the existing Form1. If the toolbox is not visible, you can display it by selecting View ⇨ Toolbox. Rename the Text properties of the controls as shown in Figure 2-17.

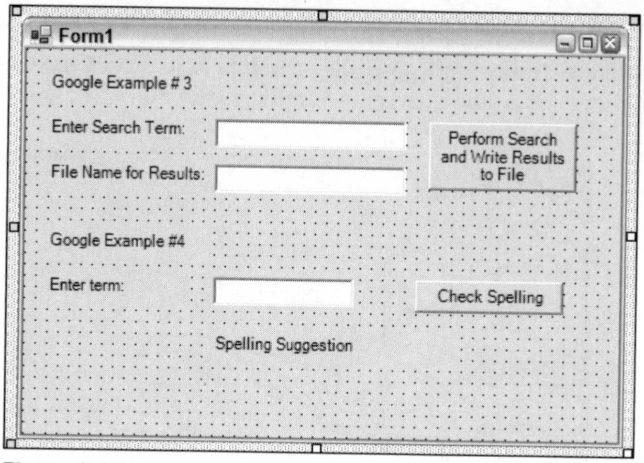

Figure 2-17

2. Change the Name property of the text box to `txtSpelling`, change the Name property of the bottom label to `lblSpelling`, and change the Name property of the button to `btnSpelling`.

3. Add the following code to the `btnSpelling_Click` event, inserting your developer key in the appropriate line of code:

```
Private Sub btnSpelling_Click(ByVal sender As System.Object, ByVal e As _
        System.EventArgs) Handles btnSpelling.Click

        'Create a Google Search object
        Dim Search As New Google.GoogleSearchService

        Dim strLicense As String
        Dim strSearchText As String
        Dim strSuggestedSpelling As String

        Try

            'set the values to pass to the Google web service
            strLicense = "YOUR KEY GOES HERE"
            'get the search string from the text box
            strSearchText = txtSpelling.Text

            'execute the doSpellingSuggestion method
            strSuggestedSpelling = _
                    Search.doSpellingSuggestion(strLicense, strSearchText)

            lblSpelling.Text = "You should also consider: " & strSuggestedSpelling

        Catch exception As System.Web.Services.Protocols.SoapException
            MsgBox(exception.Message)
        End Try

    End Sub
End Class
```

4. Save and run the program.

5. Specify one or more terms in the spelling search field and click the Check Spelling button. The suggested spelling should be displayed, similar to the examples shown in Figure 2-18.

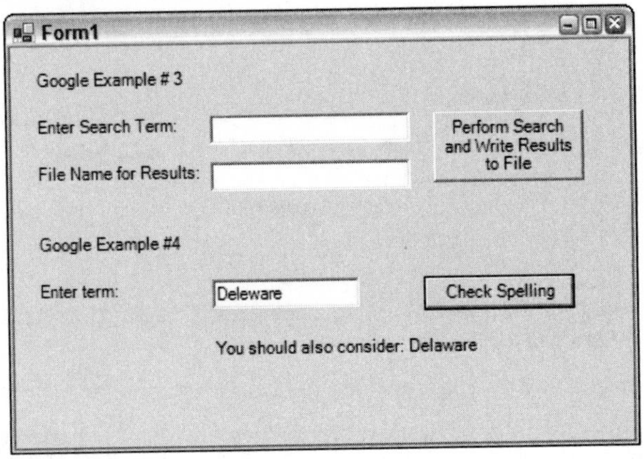

Figure 2-18

#5 — Use the Google Cache to Retrieve a Web Site That Is No Longer Available

In this final example, you use the Google cache feature to retrieve a historical Web page.

1. Create a new Web project as you did in Examples 1 and 2. Select File ⇨ New ⇨ Project. Specify ASP.NET Web Application for the Template and http://localhost/GoogleExample5 for the Location.

2. Use the toolbox to drag and drop a button control onto the form. Using the Properties Window, change the ID property of the button control to btnRetrieve and the Text property to Retrieve Page from Google Cache. The form should now look similar to the one shown in Figure 2-19.

3. Select Project ⇨ Add Web Reference. In the URL, specify the location of the Google WSDL file http://api.google.com/GoogleSearch.wsdl and click the GO button. Change the Web reference name to Google so that you can use a shorter name in your project. Select the Add Reference button to add a reference to your project.

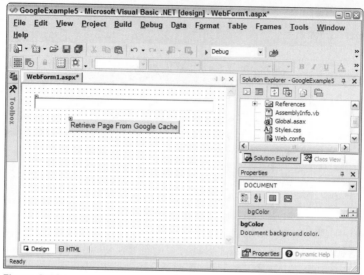

Figure 2-19

4. Add the following code to the btnRetrieve_Click event, inserting your developer code in the appropriate line of code.

```vb
Private Sub btnRetrieve_Click(ByVal sender As System.Object, ByVal e As _
        System.EventArgs) Handles btnRetrieve.Click

    'Create a Google Search object
    Dim Search As New Google.GoogleSearchService

    Dim strLicense As String
    Dim strSearchText As String

    Try

        'set the values to pass to the Google web service
        strLicense = "YOUR KEY GOES HERE"
        'specify a search term
        strSearchText = txtURL.Text

        'hide the search fields
        txtURL.Visible = False
        btnRetrieve.Visible = False

        'call the doGetCachedPage method and write the results to the
        'web browser)
        Dim bytPage() As Byte = Search.doGetCachedPage(strLicense, _
            strSearchText)
```

```
            'convert base 64 byte array returned from Google to a string
            Dim strHTML As String = _
                System.Text.ASCIIEncoding.ASCII.GetString(bytPage)

            'display the page retrieved from cache
            Response.Write(strHTML)

            Exit Sub

        Catch exception As System.Web.Services.Protocols.SoapException
            MsgBox(exception.Message)
        End Try

    End Sub
```

5. Save and run the project.

6. Specify a Web site to retrieve from cache, such as the one shown in Figure 2-20, and then click the Retrieve Page button.

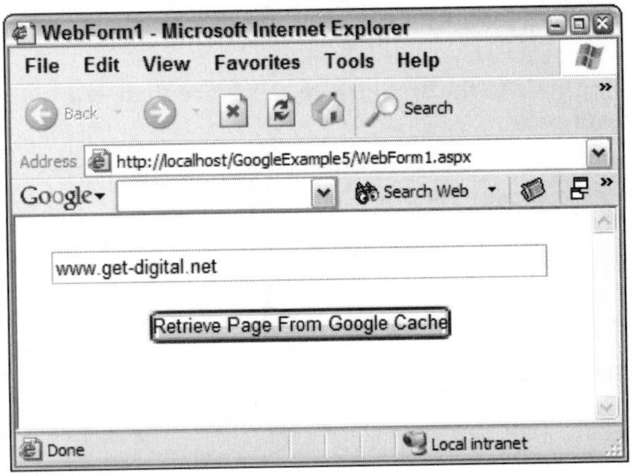

Figure 2-20

7. You should see results similar to those shown in Figure 2-21 with a notice indicating the date of the file and other information, along with the copy of the cached file itself.

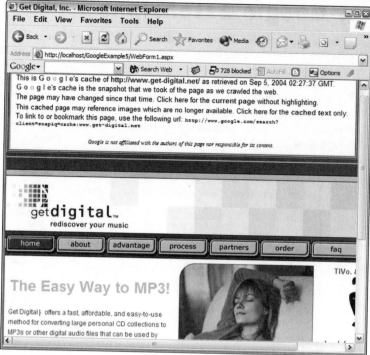

Figure 2-21

Other Ways to Use the Google API

In the previous sections, you looked at five examples to give you an idea of how you can use the Google API in your applications. Following are some additional examples of ways you might want to use the Google API. Additional examples of the Google API are also included in the later chapters and case studies at the end of this book.

❑ Build a Google box that displays the top ten results matching preprogrammed criteria that get updated periodically and/or automatically. An example of this is illustrated in Case Study 1.

❑ Restrict your search to a certain list of sites (for example: finding recipes, travel, or other data from a list of sites that you know has information you're interested in).

❑ Search for documents in a particular language only.

❑ Automatically monitor for new information on a subject.

❑ Use Google for fun, such as creating a children's story builder where you have a nursery rhyme or other story and Google fills in the blanks with random words. Remember the old MadLibs stories?

Third-Party Google Extensions

Several third parties have implemented their own solutions that use the Google API in some fashion. For example, Macromedia has a solution that allows for integrating Google results into Flash applications.

Capescience has a service called CapeMail (`http://capescience.capeclear.com/google/index.shtml`) that queries Google by e-mail. The CapeMail service allows you to retrieve Google results by sending an e-mail to google@capeclear.com with the search string. Then it returns the search results to you in an e-mail. Suppose for example that you submitted the e-mail shown in Figure 2-22 with the search criteria "Denise Gosnell google".

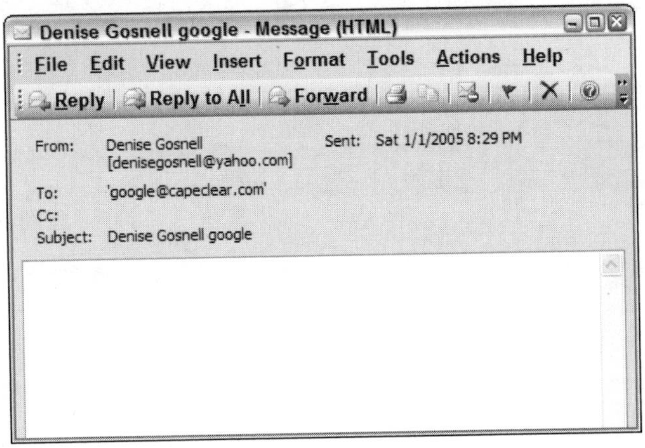

Figure 2-22

Within a short period of time after sending the e-mail, you will receive a response from the CapeMail service with the top ten results from Google that match the specified search criteria. An example of these results is shown in Figure 2-23.

At the time of this book's writing, another individual created a query Google by e-mail service similar to CapeMail and made the code available for download at `http://www.ohardt.com/mail2google/`.

Another example of a third-party utility that uses the Google API is Touch Graph (`http://www.touchgraph.com/TGGoogleBrowser.html`). This tool allows you to enter a domain, and it graphically charts all the pages related to the page you enter. An example of the pages that are related to microsoft.com is shown in Figure 2-24.

Another graphing tool that uses the Google SOAP API to build a visual Graph of page-relations can be found at `http://traumwind.de/soap/`.

Banana Slug is a search engine that uses the Google API and can be found at `http://www.bananaslug.com/`. This search engine tool runs a Google search with an additional random word to give you different results than you would otherwise get. If the 1,000 query maximum number of calls to the Google API is hit for the day, the tool just redirects you to Google.com and adds the random word in the search box. An example search on the site for *google api* is shown in Figure 2-25. Notice how the word *concert* was randomly added to the search and the results and that the results vary from what you would have gotten without the word *concert*.

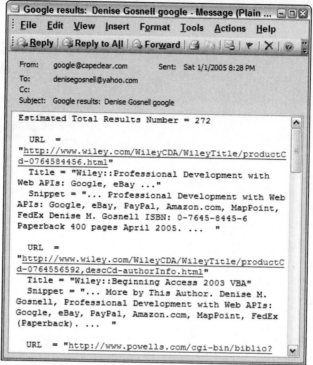

Figure 2-23

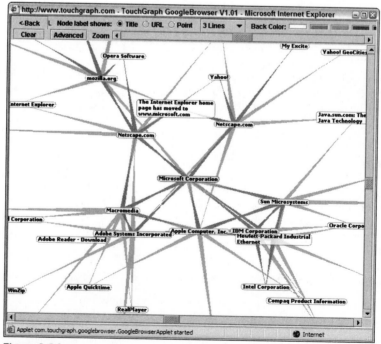

Figure 2-24

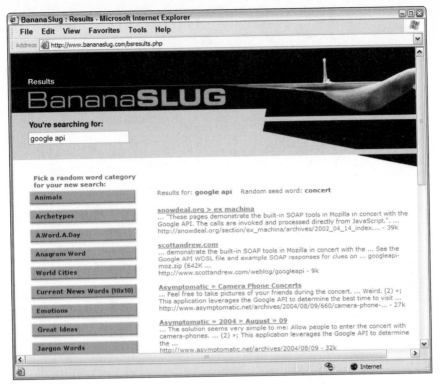

Figure 2-25

You have no doubt heard of blogs (or Web logs). One company has created a command-line tool that runs a query using the Google API and spits out an RSS feed with the top ten hits. This tool can be found at `http://www.razorsoft.net/weblog/stories/2002/04/13/google2rss.html`.

Googlematic is a tool that uses the Google API to let you search Google from MSN Messenger or AOL Messenger. This tool can be downloaded from `http://interconnected.org/googlematic/`. These are just some of the many ways that third parties are using the Google API.

Summary

In this chapter, you looked at the popular Google search engine and how to make use of the Google API in your own programs. You now have enough information to be dangerous in using Google in your own applications. For more information about using the Google API, please consult the later chapters of this book that illustrate using Web APIs from Microsoft Office, from mobile devices, and in the comprehensive case studies.

At this point, you are ready to turn your attention to Chapter 3 where you will explore the Microsoft MapPoint Web API.

Using the MapPoint API

If you have ever used a Microsoft mapping feature — such as Microsoft MapPoint, Microsoft Streets & Trips, or MSN Maps — you may have been using the MapPoint database perhaps without realizing it. Microsoft has made several of these location and mapping services available in a MapPoint API for use in your own applications. You can obtain a free trial account to use the MapPoint API; after the trial period, you pay a licensing fee. This chapter covers the following:

❑ An introduction to MapPoint as a location and mapping database

❑ How to obtain a trial version account to use the MapPoint API

❑ The syntax of MapPoint API queries

❑ How to call the MapPoint API from Visual Studio .NET

❑ How to call the MapPoint API from the .NET Framework

❑ Five detailed examples of how to use the MapPoint API

❑ Additional ideas for how you might use the MapPoint API

The MapPoint API is very comprehensive, and I could take an entire book to cover it in detail. This chapter provides you an overview of how to get up and running with the API and some examples to get you started. It then points you to more information in the detailed help documents for the MapPoint API.

MapPoint 101

MapPoint is used in various ways in the Microsoft product line. Microsoft has a software package called MapPoint that you can purchase. Microsoft also has other location services, such as Microsoft Streets and Trips and MSN Search. All these services use the same core MapPoint database for their information. An example of a Web page from MSN Search that uses MapPoint is shown in Figure 3-1.

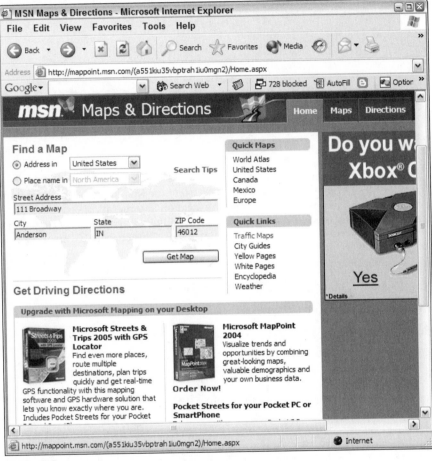

Figure 3-1

When you enter an address and click the Get Map button on Figure 3-1, you can retrieve a map of the specified location from the MapPoint database. An example of this is illustrated on Figure 3-2.

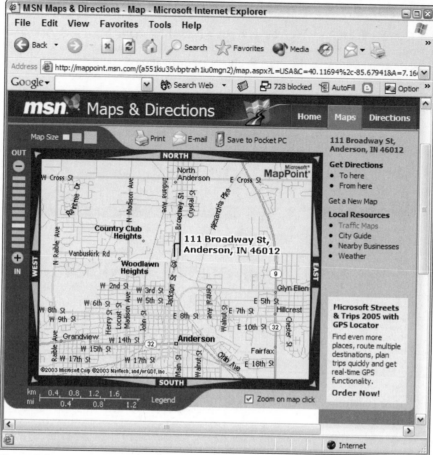

Figure 3-2

Let's now take a look at using the MapPoint API to build its features into your own custom applications.

Introduction to the MapPoint API

The MapPoint API is implemented as an XML Web service that can be called using the SOAP protocol. In this section, you look at the features supported by the MapPoint API, licensing options, as well as setting up an evaluation account.

MapPoint supports various features such as finding addresses, finding non-addressable places, reverse geocoding, address parsing, finding nearby places, custom locations, routing, map rendering, and Points of Interest (POI). These features are described in detail throughout this book.

Signing Up for an Evaluation Account

As with most Microsoft products, you have to pay a license fee to use MapPoint. Also like most Microsoft products, a free trial period is available. For details on licensing terms, contact Microsoft directly. Now let's walk through the steps to obtain an evaluation account.

First, you should visit the main MapPoint Web service site, which is currently located at `http://www.microsoft.com/mappoint/webservice/default.mspx`. This page is shown in Figure 3-3.

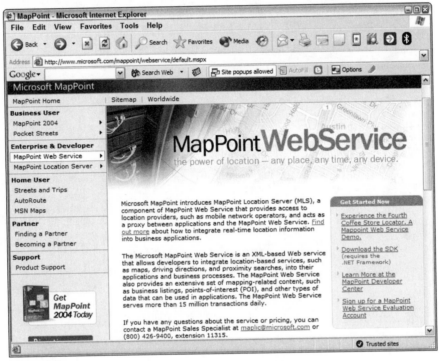

Figure 3-3

From this page, you can select the link to sign up for a MapPoint Web Service Evaluation Account, which redirects you to a signup page (such as `https://s.microsoft.com/mappoint/enterprise/webservice/seval.aspx`). An example of the signup page is shown in Figure 3-4.

After completing the signup process online, you receive a detailed e-mail within approximately two business days. The e-mail contains various IDs that you need to complete the setup of your account. The e-mail also contains detailed instructions on what to do to use the evaluation account. Look at them again here.

You must activate your account on the Microsoft extranet portal site before you can use the MapPoint API. To activate your account, go to `https://www.partners.extranet.microsoft.com/`. A screen similar to Figure 3-5 is displayed explaining installation of Microsoft root certificates.

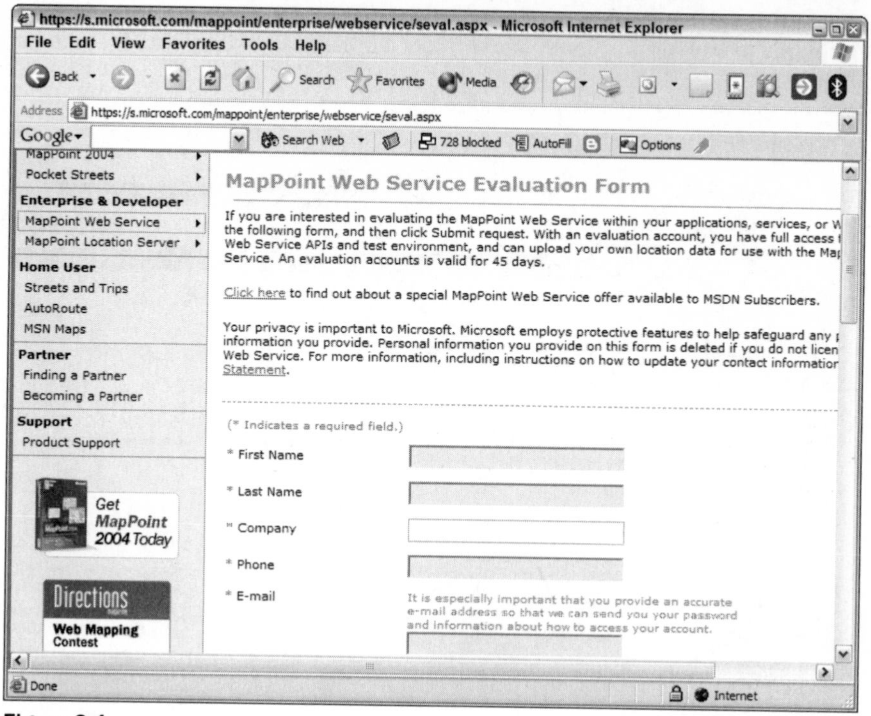

Figure 3-4

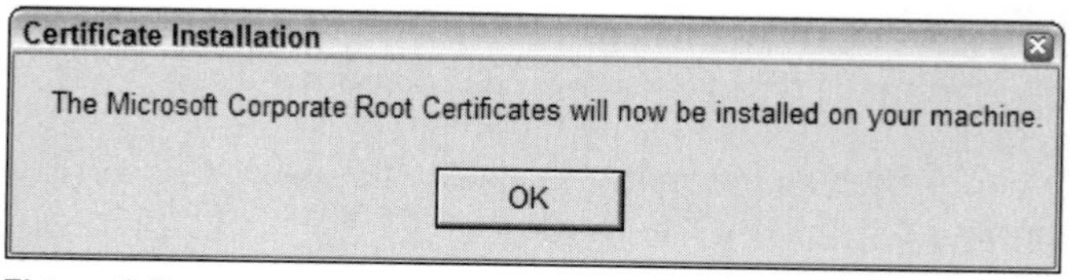

Figure 3-5

After clicking OK, you see a screen similar to the one shown in Figure 3-6.

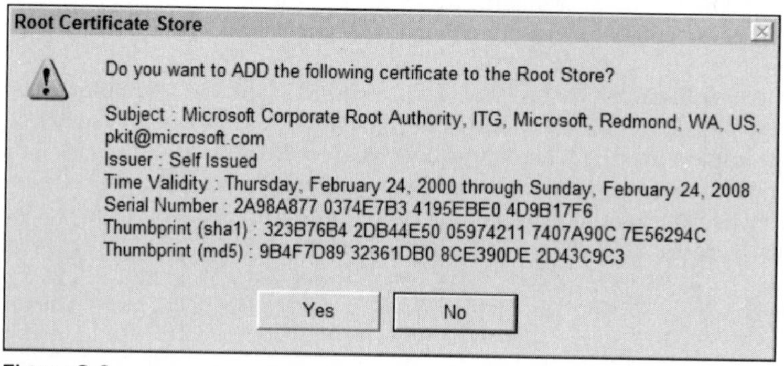

Figure 3-6

Select the Yes option on the one or more Root Certificate Store messages that appear. A screen with Partners Account Credentials displayed under Select Authentication Credentials should appear, as shown in Figure 3-7.

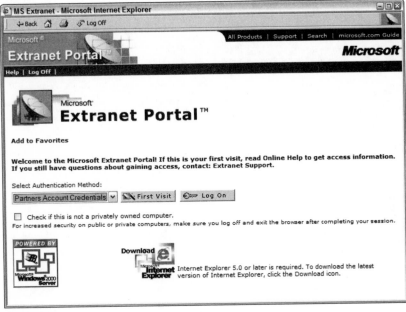

Figure 3-7

Click the First Visit button, and a screen as shown in Figure 3-8 is displayed.

After reviewing the information on the Welcome screen, click Next. A screen like the one shown in Figure 3-9 is then displayed.

Fill in the fields for log-on name, user access key, password, and password verification. The log-on name and access key are contained in the introductory e-mail mentioned previously.

After filling in the required information, click Submit. You are then prompted to type your name and accept the terms of the license agreement. After you click the Submit button, a success message is displayed to let you know your extranet portal account was set up correctly.

Before you can access the MapPoint API, you also need to access the MapPoint Web Service Customer Services site. Navigate to https://mappoint-css.partners.extranet.microsoft.com/cscV3/. Here, you are prompted to enter a username and password. Specify partners\username, with the username taken from the introductory e-mail message you received. For the password, type the password you just created during the extranet portal account setup process. After you successfully log in to the site, a screen similar to that shown in Figure 3-10 is displayed.

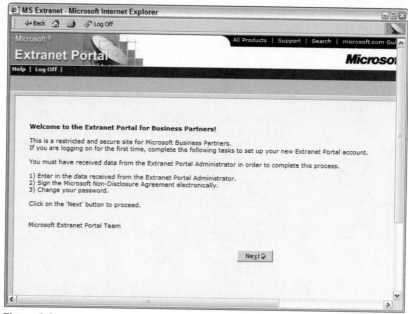

Figure 3-8

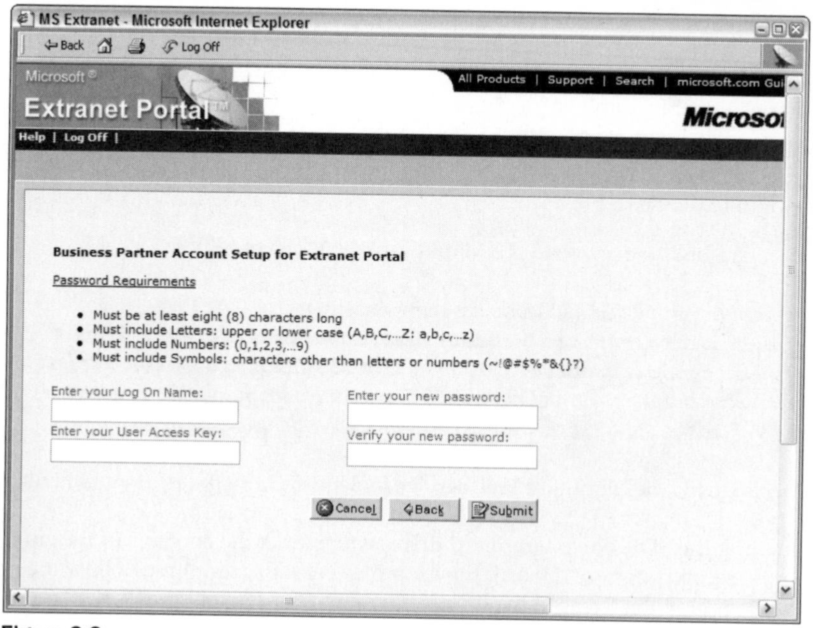

Figure 3-9

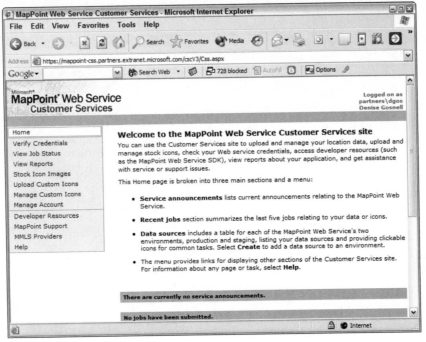

Figure 3-10

This site allows you to view and manage your MapPoint account. You can also view the online documentation, retrieve the SDK, and so on.

To obtain the MapPoint SDK, select the Developer Resources link. A screen similar to Figure 3-11 is then displayed.

Click the download link to download the MapPoint Web services SDK.

> *If the download hyperlink does not work, try going directly to*
> **http://msdn.microsoft.com/webservices/downloads/default.aspx** *or*
> **http://go.microsoft.com/fwlink/?linkid=23505&clcid=0x409**. *The link from the MapPoint Customer Service site did not work for me because Microsoft was in the process of reorganizing several Web pages. As a last resort, you can search the Microsoft site for the SDK.*

The download page for the MapPoint Web service looks similar to that shown in Figure 3-12.

After downloading the SDK file to your hard drive, you extract the contents of the zip file to a directory. You then run the setup program to install the examples on your computer. Follow the prompts on the setup program to accept the terms of the license agreement and install the SDK.

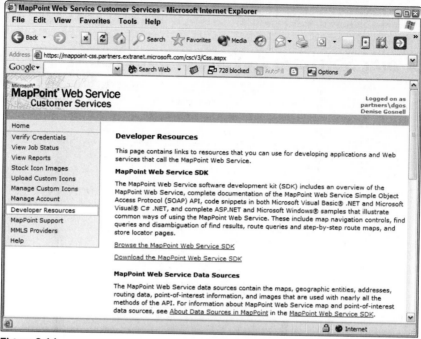

Figure 3-11

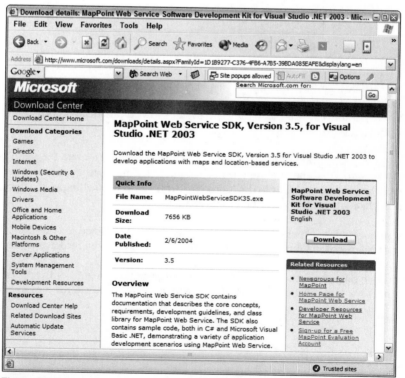

Figure 3-12

In the next section, you learn a few tips that will help you get the most value out of the SDK. For instance, it shows you how to make the SDK examples work without major hassles.

The MapPoint Software Developer's Kit (SDK)

The SDK gets installed on your hard drive at the location you specified in the setup program. If you open Visual Studio .NET, you can view the MapPoint SDK help documentation. Select Help ⇨ Contents. A screen similar to the one shown in Figure 3-13 is displayed.

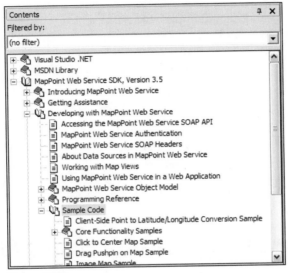

Figure 3-13

In order to get the code samples included in the SDK to work, you must make some modifications to the code. The modifications depend on what code sample you are working with. You can see in Figure 3-13 where to find the Sample Code topic in the Help system so you can locate information about the particular code sample of interest.

A common error message you might receive when you try to run a program for communicating with the MapPoint API tells you that the operation is not authorized. This typically means that you did not specify a valid set of credentials to log into the MapPoint API. The error dealing with improper credentials is explained in the Executing Query section of this chapter.

Another common problem occurs if the API methods are not recognized in your project. You have to refresh the Web reference in your project in order for the methods to be recognized on your machine.

Also, if the sample project you want to open is a Web project, you must copy the project to your inetput\ wwwroot\ directory. You must exactly match the path indicated by the error message in order for the

project to work. To avoid guessing, consult the online help documentation for the sample project to see exactly which modifications you must make.

Figure 3-14 shows an example of a help topic that illustrates how to modify a particular code sample so that it runs on your machine.

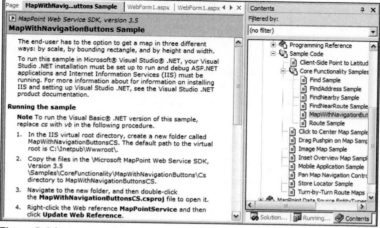

Figure 3-14

For additional developer resources not contained in the SDK, go to the main Microsoft's MapPoint Web site, which is currently located at http://www.msdn.microsoft.com/mappoint/.

Anatomy of a MapPoint API Query

In this section, you explore how a MapPoint API query is structured and learn the basics of how to execute the query and work with the results.

Available Services

The MapPoint API has four key services that you can use in your applications: FindService, RenderService, RouteService, and CommonService.

The Help documentation for the MapPoint API SDK has a complete object model of all the properties and methods available for each service, as well as code samples. To view the object model, navigate to the MapPoint Web Service Object Model node in the Help documentation as illustrated in Figure 3-15.

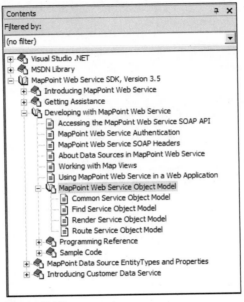

Figure 3-15

Let's now look briefly at each of the methods available for these services because these methods execute the queries against the MapPoint API.

FindServiceSoap Service

The FindServiceSoap service has several methods that deal with finding addresses and related information, as described briefly in the sections that follow.

Find Method

This method can be used to locate places based on the Find options included in the specification.

```
Find(specification As FindSpecification) As FindResults
```

FindAddress Method

This method can be used to find a list of addresses that match the specified address.

```
FindAddress(specification As FindAddressSpecification) As FindResults
```

FindById Method

This method can be used to find points of interest for a given entity.

```
FindByID(specification As FindByIDSpecification) As FindResults
```

FindByProperty Method

This method can be used to find points of interest based on various properties.

```
FindByProperty(specification As FindByPropertySpecification) As FindResults
```

FindNearby Method

This method can be used to find a list of points of interest within a circle of a particular latitude and longitude radius. In other words, this method finds points of interest near to the geocode address you specify.

```
FindNearby(specification As FindNearbySpecification) As FindResults
```

FindNearRoute Method

This method can be used to find points of interest that are within a specified distance from a particular route.

```
FindNearRoute(specification As FindNearRouteSpecification) As FindResults
```

GetLocationInfo Method

This method can be used to find nearest addresses and companies to a given latitude and longitude location.

```
GetLocationInfo(location As LatLong, dataSourceName As string, options As
GetInfoOptions) As ArrayOfLocation
```

ParseAddress Method

This method can be used to parse an address into its components.

```
ParseAddress(inputAddress As string, countryRegion As string) As Address
```

RenderServiceSoap Service

The `RenderServiceSoap` service is used to work with maps and has several methods, as described briefly in the sections that follow.

ConvertToLatLong Method

This method converts pixel coordinates of a specified map to latitude and longitude coordinates.

```
ConvertToLatLong (pixels As PixelCoord(), view As MapView, width As Integer, height
As Integer) As LatLong()ConvertToPoint
```

ConvertToPoint Method

This method converts latitude and longitude coordinates to pixel coordinates on a specified map.

```
ConvertToPoint (latLong As LatLong(),view As MapView, width As Integer, height As
Integer ) As PixelCoord()
```

GetBestMapView Method

This method creates a MapView for the specified location.

```
GetBestMapView(locations As ArrayOfLocation, dataSourceName As string) As
MapViewRepresentations
```

GetMap Method

This method returns map images of the specified MapViews.

```
GetMap(specification As MapSpecification) As ArrayOfMapImage
```

RouteServiceSoap Service

The RouteServiceSoap service has two methods used for obtaining point-to-point directions, as described briefly in the sections that follow.

CalculateRoute Method

This method calculates a route based on a particular route specification.

```
CalculateRoute(specification As RouteSpecification) As Route
```

CalculateSimpleRoute Method

This method calculates a simple route based on a series of coordinates and a specified segment preference.

```
CalculateSimpleRoute(latLongs As ArrayOfLatLong, dataSourceName As string,
preference As SegmentPreference) As Route
```

CommonServiceSoap Service

The CommonServiceSoap service has several methods, which are described briefly in the sections that follow. The CommonServiceSoap service can be used to look up details that you might use for working with the other MapPoint API methods, such as a list of data sources that can be used in your queries. Much of the information provided by the CommonServiceSoap is also described under various topics in the Help documentation, so you need not use these methods if all you want to do is view the data values already displayed in the Help document.

GetCountryRegionInfo Method

This method retrieves information about countries or national regions.

```
GetCountryRegionInfo(entityIDs As ArrayOfInt) As ArrayOfCountryRegionInfo
```

GetDataSourceInfo Method

This method retrieves a general description of the data sources you can use in your MapPoint API queries.

```
GetDataSourceInfo(dataSourceNames As ArrayOfString) As ArrayOfDataSource
```

GetEntityTypes Method

This method retrieves a list of types that can be used in your MapPoint API queries.

```
GetEntityTypes(dataSourceName As string) As ArrayOfEntityType
```

GetGreatCircleDistances Method

This method calculates pair-wise distances.

```
GetGreatCircleDistances(latLongs As ArrayOfLatLong) As ArrayOfDouble
```

GerVersionInfoMethod

This method retrieves the version of the MapPoint Web service.

```
GetVersionInfo() As ArrayOfVersionInfo
```

Using the Test Environment versus Production

MapPoint has a test environment and a production environment. In your projects that use the MapPoint API, you must add a Web reference to the location of the WSDL file for the respective environment you want to use. As you should recall from Chapter 1, the WSDL file of a Web service explains the features that are available in the service.

You can find the staging (or test) environment WSDL file for version 3 of the API at this location:

```
http://staging.mappoint.net/standard-30/mappoint.wsdl
```

You can find the production WSDL file for version 3 of the API at this address:

```
http://service.mappoint.net/standard-30/mappoint.wsdl
```

All the examples in this chapter use the test environment. These concepts are illustrated in more detail in following sections.

Executing a MapPoint Query

In this section, I walk through a simple example of how to execute a MapPoint query. As you can see in the example, you must specify your customer ID and password before you can communicate with the MapPoint API.

> In the information e-mail, the customer ID and password values are called **web service (soap) account id** and **web service (soap) password**.

You have multiple ways to specify your credentials. The first is to specify the credentials one time in a config file, such as a Web configuration file or appsettings configuration file. Doing so applies them to

the entire application. The second option is to include lines of code each time you use any of the FindService, RenderService, RouteService, or CommonService services. I decided to explicitly include lines of code for each instance in this chapter to make the examples less dependent on other files. However, if you want to learn how to modify a configuration file, consult the code samples that are included in the SDK and described in the Help documentation.

> *A common error message that you see when credentials are not specified correctly tells you that the operation was not authorized. For a knowledge-based article on troubleshooting this error, see* **http:// support.microsoft.com/default.aspx?scid=kb;en-us;814307**. *This error has other causes, as well, but the most common cause is improper credentials.*

Let's turn now to an example that illustrates how to execute a MapPoint query using Visual Studio.NET.

Executing a MapPoint Query Using Visual Studio .NET

You now create a new Windows application using Visual Studio .NET that calls the MapPoint API.

1. Open Visual Studio .NET and select File ➪ New ➪ Project.

2. Select Visual Basic Project as the Project Type and Windows Application as the Template. For the project name, specify `MapPointSearch`, or another suitable name; for the path specify the location where you want the project to be created. Click OK to create the new project.

3. Add a reference to the MapPoint API in the staging environment by selecting Project ➪ Add Web Reference. For the URL field, specify `http://staging.mappoint.net/standard-30/ mappoint.wsdl`.

4. Click the GO button to make Visual Studio locate the MapPoint service.

5. Change the Web Reference Name to `MapPoint` so that you can use a shorter name in your project. A screen similar to that shown in Figure 3-16 should be displayed.

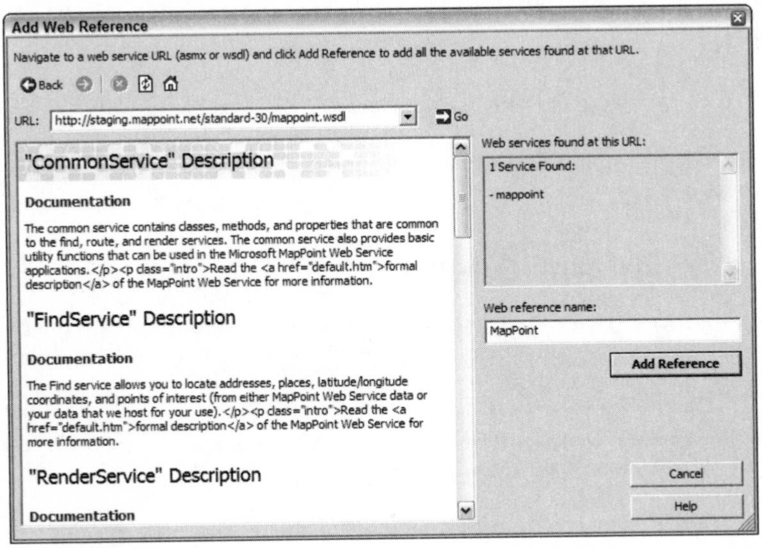

Figure 3-16

6. Click the Add Reference button to add the reference to your project. Visual Studio .NET uses the WSDL file to identify the methods that you can use to execute your project.

7. Use the toolbox to drag and drop three labels, two text boxes, and one button control on the form. Change the Name property of the first text box to `txtAddress`, rename the Name property of the second text box `txtCity`, rename the Name property of the label `lblCompleteAddress`, and change the Name property of the button to `btnGetAddress`. Modify the Text properties of each control as shown in Figure 3-17.

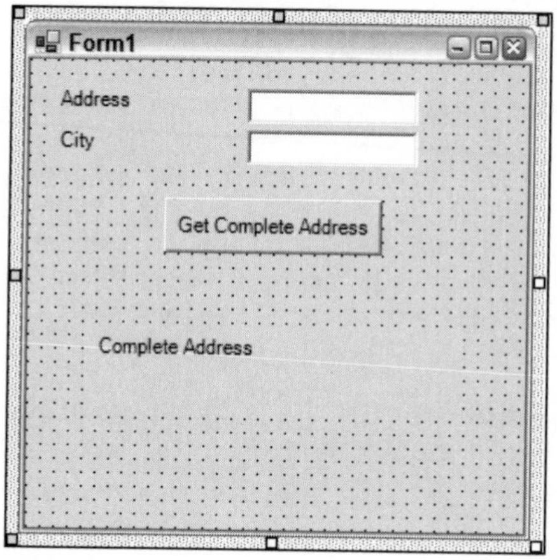

Figure 3-17

8. Add the following imports statement to the top of the `Form1` code section of your project, prior to all other code:

```
Imports MapPointSearch.MapPoint
```

9. Add the following procedure to `Form1`:

```
Private Sub btnGetAddress_Click(ByVal sender As System.Object, ByVal e As _
    System.EventArgs) Handles btnGetAddress.Click

        'Purpose: Use the Find method of the FindServiceSoap service to
        'look up a complete address from a partial address provided

        'NOTE: Make sure to include imports statement for MapPoint
        'Web service for abbreviated declarations below to work

        'Specify the credentials for the find service
        'Use the customer id and password you were provided
        Dim findService As New FindServiceSoap
        findService.Credentials = _
            New System.Net.NetworkCredential("YOUR CUSTOMER ID", _
            "YOUR PASSWORD")
        findService.PreAuthenticate = True

        'populate the address with the values on the form
        Dim myAddress As New Address
```

```
        myAddress.AddressLine = txtAddress.Text
        myAddress.PrimaryCity = txtCity.Text

        'declare the FindAddressSpecification details
        Dim findAddressSpec As New FindAddressSpecification
        findAddressSpec.InputAddress = myAddress
        'specify which MapPoint data source to use
        'consult the on-line documentation for a complete list
        findAddressSpec.DataSourceName = "MapPoint.NA"

        'call the FindAddress method
        Dim foundAddressResults As FindResults
        foundAddressResults = findService.FindAddress(findAddressSpec)

        'display the result of the FindAddress method
        If (foundAddressResults.NumberFound = 1) Then
            lblCompleteAddress.Text = _
                foundAddressResults.Results(0).FoundLocation.Entity.DisplayName
        ElseIf (foundAddressResults.NumberFound = 0) Then
            lblCompleteAddress.Text = "Zero results were returned."
        Else
            lblCompleteAddress.Text = "Multiple results were returned."
        End If

End Sub
```

10. Input your customer ID and password on the appropriate lines of code. As I mentioned previously, these values are provided in the information e-mail you receive when you set up your account. In the e-mail, these values are called web service (soap) account id and web service (soap) password.

11. Select File ⇨ Save All to save all changes to the project.

12. Select Debug ⇨ Start (or press F5) to run the project.

13. Type an address and city in the text boxes on the form.

14. You should see a window similar to Figure 3-18 that displays the complete address retrieved using the MapPoint API. If no address was returned, the address and city you used may be located in more than one state.

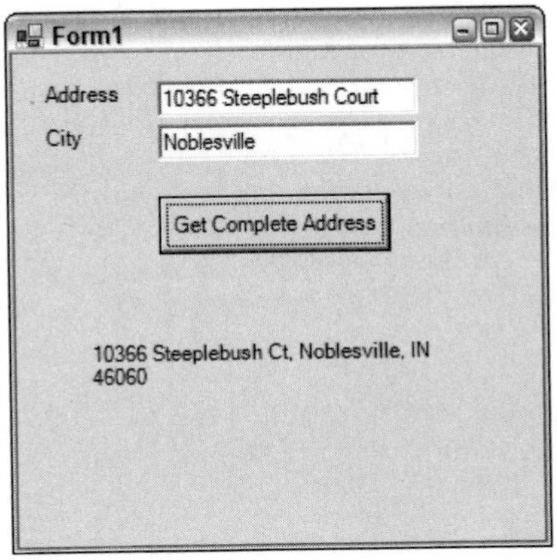

Figure 3-18

The essence of this example is included in the `btnGetAddress_Click` procedure, so let's see how it works.

First, you declared a new `FindServiceSoap` service and then specified your MapPoint login credentials.

```
'Specify the credentials for the find service
'Use the customer id and password you were provided
Dim findService As New FindServiceSoap
findService.Credentials = _
    New System.Net.NetworkCredential("YOUR CUSTOMER ID", _
    "YOUR PASSWORD")
findService.PreAuthenticate = True
```

Next, you populated the address variable with the values from the text boxes on the form.

```
'populate the address with the values on the form
Dim myAddress As New Address
myAddress.AddressLine = txtAddress.Text
myAddress.PrimaryCity = txtCity.Text
```

Next, you set up the details of the address and where to look for the address.

```
'declare the FindAddressSpecification details
Dim findAddressSpec As New FindAddressSpecification
findAddressSpec.InputAddress = myAddress
'specify which MapPoint data source to use
'consult the on-line documentation for a complete list
findAddressSpec.DataSourceName = "MapPoint.NA"
```

The next line of code then calls the `FindAddress` method to get the complete address of the location specified on the form.

```
'call the FindAddress method
Dim foundAddressResults As FindResults
foundAddressResults = findService.FindAddress(findAddressSpec)
```

The results of the address lookup are then displayed on the form.

```
'display the result of the FindAddress method
If (foundAddressResults.NumberFound = 1) Then
    lblCompleteAddress.Text = _
        foundAddressResults.Results(0).FoundLocation.Entity.DisplayName
ElseIf (foundAddressResults.NumberFound = 0) Then
    lblCompleteAddress.Text = "Zero results were returned."
Else
    lblCompleteAddress.Text = "Multiple results were returned."
End If

End Sub
```

Now that you know how to call the MapPoint API using Visual Studio .NET, you learn how to generate this exact same example using just the .NET Framework.

Executing a MapPoint Query Using the .NET Framework

In this section, you execute the same MapPoint query using the .NET Framework directly without using Visual Studio .NET.

1. Add the following code to a new file called `MapPointSearch.vb` (using Notepad or another text editor).

```
Imports System
Imports MapPointSearch.MapPoint

Public Class Form1
    Inherits System.Windows.Forms.Form

    Public Sub New()
        MyBase.New()

        'This call is required by the Windows Form Designer.
        InitializeComponent()

        'Add any initialization after the InitializeComponent() call

    End Sub

    'Form overrides dispose to clean up the component list.
    Protected Overloads Overrides Sub Dispose(ByVal disposing As Boolean)
        If disposing Then
            If Not (components Is Nothing) Then
                components.Dispose()
            End If
        End If
        MyBase.Dispose(disposing)
    End Sub

    'Required by the Windows Form Designer
    Private components As System.ComponentModel.IContainer

    'NOTE: The following procedure is required by the Windows Form Designer
    'It can be modified using the Windows Form Designer.
    'Do not modify it using the code editor.
    Friend WithEvents btnGetAddress As System.Windows.Forms.Button
    Friend WithEvents Label1 As System.Windows.Forms.Label
    Friend WithEvents Label2 As System.Windows.Forms.Label
    Friend WithEvents txtAddress As System.Windows.Forms.TextBox
    Friend WithEvents txtCity As System.Windows.Forms.TextBox
    Friend WithEvents lblCompleteAddress As System.Windows.Forms.Label
    <System.Diagnostics.DebuggerStepThrough()> Private Sub InitializeComponent()
        Me.btnGetAddress = New System.Windows.Forms.Button
        Me.txtAddress = New System.Windows.Forms.TextBox
        Me.txtCity = New System.Windows.Forms.TextBox
        Me.Label1 = New System.Windows.Forms.Label
        Me.Label2 = New System.Windows.Forms.Label
        Me.lblCompleteAddress = New System.Windows.Forms.Label
        Me.SuspendLayout()
        '
        'btnGetAddress
```

```
'
Me.btnGetAddress.Location = New System.Drawing.Point(80, 80)
Me.btnGetAddress.Name = "btnGetAddress"
Me.btnGetAddress.Size = New System.Drawing.Size(128, 32)
Me.btnGetAddress.TabIndex = 0
Me.btnGetAddress.Text = "Get Complete Address"
'
'txtAddress
'
Me.txtAddress.Location = New System.Drawing.Point(80, 16)
Me.txtAddress.Name = "txtAddress"
Me.txtAddress.Size = New System.Drawing.Size(144, 20)
Me.txtAddress.TabIndex = 1
Me.txtAddress.Text = ""
'
'txtCity
'
Me.txtCity.Location = New System.Drawing.Point(80, 40)
Me.txtCity.Name = "txtCity"
Me.txtCity.Size = New System.Drawing.Size(144, 20)
Me.txtCity.TabIndex = 2
Me.txtCity.Text = ""
'
'Label1
'
Me.Label1.Location = New System.Drawing.Point(16, 16)
Me.Label1.Name = "Label1"
Me.Label1.Size = New System.Drawing.Size(48, 23)
Me.Label1.TabIndex = 3
Me.Label1.Text = "Address"
'
'Label2
'
Me.Label2.Location = New System.Drawing.Point(16, 40)
Me.Label2.Name = "Label2"
Me.Label2.Size = New System.Drawing.Size(48, 23)
Me.Label2.TabIndex = 4
Me.Label2.Text = "City"
'
'lblCompleteAddress
'
Me.lblCompleteAddress.Location = New System.Drawing.Point(40, 160)
Me.lblCompleteAddress.Name = "lblCompleteAddress"
Me.lblCompleteAddress.Size = New System.Drawing.Size(216, 80)
Me.lblCompleteAddress.TabIndex = 5
Me.lblCompleteAddress.Text = "Complete Address"
'
'Form1
'
Me.AutoScaleBaseSize = New System.Drawing.Size(5, 13)
Me.ClientSize = New System.Drawing.Size(292, 273)
Me.Controls.Add(Me.lblCompleteAddress)
Me.Controls.Add(Me.Label2)
Me.Controls.Add(Me.Label1)
Me.Controls.Add(Me.txtCity)
```

```
            Me.Controls.Add(Me.txtAddress)
            Me.Controls.Add(Me.btnGetAddress)
            Me.Name = "Form1"
            Me.Text = "Form1"
            Me.ResumeLayout(False)

    End Sub


Private Sub btnGetAddress_Click(ByVal sender As System.Object, ByVal e As _
        System.EventArgs) Handles btnGetAddress.Click

        'Purpose: Use the Find method of the FindServiceSoap service to
        'look up a complete address from a partial address provided

        'NOTE: Make sure to include imports statement for MapPoint
        'Web service for abbreviated declarations below to work

        'Specify the credentials for the find service
        'Use the customer id and password you were provided
        Dim findService As New FindServiceSoap
        findService.Credentials = _
            New System.Net.NetworkCredential("YOUR CUSTOMER ID", _
            "YOUR PASSWORD")
        findService.PreAuthenticate = True

        'populate the address with the values on the form
        Dim myAddress As New Address
        myAddress.AddressLine = txtAddress.Text
        myAddress.PrimaryCity = txtCity.Text

        'declare the FindAddressSpecification details
        Dim findAddressSpec As New FindAddressSpecification
        findAddressSpec.InputAddress = myAddress
        'specify which MapPoint data source to use
        'consult the on-line documentation for a complete list
        findAddressSpec.DataSourceName = "MapPoint.NA"

        'call the FindAddress method
        Dim foundAddressResults As FindResults
        foundAddressResults = findService.FindAddress(findAddressSpec)

        'display the result of the FindAddress method
        If (foundAddressResults.NumberFound = 1) Then
            lblCompleteAddress.Text = _
                foundAddressResults.Results(0).FoundLocation.Entity.DisplayName
        ElseIf (foundAddressResults.NumberFound = 0) Then
            lblCompleteAddress.Text = "Zero results were returned."
        Else
            lblCompleteAddress.Text = "Multiple results were returned."
        End If

    End Sub
End Class
```

In addition to the click event that calls the MapPoint Web service, this code also contains the graphical user interface code, which was created automatically for you in the prior example. Because the .NET Framework does not have a graphical user interface to enable you to design forms, you have to specify any graphical elements in the code. Often, this can be quite difficult. The previous code also includes the imports statement required to use the System library.

2. Next, you have to link the code to the MapPoint staging environment WSDL file (that is, per-form the equivalent of adding a Web reference and generating the necessary files to communi-cate with the Web service). Visual Studio .NET does this automatically. To do so manually, you must open a command window and navigate to the directory where your code is located. This step is easiest to perform if you open the command window using the Visual Studio .NET Command Prompt. Then, execute the following command.

```
wsdl.exe /l:vb http://staging.mappoint.net/standard-30/mappoint.wsdl
```

If you receive an error indicating that the WSDL.exe file could not be located, make sure Windows knows where to find the WSDL.exe file. One way is to open the Command Window from Start ➪ Programs ➪ Visual Studio.NET ➪ Visual Studio .NET Tools ➪ Visual Studio .NET Command Prompt so that the proper path settings are included automatically. Another way is to specify the com-plete path to the WSDL.exe file in the command. One example of where you might find the WSDL.exe file is C:\Program Files\Microsoft Visual Studio .NET 2003\SDK\v1.1\Bin.

3. Instead of specifying the long path to the WSDL file on the MapPoint server, you can alterna-tively copy the WSDL file to your working directory and then use a command such as this:

```
wsdl.exe /l:vb mappoint.wsdl
```

4. A new vb file is created in your directory after you run the wsdl.exe utility, which contains the SOAP proxy client information needed to call the MapPoint Web API.

5. You are now ready to compile the application using the vbc.exe compiler with the following command:

```
vbc /out:MapPointSearch.exe *.vb
```

Depending on the environment on your computer, you may also need to specify the complete path to the vbc.exe file that comes with Visual Studio .NET and the .NET Framework.

6. Run the MapPointSearch.exe program.

Although you have fewer files to work with when you use the command line tools versus the Visual Studio .NET graphical user interface, you still have to manually generate the SOAP proxy client and compile the program. The remaining examples in this chapter are implemented using Visual Studio .NET so you can see how the forms and features look.

Five Creative Ways to Use the MapPoint API

In this section, you will look at five ways to use the MapPoint API. Let's jump right in with the first example.

#1 — Obtain Driving Directions

In this example, you implement a Web feature that obtains driving directions from one address to another using the CalculateRoute method of the Route service.

1. From Visual Studio.NET, select File ⇨ New ⇨ Project and select ASP.NET Web Application as the template. Specify http://localhost/MapPointExamples1and2 or any other suitable name/location for the Location.

2. Use the toolbox to drag and drop two labels, two text boxes, and a button control onto web-form1.aspx.

3. Using the Properties Window, rename the ID property of the first text box txtStartingAddress, the ID of the second text box txtEndingAddress, and the ID of the button btnRetrieve. Rename the Text property of the labels as shown in Figure 3-19.

Figure 3-19

4. Select Project ⇨ Add Web Reference. In the URL, specify the location of the MapPoint WSDL file (http://staging.mappoint.net/standard-30/mappoint.wsdl) and click the GO button.

5. Change the Web Reference Name to MapPoint so that you can use a shorter name in your project.

6. Click the Add Reference button to add a reference to your project.

7. Add the following imports statement to the top of the webform1.aspx code segment (before the Public Class webform1 statement) so that you can refer to the MapPoint service in the project in shorthand mode.

```
Imports MapPointExamples1and2.MapPoint
```

8. Add the following Example1 procedure to the Web form, inserting your customer ID and password in two places in the appropriate lines of code:

```
Sub Example1()

    'Purpose: Obtain Driving Directions from one address to
    'another

    'NOTE: Make sure to include imports statement for MapPoint
    'Web service for abbreviated declarations below to work

    'Specify the credentials for the find service
    'Use the customer id and password you were provided
    Dim findService As New FindServiceSoap
    findService.Credentials = New _
        System.Net.NetworkCredential("YOUR CUSTOMER ID", "YOUR PASSWORD")
    findService.PreAuthenticate = True
```

```vb
Dim findSpec As New FindSpecification
findSpec.DataSourceName = "MapPoint.NA"
'specify and obtain details for the starting address
findSpec.InputPlace = txtStartingAddress.Text
Dim StartingAddress As FindResults = findService.Find(findSpec)

'specity and obtain details for the ending address
findSpec.InputPlace = txtEndingAddress.Text
Dim EndingAddress As FindResults = findService.Find(findSpec)

'specify the route segment details
Dim rteSegmentSpec(1) As SegmentSpecification
rteSegmentSpec(0) = New SegmentSpecification
rteSegmentSpec(0).Waypoint = New Waypoint
rteSegmentSpec(0).Waypoint.Name = _
StartingAddress.Results(0).FoundLocation.Entity.Name
rteSegmentSpec(0).Waypoint.Location = _
    StartingAddress.Results(0).FoundLocation
rteSegmentSpec(1) = New SegmentSpecification
rteSegmentSpec(1).Waypoint = New Waypoint
rteSegmentSpec(1).Waypoint.Name = _
    EndingAddress.Results(0).FoundLocation.Entity.Name
rteSegmentSpec(1).Waypoint.Location = _
    EndingAddress.Results(0).FoundLocation

'specify the route specification details
Dim routeSpec As New RouteSpecification
routeSpec.DataSourceName = "MapPoint.NA"
routeSpec.Segments = rteSegmentSpec

'Specify the credentials for the route service
'Use the customer id and password you were provided
Dim routeService As New RouteServiceSoap
routeService.Credentials = New _
    System.Net.NetworkCredential("YOUR CUSTOMER ID", "YOUR PASSWORD")
routeService.PreAuthenticate = True

'call the calculate route method to retrieve the route
Dim Route As Route
Route = routeService.CalculateRoute(routeSpec)

Dim intCount As Integer

'display some line feeds in the browser so the results will not
'be printed over the search controls
Response.Write("<br><br><br><br><br><br><br><br>")

'loop through the results returned to display the route returned
'in the web browser
For intCount = 0 To Route.Itinerary.Segments(0).Directions.Length - 1
    Response.Write _
        (Route.Itinerary.Segments(0).Directions(intCount).Instruction)
Next intCount

End Sub
```

9. Add the following btnRetrieve_Click event to the Web form. Note that you can double-click on the command button to have an empty procedure created automatically.

```
Private Sub btnRetrieve_Click(ByVal sender As System.Object, ByVal e As _
    System.EventArgs) Handles btnRetrieve.Click

        'Use this procedure for examples 1 and 2
        'Example 1 uses both starting and ending
        'addresses, while Example 2 uses just the
        'starting address (single address)

        If txtEndingAddress.Text <> "" Then
            'call the code to run the first example
            Example1()
        End If

End Sub
```

10. Save and run the program.

11. Type in your search command in the text box on the Web page and click the Retrieve button. You should see driving directions based on the address you entered, such as those shown in Figure 3-20.

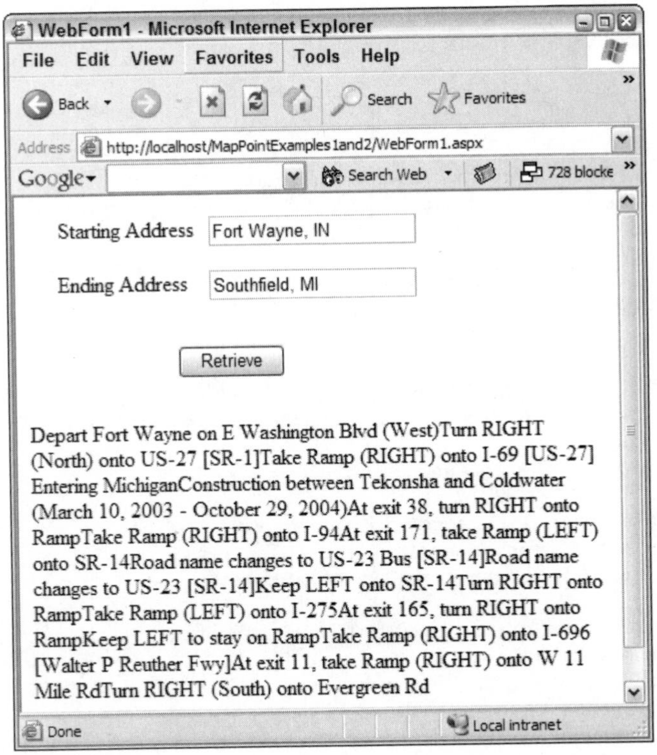

Figure 3-20

A nice modification you can make to this code on your own is to change the code in the Example1 procedure to display the directions on separate numbered lines.

#2—Retrieve a Map

In this example, you use the `GetMap` method of the Render service to obtain a map of a given area. You expand upon the project that you created in the prior example.

1. Add the following `Example2` procedure to the Web form, inserting your customer ID and password in two places in the appropriate lines of code:

```
Sub Example2()

        'Purpose: Retrieve a map for a given address

        'NOTE: Make sure to include imports statement for MapPoint
        'Web service for abbreviated declarations below to work

        'Specify the credentials for the find service
        'Use the customer id and password you were provided
        Dim findService As New FindServiceSoap
        findService.Credentials = New _
            System.Net.NetworkCredential("YOUR CUSTOMER ID", "YOUR PASSWORD")
        findService.PreAuthenticate = True

        'Get a map of a specified address
        Dim findSpec As New FindSpecification
        findSpec.DataSourceName = "MapPoint.NA"
        findSpec.InputPlace = txtStartingAddress.Text

        Dim foundResults As FindResults
        foundResults = findService.Find(findSpec)

        Dim Views(0) As ViewByHeightWidth
        Views(0) = foundResults.Results(0).FoundLocation.BestMapView.ByHeightWidth

        'Specify the credentials for the render service
        'Use the customer id and password you were provided
        Dim renderService As New RenderServiceSoap
        renderService.Credentials = New _
            System.Net.NetworkCredential("YOUR CUSTOMER ID", "YOUR PASSWORD")
        renderService.PreAuthenticate = True

        Dim mapSpec As New MapSpecification
        mapSpec.DataSourceName = "MapPoint.NA"
        mapSpec.Views = Views

        Dim mapImages() As MapImage
        mapImages = renderService.GetMap(mapSpec)

        'display the map in the web browser
        Response.Clear()
        Response.ContentType = mapImages(0).MimeData.MimeType
        Response.BinaryWrite(mapImages(0).MimeData.Bits)
        Response.End()

End Sub
```

2. Add the following code to replace the code in the `btnRetrieve_Click` event:

```
Private Sub btnRetrieve_Click(ByVal sender As System.Object, ByVal e As _
    System.EventArgs) Handles btnRetrieve.Click

        'Use this procedure for examples 1 and 2
        'Example 1 uses both starting and ending
        'addresses, while Example 2 uses just the
        'starting address (single address)

        If txtEndingAddress.Text <> "" Then
            'call the code to run the first example
            Example1()
        Else
            'call the code to run the second example
            Example2()

        End If

    End Sub
```

3. Save and run the program.

4. Enter a value for the starting address field, such as a city and a state. An example is shown in Figure 3-21.

Figure 3-21

5. Click the Retrieve button. A map of the starting address you specified should be displayed, such as the one shown in Figure 3-22.

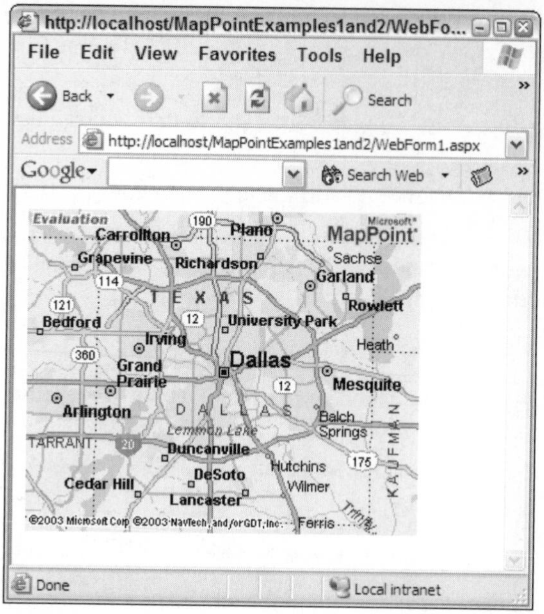

Figure 3-22

#3 — Perform a Geocode Lookup

In this example, you look up the latitude and longitude coordinates of a given address using the FindAddress method of the Find service. This project will also be used in Examples 4 and 5.

1. From Visual Studio .NET, select File ⇨ New ⇨ Project and select ASP.NET Web Application as the template. Specify http://localhost/MapPointExamples3to5 for the Location.

2. Use the toolbox to drag and drop four labels, four text boxes, and a button control onto webform1.aspx.

3. Using the Properties window, rename the ID property of the first text box txtAddress, the ID property of the second text box txtCity, the ID property of the third text box txtRegion, the ID property of the fourth text box txtPostalCode, and the ID property of the button btnRetrieve. Rename the Text property of the labels as shown in Figure 3-23.

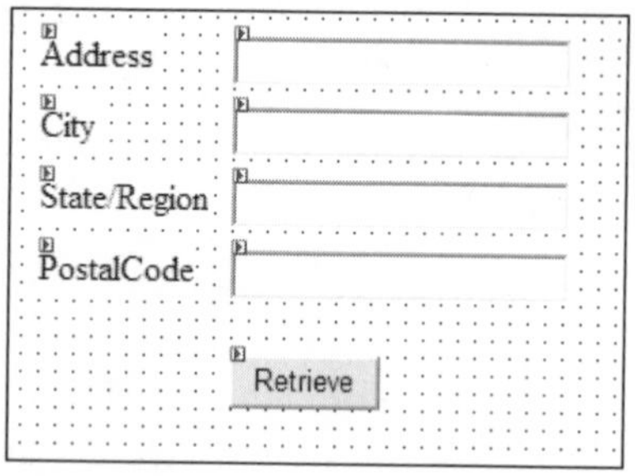

Figure 3-23

4. Select Project ⇨ Add Web Reference. In the URL, specify the location of the MapPoint WSDL file (`http://staging.mappoint.net/standard-30/mappoint.wsdl`) and click the GO button.

5. Change the Web Reference Name to `MapPoint` so that you can use a shorter name in your project.

6. Click the Add Reference button to add a reference to your project.

7. Add the following imports statement to the top of the webform1.aspx code segment (before the `Public Class webform1` statement) so that you can refer to the MapPoint service in the project in shorthand mode.

```
Imports MapPointExamples3to5.MapPoint
```

8. Add the following `Example3` procedure to the Web form, inserting your customer ID and password in the appropriate lines of code:

```
Sub Example3(ByRef dblLatitude As Double, ByRef dblLongitude As Double)

    'Purpose: perform a Geocode lookup to lookup latitude and
    'longitude based on a specified address

    'NOTE: Make sure to include imports statement for MapPoint
    'Web service for abbreviated declarations below to work

    'Specify the credentials for the find service
    'Use the customer id and password you were provided
    Dim findService As New FindServiceSoap
    findService.Credentials = New _
        System.Net.NetworkCredential("YOUR CUSTOMER ID", "YOUR PASSWORD")
    findService.PreAuthenticate = True

    'set up the Address
    Dim StartingAddress As New Address
    StartingAddress.AddressLine = txtAddress.Text
    StartingAddress.PrimaryCity = txtCity.Text
    StartingAddress.Subdivision = txtRegion.Text
    StartingAddress.PostalCode = txtPostalCode.Text

    'set up the FindAddressSpecification
    Dim findAddressSpec As New FindAddressSpecification
    findAddressSpec.InputAddress = StartingAddress
    findAddressSpec.DataSourceName = "MapPoint.NA"

    'call the FindAddress method to look up the address
    Dim foundResults As FindResults
    foundResults = findService.FindAddress(findAddressSpec)
```

```
                    'set the values for the return variables
                    If (foundResults.NumberFound = 1) Then
                        dblLatitude = foundResults.Results(0).FoundLocation.LatLong.Latitude
                        dblLongitude = foundResults.Results(0).FoundLocation.LatLong.Longitude
                    Else
                        dblLatitude = 0
                        dblLongitude = 0
                    End If

                End Sub
```

9. Add the following `btnRetrieve_Click` event to the Web form:

```
Private Sub btnRetrieve_Click(ByVal sender As System.Object, ByVal e As _
    System.EventArgs) Handles btnRetrieve.Click

        'This variable specifies which example to run
        Dim intExample As Integer
        '**Change this value to run a different example.
        intExample = 3

        If intExample = 3 Then
            '**This code section is used for Example 3
            Dim dblLatitude As Double
            Dim dblLongitude As Double
            'run example 3
            Example3(dblLatitude, dblLongitude)
            'insert line feeds so the results to not print over the controls
            Response.Write("<br><br><br><br><br><br><br><br><br><br><br><br>")
            'display the results
            Response.Write("Latitude: " & dblLatitude & "  Longitude: " & _
                    dblLongitude)
        ElseIf intExample = 4 Then
            'run example 4
            Example4()
        ElseIf intExample = 5 Then
            'run example 5
            Example5()
        End If

    End Sub
```

10. Save and run the program.

11. Type in an address in the various fields and click the Retrieve button. You should see latitude and longitude coordinates of the address you entered, similar to those shown in Figure 3-24.

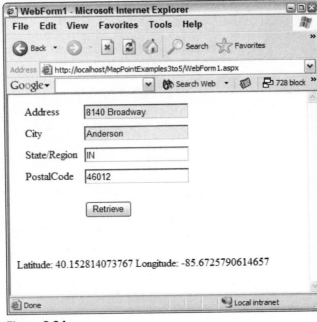

Figure 3-24

There is no particular reason why the Address and City fields in the figure are displayed in a different color than the other fields. This appears to be a bug in Internet Explorer.

#4 — Find Nearby Places

In this example, you look up restaurants that are near to a specified address using the `FindNearby` method of the Find service. You will continue to work with the Web project you created in Example 3.

1. Add the following `Example4` procedure to the Web form, inserting your customer ID and password in the appropriate lines of code:

```
Sub Example4()

    'Purpose:  Retrieve nearby restaurants to a given address

    'NOTE: Make sure to include imports statement for MapPoint
    'Web service for abbreviated declarations below to work

    'NOTE: The FindNearby method is valid only with data sources
    'that have a CanFindNearby capability

    'retrieve the latitude and longitude of the address present
    'on the web page as set up in Example 3 - to be used in
    'getting list of nearby places (which uses latitude and
    'longitude and not an address)
    Dim dblLatitude As Double
```

```
        Dim dblLongitude As Double
        Example3(dblLatitude, dblLongitude)

        'Specify the credentials for the find service
        'Use the customer id and password you were provided
        Dim findService As New FindServiceSoap
        findService.Credentials = New _
            System.Net.NetworkCredential("YOUR CUSTOMER ID", "YOUR PASSWORD")
        findService.PreAuthenticate = True

        'Output a property value (the phone number) for each
        'MapPoint.FourthCoffeeSample store nearby
        Dim findNearbySpec As New FindNearbySpecification
        findNearbySpec.DataSourceName = "NavTech.NA"
        findNearbySpec.Distance = 1
        findNearbySpec.LatLong = New LatLong
        findNearbySpec.LatLong.Latitude = dblLatitude
        findNearbySpec.LatLong.Longitude = dblLongitude

        'set filter to restaurants
        findNearbySpec.Filter = New FindFilter
        'consult the MapPoint help document for list of codes
        findNearbySpec.Filter.EntityTypeName = "SICMaj58"

        'call the FindNearby method to lookup nearby restaurants
        Dim foundResults As FindResults
        foundResults = findService.FindNearby(findNearbySpec)

        Dim findres As FindResult

        'insert line feeds so the results to not print over the controls
        Response.Write("<br><br><br><br><br><br><br><br><br><br>")

        'if no results were found, then display msg and exit
        If foundResults.NumberFound = 0 Then
            Response.Write("No results match your specified request.")
            Exit Sub
        End If

        'write the results to the web browser, including line breaks for
        'formatting
        For Each findres In foundResults.Results
            Response.Write(findres.FoundLocation.Entity.Name + "<br>")

        Response.Write _
          (findres.FoundLocation.Entity.Properties(3).Value.ToString() + _
           " " + findres.FoundLocation.Entity.Properties(4).Value.ToString() + _
           " " + findres.FoundLocation.Entity.Properties(5).Value.ToString() + _
           " " + findres.FoundLocation.Entity.Properties(6).Value.ToString())
          Response.Write("<br><br>")
        Next

    End Sub
```

2. Modify the `btnRetrieve_Click` event to change the `intExample` variable to 4.

3. Save and run the program.

4. Type in an address in the various fields and click the Retrieve button. You should see a list of restaurants in the city you specified, similar to those shown in Figure 3-25.

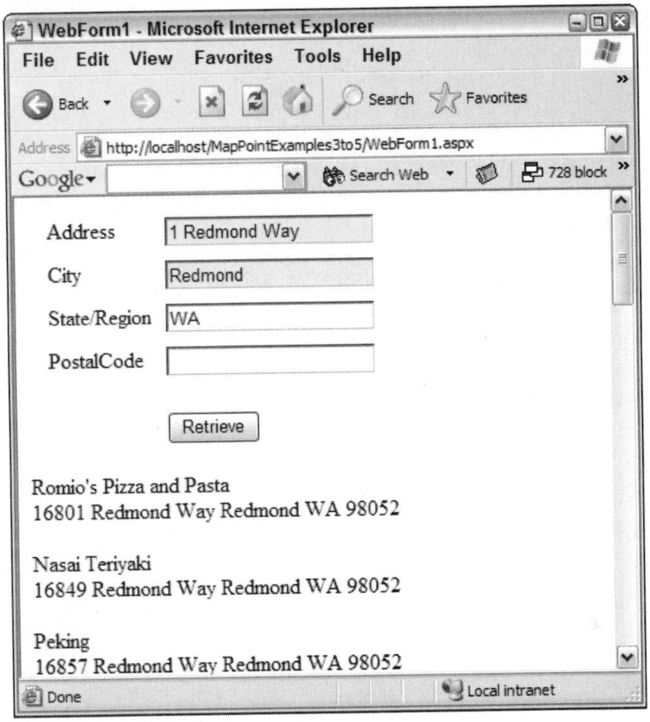

Figure 3-25

Again, the Address and City fields are not supposed to be displayed in a different color than the other fields. This appears to be a bug in Internet Explorer.

#5 — Obtain Information on Points of Interests

In this example, you look up all the Fourth Coffee Shops present in a given city. This example uses the `FindByProperty` method of the Find service and accesses the `MapPoint.FourthCoffeeSample` data source. You continue to work with the Web project you created in Example 3.

1. Add the following `Example5` procedure to the Web form, inserting your customer ID and password in the appropriate lines of code:

```
Sub Example5()

    'Purpose: Retrieves list of Fourth Coffee Shops in
    'specified US city (Uses City and State/Region fields)
    'NOTE: Make sure to include imports statement for MapPoint
    'Web service for abbreviated declarations below to work
```

```
'Specify the credentials for the find service
'Use the customer id and password you were provided
Dim findService As FindServiceSoap = New FindServiceSoap
findService.Credentials = New _
    System.Net.NetworkCredential("YOUR CUSTOMER ID", "YOUR PASSWORD")
findService.PreAuthenticate = True

Dim entityPropertyValues As EntityPropertyValue() = New _
    EntityPropertyValue(1) {}
entityPropertyValues(0) = New EntityPropertyValue
entityPropertyValues(0).Name = "PrimaryCity"
entityPropertyValues(0).Value = txtCity.Text
entityPropertyValues(1) = New EntityPropertyValue
entityPropertyValues(1).Name = "SubDivision"
entityPropertyValues(1).Value = txtRegion.Text

Dim findByPropertySpecification As FindByPropertySpecification = _
    New FindByPropertySpecification
findByPropertySpecification.DataSourceName = "MapPoint.FourthCoffeeSample"
findByPropertySpecification.Filter = New FindFilter
findByPropertySpecification.Filter.EntityTypeName = "FourthCoffeeShops"
findByPropertySpecification.Filter.WhereClause = New WhereClause
findByPropertySpecification.Filter.WhereClause.SearchProperties = _
    entityPropertyValues
findByPropertySpecification.Filter.WhereClause.SearchOperator = _
    SearchOperatorFlag.And
Dim findResults As FindResults = _
    findService.FindByProperty(findByPropertySpecification)

Dim findres As FindResult

'insert line feeds so the results to not print over the controls
Response.Write("<br><br><br><br><br><br><br><br><br><br>")

'if no results were found, then display msg and exit
If findResults.NumberFound = 0 Then
    Response.Write("No results match your specified request.")
    Exit Sub
End If

'write the results to the web browser, including line breaks for
'formatting
For Each findres In findResults.Results
    Response.Write(findres.FoundLocation.Entity.Name + "<br>")
    Response.Write _
      (findres.FoundLocation.Entity.Properties(0).Value.ToString() + _
      " " + findres.FoundLocation.Entity.Properties(1).Value.ToString() + _
      " " + findres.FoundLocation.Entity.Properties(2).Value.ToString() + _
      " " + findres.FoundLocation.Entity.Properties(3).Value.ToString())
    Response.Write("<br><br>")
Next

End Sub
```

2. Modify the `btnRetrieve_Click` event to change the `intExample` variable to 5 so that Example 5 will be executed.

3. Save and run the program.

4. Type in a city and a state/region value and click the Retrieve button. You should see a list of Fourth Coffee Stores in the city you specified, similar to that shown in Figure 3-26.

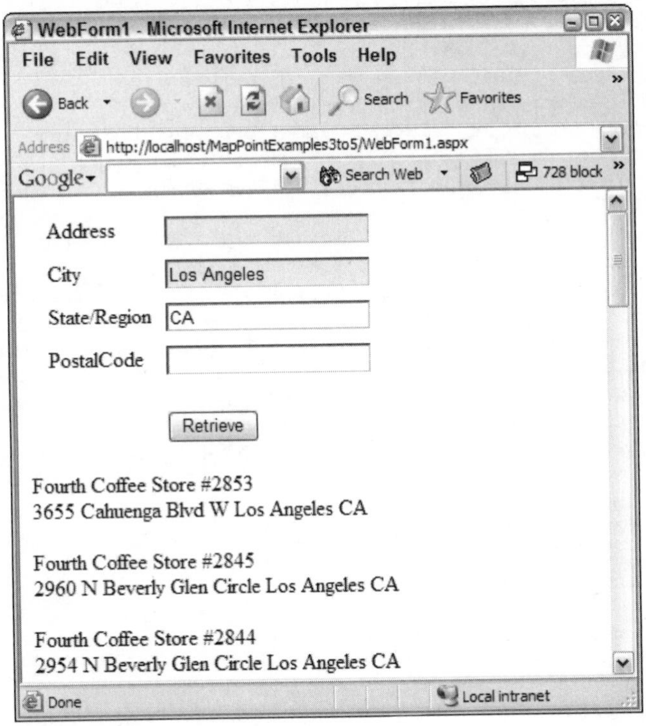

Figure 3-26

Other Ways to Use the MapPoint API

In the previous sections, you looked at five examples to give you an idea of how you can use the MapPoint API in your applications. Following are some additional examples of ways you might want to use the MapPoint API. Additional examples of the MapPoint API are also included in the later chapters and case studies at the end of this book.

Here are examples of other ways to use the MapPoint API:

❑ Create a map that allows you to zoom in and out to see different views of the map.

- ❏ Create and use custom locations that are uploaded to a custom database for use with the MapPoint Web service. For example, you might upload locations of all your facilities or of all your customers.

- ❏ Parse an address to identify which elements are Street, City, State, Zip, Country, and so on.

Third-Party MapPoint Extensions

Various third parties have discovered creative ways to use the MapPoint API in their own solutions. These companies found it cheaper to pay Microsoft the licensing fees for the service than to create their own geography services. Microsoft describes several of these solutions on its Web site at http://www.microsoft.com/net/business/msuses_mappoint.asp.

For example, Zone Labs Inc., a maker of Internet security software, uses the MapPoint API in its Zone Alarm security products. When Zone Labs' software identifies a security threat, the software collects IP addresses, port numbers, and other information identifying the threat. The software then calls the MapPoint API and displays a map showing the geographic location of the threat. More information about these products can be found at www.zonealarm.com.

Apptera has announced that it uses the MapPoint API in its voice-driven ATM/branch locator software. The Apptera Locator software allows users to say a street address, cross street, phone number, or other values to locate the nearest banking locations. More information about Apptera can be found at www.apptera.com.

Summary

In this chapter, you learned about the MapPoint database engine and how to make use of the MapPoint API in your own programs. The MapPoint API has a very robust set of features that are beyond the scope of this chapter and this book. One or more additional examples of MapPoint are included in some later chapters, such as in one or more of the chapters that illustrate using Web APIs from Microsoft Office, from mobile devices, and in the comprehensive case studies.

Let's move on to Chapter 4 where you will learn about another popular Web API from Amazon.

Using the Amazon.com APIs

You are no doubt familiar with Amazon.com as a shopping resource, and probably have purchased items from Amazon.com yourself. Amazon has made several of these shopping features available in a Web API for use in your own applications. What you may not know is that Amazon has also expanded its horizons by forming new companies, including one called Alexa Internet, Inc. Alexa offers a Web crawler that is currently the largest on the Web. Amazon has released a Web API that you can use to search Alexa. Amazon has also recently released a new Web API that allows you to create distributed queues for your applications. You can obtain a free subscriber ID that can be used with these Amazon APIs. This chapter will cover the following:

- ❑ An introduction to Amazon.com as an online shopping resource
- ❑ An introduction to Alexa Internet, Inc., an Amazon Company that provides Web crawling features
- ❑ An introduction to A9.com, Inc., an Amazon Company that provides a search engine that uses Amazon.com, Alexa technology, and Google technology
- ❑ How to obtain a subscriber ID to use the Amazon APIs (E-Commerce Service and Alexa Web Information Service)
- ❑ The syntax of Amazon API queries
- ❑ How to call the Amazon APIs using HTTP-GET (REST)
- ❑ How to call the Amazon APIs from Visual Studio .NET
- ❑ Five examples of how to use the Amazon APIs
- ❑ Additional ideas for how you might use the Amazon APIs

The Amazon APIs are very comprehensive and would take numerous chapters or perhaps an entire book to cover fully. This chapter serves as an overview that will help you get you up and running quickly with the APIs, walking you through numerous examples to get you started. You can then consult the online documentation on the Amazon.com API Web site for additional information.

Amazon 101

As you are probably already aware, Amazon.com is an online seller of books, as well as of various other merchandise. Amazon started as an online bookstore and has expanded over the years to sell various items, including acting as a virtual store front to hundreds or perhaps thousands of third-party merchants. An example of a product search on Amazon is shown in Figure 4-1.

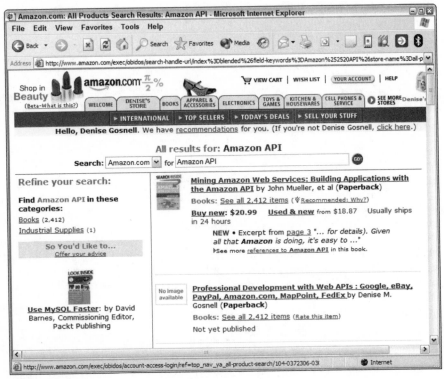

Figure 4-1

In addition to serving as an online shopping resource, Amazon has expanded its horizons to offering Web crawling and Web searching services. For example, Alexa Internet, Inc. is an Amazon.com Company that, at the time of this book's writing, is alleged to have the world's largest Web crawl with more than 100 terabytes of data from over 4 billion pages. Alexa offers various services, such as:

❑ Web searching features that use Alexa's index created from Web crawls

❑ Access to Web pages by categories and subcategories

❑ Access to Web site statistics gathered from Alexa's Web crawls

❑ Web page metadata gathered from Alexa's Web crawls

❑ Links to or from a specified URL

The main Web site for Alexa Internet, Inc. is located at http://www.alexa.com, as shown in Figure 4-2.

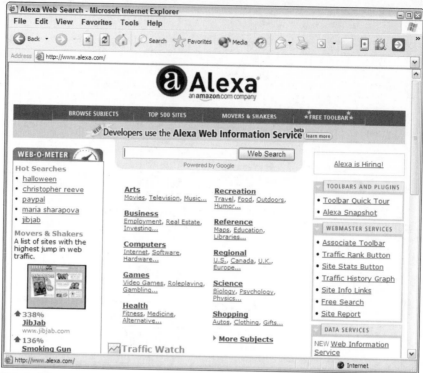

Figure 4-2

Another Amazon.com company is A9.com, Inc. A9.com offers a search engine that uses the Alexa search technology, Amazon's product catalogs, and Google, among other sources in a customizable, multicolumn results format. A9.com's main Web site is—you guessed it—`http://www.a9.com`. A9.com uses the Alexa Web service discussed later in this chapter for a portion of its results. A9.com may also use the Amazon E-Commerce Web service API and/or the Google Web service API behind the scenes, but I do not know for sure.

A9.com does not currently have its own Web API, but I'm mentioning A9.com here briefly for two reasons. First, I think A9.com is a really cool search engine that epitomizes the power of bringing together resources from multiple vendors, such as through Web services. Second, it is an Amazon Company that uses at least part of the technology discussed in the remainder of this chapter on Amazon APIs.

I definitely recommend that you spend five minutes now to check A9.com out, if you are not already familiar with it. It amazed me how, when I ran a search with my own name as shown in the example of Figure 4-3, it gathered those old photos from all over the Web and displayed them in a separate pane from the Web sites talking about me and the books I have written. I didn't have to navigate through dozens of search results to find those photos or books. Actually, some of those old photos of me are scary, so I am sorry that A9.com found them so easily!

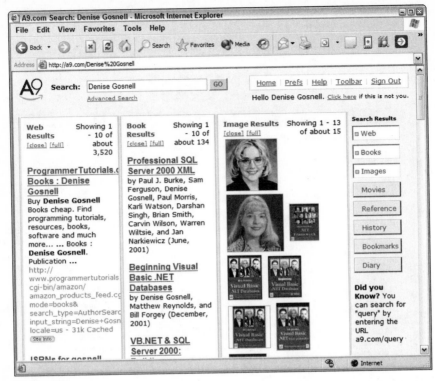

Figure 4-3

What is also cool about A9.com is that you can toggle the different panes on and off from the Search Results filter, as shown in the right portion of the screen in Figure 4-3.

Introduction to the Amazon APIs

Now that you have a basic idea of the services offered by Amazon.com and its Alexa company, it's time to learn about the Web APIs. The first Amazon Web API is called Amazon E-Commerce Service (ECS). The second Amazon Web API is called Alexa Web Information Service (AWIS). A third Amazon Web API is called the Simple Queue Service. All these APIs are XML Web services that can be called using the SOAP protocol or using HTTP-GET (REST). Let's briefly look at the features that are supported in each of these APIs and then walk through the steps for obtaining a subscription ID so you can use these APIs in your own programs.

Supported Features

The *Amazon E-Commerce Service (ECS) Web API* allows you to work with the most popular Amazon.com features from your own programs, such as:

❑ Retrieving product and pricing information

❑ Retrieving customer reviews of a product

- ❏ Retrieving product images
- ❏ Performing simple and advanced searches
- ❏ Retrieving wish lists by name, e-mail, and other identifiers
- ❏ Creating and updating remote shopping carts

More details about the features supported by ECS can be found later in this chapter, as well as from the Amazon.com Web site. Currently, the page is located at `http://www.amazon.com/gp/browse.html/ 104-0372306-0302351?node=12738641`.

The *Alexa Web Information Service (AWIS) API* supports the same features that you can access interactively on alexa.com:

- ❏ Performing Web searches
- ❏ Accessing Web pages by categories and subcategories
- ❏ Accessing Web site statistics gathered from Alexa's Web crawls
- ❏ Accessing Web page metadata gathered from Alexa's Web crawls
- ❏ Retrieving links to or from a specified URL

More details about the features supported by AWIS can be found later in this chapter, as well as from Amazon.com Web site. Currently, the page is located at `http://www.amazon.com/gp/browse.html/ 104-0372306-0302351?node=12782661`.

The *Amazon Simple Queue Service* was released in November 2004 by Amazon in beta form. The Amazon Simple Queue Service provides the following features:

- ❏ It offers a hosted queue for buffering messages between distributed application components.
- ❏ It enables you to decouple components of your application so that they run independently. Any component of a distributed application can store any type of data in a reliable queue at Amazon.com.
- ❏ Once the component is stored in the queue, any other procedure or application can then later retrieve the data. A single queue can be used simultaneously by multiple applications or components without the need for them to communicate with each other.
- ❏ What is terrific about this new Simple Queue Service API is that your application does not have to be based on other Amazon.com features in any fashion for you to take advantage of it.

More details about the features supported by the Simple Queue Service can be found later in this chapter, as well as from the Amazon.com Web site. Currently, the page is located at `http://www.amazon. com/gp/browse.html/102-4350568-9295354?node=3435361&`.

Signing Up for a Subscription ID

Before you can work with EWS or AWIS, you must first obtain a subscription ID. In prior versions of EWS, this was referred to as a developer token. Developer tokens are no longer used beginning with version 4.0 of EWS.

The subscription ID is different from an associates ID, which enables you to earn credit for sales made with your ID.

What is really great is that you can sign up for one subscription ID and use it for both EWS and AWIS. What is even better is that signing up for a subscription ID is really easy. First, you navigate to the registration page on Amazon.com, which is currently located at `http://www.amazon.com/gp/aws/registration/registration-form.html/104-0372306-0302351?`, as shown in Figure 4-4.

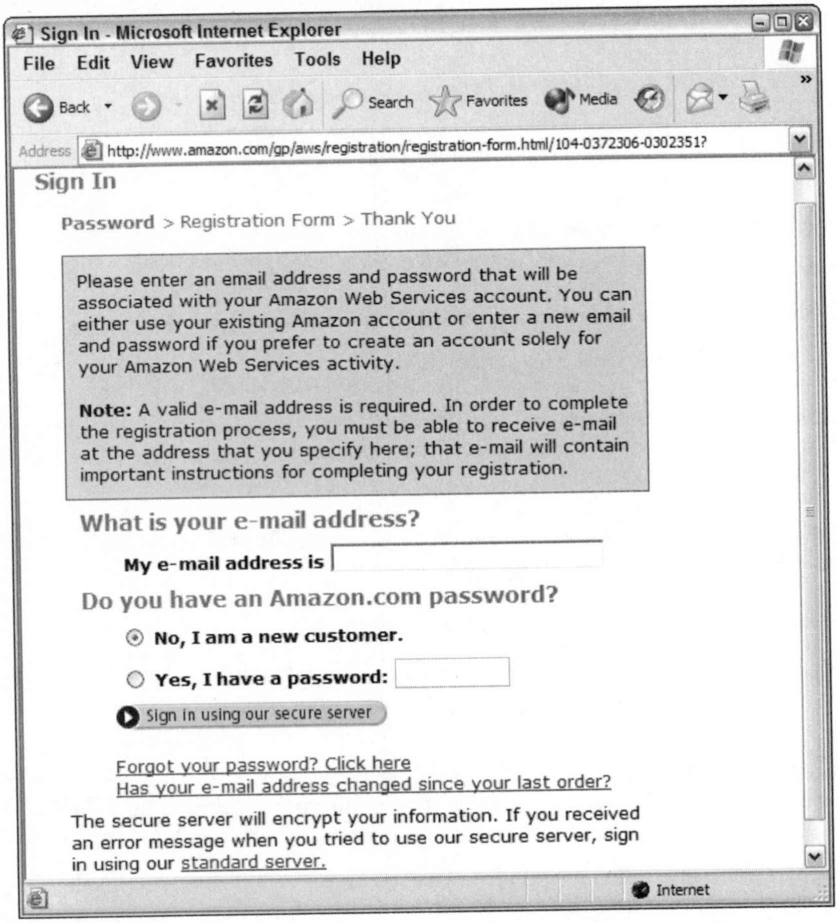

Figure 4-4

If you already have an Amazon.com account that you have used for making purchases online, you can specify the e-mail address and password associated with that account. You then are prompted to accept a license agreement and are sent an e-mail that contains a hyperlink for activating your subscriber ID.

If you do not already have an Amazon.com account, then creating an account just to use with the Web APIs is also very easy. You first select "No, I am a new customer." and then select "Sign in using our secure server" as shown on Figure 4-4. A registration form as shown in Figure 4-5 is then displayed.

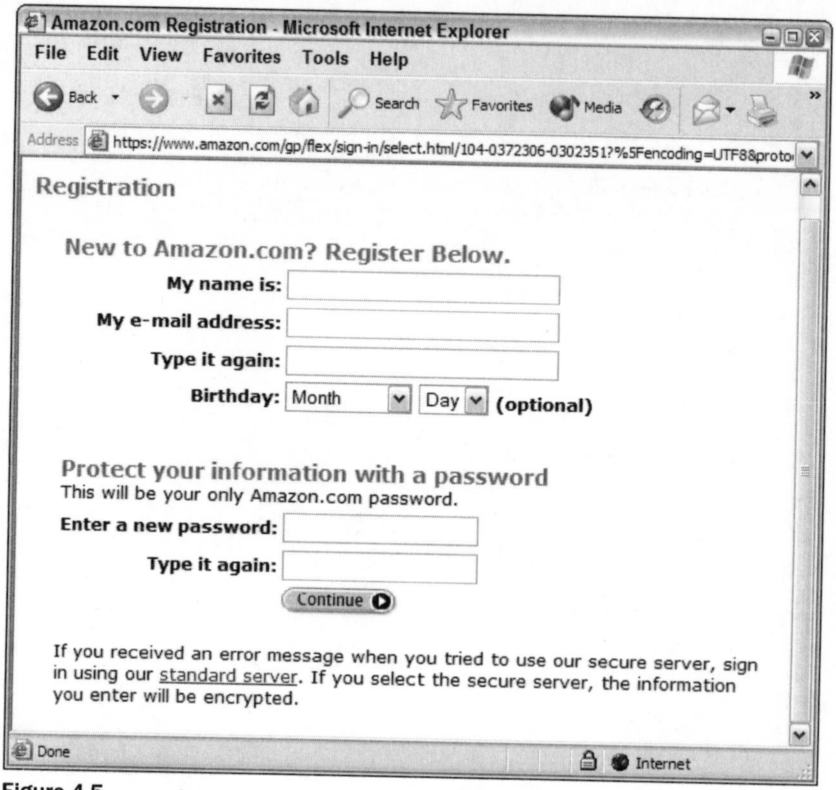

Figure 4-5

After you fill in the requested information shown in Figure 4-5, you click Continue. You are prompted to provide some additional information, such as your mailing address, as shown in Figure 4-6.

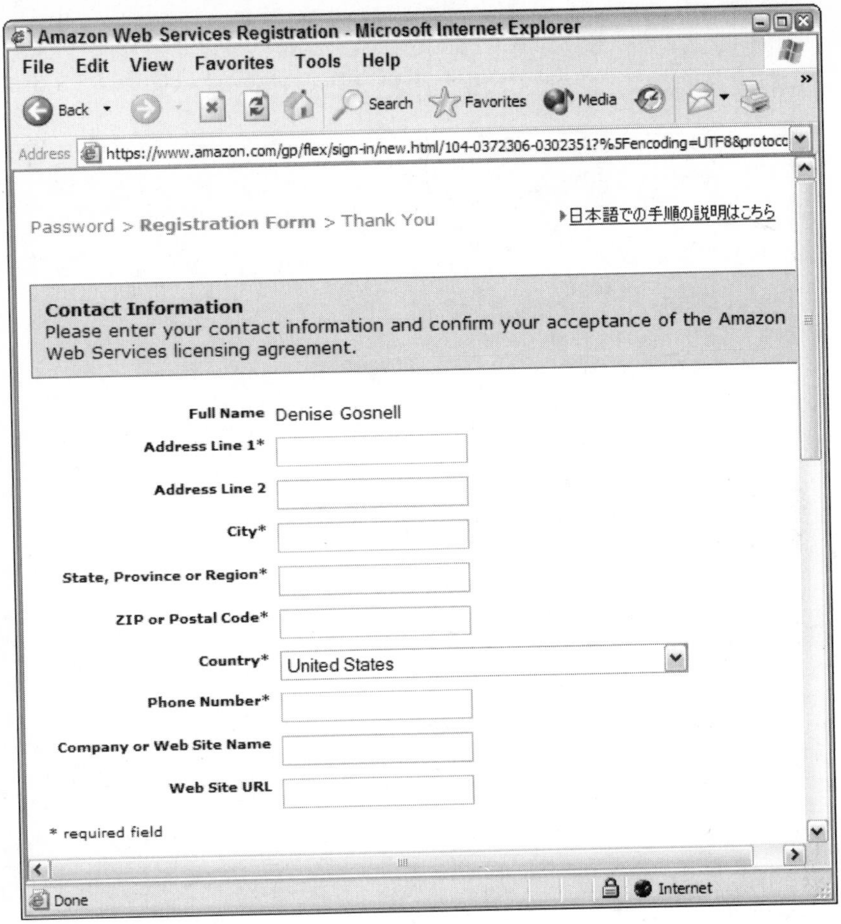

Figure 4-6

You must scroll down farther and fill in where you learned about the Web API and accept the terms of the license agreement, as shown in Figure 4-7.

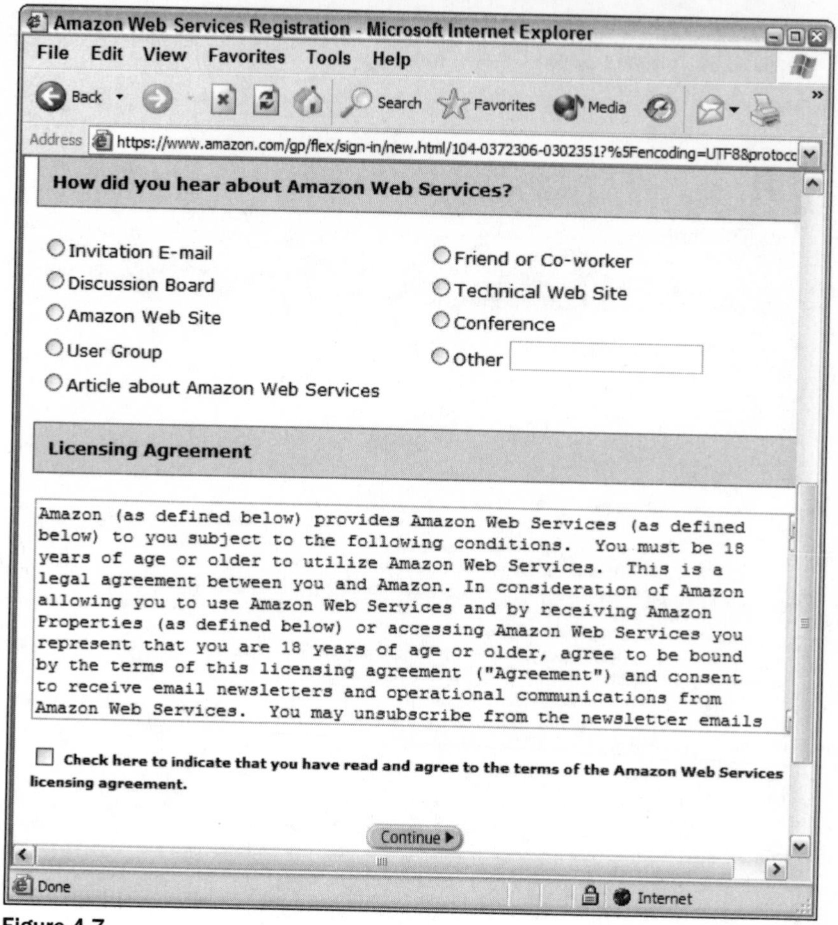

Figure 4-7

You then click Continue to complete the first part of the process. A confirmation screen is displayed, as shown in Figure 4-8. The confirmation screen indicates that you will receive an e-mail at the address you provided with final instructions when you complete the registration.

Figure 4-8

Upon receipt of the e-mail, you are directed to visit a particular page to activate your subscription ID. You then receive an e-mail that contains your actual subscription ID, as well as hyperlinks to online documentation and other useful information. For example, for the ECS Web API, you can currently obtain various code examples in Java, Perl, and others languages and can view the complete API reference and programmer's guide at `http://www.amazon.com/gp/aws/sdk/104-0372306-0302351?`.

For the AWIS Web API, you can currently obtain code examples and view the complete API reference and programmer's guide at `http://www.amazon.com/gp/aws/sdk/104-0372306-0302351?s=AlexaWebInfoService&v=1%2d0`.

Anatomy of Amazon API Queries

You begin this section by exploring how both the Amazon E-Commerce Service queries and Alexa Web Information Service queries are structured. You then look at some simple examples of how to execute the queries and work with the results.

Amazon.com E-Commerce Service API Query Syntax

The ECS API has one service called `AWSECommerceService` that you can use in your applications to execute various e-commerce–related methods, which Amazon.com refers to as operations. Although using the API is free, you can send no more than one query call per second with your subscription ID, so Amazon can control server resources. For more information on these limitations, consult the licensing agreement.

All ECS queries require that the following parameters be specified:

❏ **Service** — AWSEcommerceService, which is the ECS service

❏ **SubscriptionId** — Your subscription ID

❏ **Operation** — The method/operation you want to execute

In addition to these required parameters, all ECS queries can also optionally include one or more of the following:

❏ **AssociateTag** to indicate whom you want to receive credit for the sale

❏ **ResponseGroup** to indicate what data should be returned

❏ **Style**, **ContentType**, or **Version** of the XSL style sheet you want Amazon to use to format the returned data

❏ **XMLEscaping** to specify whether responses are XML-encoded in a single pass or a double pass

❏ **Validate**, which when set to True, only tests the query but does not return results

You now briefly look at each operation you can use in an ECS query, with the HTTP-GET (REST) syntax provided to illustrate each of the required parameters. For the optional parameters, which are numerous, and/or for additional information on the syntax for using these operations with SOAP, please consult the online documentation.

Item Operations

The following item operations allow you to search and retrieve information about products available from Amazon.com.

ItemLookup

The `ItemLookup` operation enables you to retrieve catalog information such as pricing, availability, images, customer reviews, product similarities, and so on. This operation is limited to ten products or restaurants at a time.

```
http://webservices.amazon.com/onca/xml?Service=AWSECommerceService
&SubscriptionId=[Your Subscription ID]
&Operation=ItemLookup
&ItemId=[Up to 10 ID's separated by commas, assumed to be ASIN unless ItemType
parameter used]
```

These REST examples are provided on multiple lines for clarity purposes. If you want to paste these into your Web browser to test them, you remove the carriage returns and type them as a continuous URL.

ItemSearch

The `ItemSearch` operation allows you to search for products or restaurants.

```
http://webservices.amazon.com/onca/xml?Service=AWSECommerceService
&SubscriptionId=[Your Subscription ID Here]
&Operation=ItemSearch&Keywords=[Keywords]
&SearchIndex=[Search Index]
```

SimilarityLookup

The `SimilarityLookup` operation allows you to retrieve products that are similar to a particular Amazon product.

```
http://webservices.amazon.com/onca/xml?Service=AWSECommerceService
&SubscriptionId=[YourSubscription ID Here]
&Operation=SimilarityLookup
&ItemId=[Up to 10 ASINs separated by commas]
```

Customer Content-Related Operations

The customer content operations allow you to identify and retrieve customer-created content such as product reviews, wish lists, Listmania lists, and "About You" information submitted by the customer.

CustomerContentLookup

The `CustomerContentLookup` operation retrieves information submitted by customers that is available to the public, such as reviews, wish lists, and so on.

```
http://webservices.amazon.com/onca/xml?Service=AWSECommerceService
&SubscriptionId=[Your Subscription ID Here]
&Operation=CustomerContentLookup
&CustomerId=[The Customer Id you want to look up]
```

*If you are not using **CustomerContentSearch** in conjunction with **CustomerContentLookup** to look up a customer ID, you may need to look up a customer ID from Amazon.com.*

CustomerContentSearch

The `CustomerContentSearch` operation will look up the Customer ID for the person you specify by name or e-mail address.

```
http://webservices.amazon.com/onca/xml?Service=AWSECommerceService
&SubscriptionId=[Your Subscription ID Here]
&Operation=CustomerContentSearch
&Name=[name of person – such as Denise%20Gosnell]
```

or

```
http://webservices.amazon.com/onca/xml?Service=AWSECommerceService
&SubscriptionId=[Your Subscription ID Here]
&Operation=CustomerContentSearch
&Email=[email of person]
```

List Retrieval Operations

The list retrieval operations allow you to identify and retrieve wish lists, wedding registries, baby registries, or Listmania lists.

ListLookup

The `ListLookup` operation retrieves all products in a specified wish list or Listmania.

```
http://webservices.amazon.com/onca/xml?Service=AWSECommerceService
&SubscriptionId=[Your Subscription ID Here]
&Operation=ListLookup
&ListType=[Type of list]
&ListId=[Wishlist ID you want to retrieve]
```

ListSearch

The `ListSearch` operation allows you to search for a wish list, wedding registry, or baby registry by name, first name, last name, e-mail, and other combinations. It returns information that includes one or more `ListId`'s you can use with `ListLookup`. The example that follows illustrates searching by name.

```
http://webservices.amazon.com/onca/xml?Service=AWSECommerceService
&SubscriptionId=[Your Subscription ID Here]
&Operation=ListSearch
&ListType=[Type of List]
&Name=[Name of person - such as Denise%20Gosnell]
```

Remote Shopping Cart Operations

The remote shopping cart operations allow you to create and manage Amazon shopping carts from your own Web sites, where you can later transfer your customer to Amazon.com to complete the checkout process.

CartAdd

The `CartAdd` operation allows you to add items to a remote shopping cart that was previously created with the `CartCreate` operation.

```
http://webservices.amazon.com/onca/xml?Service=AWSECommerceService
&SubscriptionId=[Your Subscription ID Here]
&Operation=CartAdd
&CartId=[Existing Cart ID to add products to]
&HMAC=[An HMAC Shopping Cart Token for the cart you want to add products to]
&Item.1.ASIN=[An ASIN to add to the cart]
&Item.1.Quantity=[numeric quantity to add to the cart]
```

CartClear

The `CartClear` operation enables you to clear a remote shopping cart.

```
http://webservices.amazon.com/onca/xml?Service=AWSECommerceService
&SubscriptionId=[Your Subscription ID Here]
&Operation=CartClear
&CartId=[Existing Cart ID to clear]
&HMAC=[An HMAC Shopping Cart Token for the cart you want to clear]
```

CartCreate

The `CartCreate` operation allows you to create a new remote shopping cart.

```
http://webservices.amazon.com/onca/xml?Service=AWSECommerceService
&SubscriptionId=[Your Subscription ID Here]
&Operation=CartCreate
&Item.1.ASIN=[An ASIN to add to the cart]
&Item.1.Quantity=[the quantity, likely 1]
```

Or, for multiple items:

```
http://webservices.amazon.com/onca/xml?Service=AWSECommerceService
&SubscriptionId=[Your Subscription ID Here]
&Operation=CartCreate
&Item.1.ASIN=[A first ASIN to add to the cart]
&Item.1.Quantity=[the quantity, likely 1]
&Item.2.ASIN=[A second ASIN to add to the cart]
&Item.2.Quantity=[the quantity, likely 1]
&Item.3.ASIN=[A third ASIN to add to the cart]
&Item.3.Quantity=[the quantity, likely 1]
```

CartGet

The `CartGet` operation allows you to retrieve the contents of a remote shopping cart.

```
http://webservices.amazon.com/onca/xml?Service=AWSECommerceService
&SubscriptionId=[Your Subscription ID Here]
&Operation=CartGet&CartId=[A Cart ID for the cart you want to retrieve]
&HMAC=[An HMAC Shopping Cart Token for the cart you want to retrieve]
```

CartModify

The `CartModify` operation allows you to modify the contents of a remote shopping cart. You can either change the quantity, or switch the item from the shopping cart to the `SaveforLater` category.

```
http://webservices.amazon.com/onca/xml?Service=AWSECommerceService
&SubscriptionId=[Your Subscription ID Here]
&AssociateTag=[Your Associate ID Here]
&Operation=CartModify
&CartId=[A Cart ID]
&HMAC=[An HMAC Shopping Cart Token]
&Item.1.CartItemId=[The CartItemId of the item you want to modify]
&Item.1.Quantity=[number from 0 on up]
```

The following example illustrates how to modify the quantity for a first item to 0 and the second item to 3, and to save the third item for later.

```
http://webservices.amazon.com/onca/xml?Service=AWSECommerceService
&SubscriptionId=[Your Subscription ID Here]
&AssociateTag=[Your Associate ID Here]
&Operation=CartModify
&CartId=[A Cart ID]
&HMAC=[An HMAC Shopping Cart Token]
&Item.1.CartItemId=[The CartItemId of the item you want to modify]
&Item.1.Quantity=0
&Item.2.CartItemId=[The CartItemId of the item you want to modify]
&Item.2.Quantity=3
&Item.3.CartItemId=[The CartItemId of the item you want to modify]
&Item.3.Action=SaveForLater
```

Seller Lookup Operation

The SellerLookup operation allows you to retrieve feedback about specific sellers, such as location, customer feedback, average ratings, and so on.

```
http://webservices.amazon.com/onca/xml?Service=AWSECommerceService
&SubscriptionId=[Your Subscription ID Here]
&Operation=SellerLookup
&SellerId=[Seller ID's separated by commas]
```

Seller Listing Lookup Operation

The SellerListingLookup operation allows you to look up information about Amazon zShops and Marketplace products, such as seller information, product descriptions, and condition information.

```
http://webservices.amazon.com/onca/xml?Service=AWSECommerceService
&SubscriptionId=[Your Subscription ID Here]
&Operation=SellerListingLookup
&IdType=[Listing or Exchange]
&Id=[Offer Listing ID you want to retrieve information for]
```

SellerListingSearch

The SellerListingSearch operation allows you to search for Amazon zShops and Marketplace listings.

```
http://webservices.amazon.com/onca/xml?Service=AWSECommerceService
&SubscriptionId=[Your Subscription ID Here]
&Operation=SellerListingSearch
&SearchIndex=[Marketplace or zShops]
&Keywords=[Keywords to use in search]
&Sort=+price
&OfferStatus=Open
```

Help Operation

The Help operation enables you to retrieve help information about operations and response groups. This operation can be used to help document your programs.

```
http://webservices.amazon.com/onca/xml?Service=AWSECommerceService
&SubscriptionId=[Your Subscription ID Here]
&Operation=Help
&HelpType=[Operation or ResponseGroup]
&About=[Topic for which you want help with]
```

Transaction Operation

The TransactionLookup operation allows you to look up limited information about all Amazon transactions, such as order status and total price. For confidentiality reasons, customer information and details about each item in the order are not available.

```
http://webservices.amazon.com/onca/xml?Service=AWSECommerceService
&SubscriptionId=[Your Subscription ID Here]
&Operation=TransactionLookup
&TransactionId=[Transaction ID you wish to lookup information for]
```

Alexa Web Information Service API Query Syntax

The Alexa Web Information Service is in beta version at the time of this book's writing. Thus, the format discussed herein could change drastically in the final release. Using AWIS is currently free, but you are limited to 10,000 calls per day. For more information on these limitations, consult the licensing agreement. Amazon indicates that they may charge for using the service in the future.

The AWIS API has one service called AWSAlexa that you can use in your applications to execute various methods, which are also called operations. As I did with the EWS, I now briefly look at each operation you can use in an AWIS query, with the HTTP-GET (REST) syntax provided to illustrate each of the required parameters. For the optional parameters, which are numerous, and/or for additional information on the syntax for using these operations with SOAP, please consult the online documentation.

Category

The category operation is a directory service based on the dmoz.org Open Directory and returns a list of subcategories, site listings, and top sites for a given category.

```
http://aws-beta.amazon.com/onca/xml?Service=AlexaWebInfoService
&Operation=Category
&SubscriptionId=[Your Subscription ID]
&ResponseGroup=[Response Group - currently only Browse available]
&Path=[Directory Path]
```

Crawl

The `crawl` operation returns a list of information about a specified URL from the most recent Alexa Web crawl.

```
http://aws-beta.amazon.com/onca/xml?Service=AlexaWebInfoService
&Operation=Crawl
&SubscriptionId=[Your Subscription ID]
&ResponseGroup=[Response Group, currently MetaData]
&Url=[URL]
```

Search

The `search` operation returns a list of results that match one or more keywords specified.

```
http://aws-beta.amazon.com/onca/xml?Service=AlexaWebInfoService
&Operation=Search
&SubscriptionId=[Your Subscription ID]
&ResponseGroup=[Response Group, currently Web]
&Query=[Search terms]
```

UrlInfo

The `urlinfo` operation returns information about a specified URL, such as popularity, related sites, and so on.

```
http://aws-beta.amazon.com/onca/xml?Service=AlexaWebInfoService
&Operation=UrlInfo
&SubscriptionId=[Your Subscription ID]
&Url=[URL to retrieve information for]
&ResponseGroup=[Comma Separated List of Response Groups]
```

WebMap

The `webmap` operation returns a list of links that connect to or from a specified URL.

```
http://aws-beta.amazon.com/onca/xml?Service=AlexaWebInfoService
&Operation=WebMap
&SubscriptionId=[Your Subscription ID]
&Url=[URL]
&ResponseGroup=[ Response Group, currently LinksIn or LinksOut]
```

Simple Queue Service API Query Syntax

As with the Alexa Web Information Service, the Simple Queue Service API is in beta version at the time of this book's writing. Thus, the format discussed here could change drastically in the final release. Amazon is currently allowing developers to access the Simple Queue Service for free during the beta. The limit is 4,000 queue entries per developer.

The Simple Queue Service supports the following operations:

❑ **ConfigureQueue** — Allows you to modify the properties of an existing queue.

❑ **CreateQueue** — Allows you to create queues.

❑ **DeleteQueue** — Allows you to delete one of your queues.

❑ **Dequeue** — Allows you to remove a specified piece of data from a specified queue.

❑ **Enqueue** — Allows you to add any data entries up to 4 KB in size to a specified queue.

❑ **ListMyQueues** — Allows you to list your existing queues.

❑ **Read** — Allows you to read data from a specified queue. Data is returned in approximately the same order it was added.

Executing a Query Using HTTP-GET (REST)

Now that you have a basic idea of the types of operations supported by the Amazon APIs, let's look at some simple examples of how to execute queries against these APIs. Both ECS and AWIS can be executed using SOAP or HTTP-GET (REST). In this section, you walk through the basics of executing queries against the Amazon APIs using HTTP-GET (REST).

As you learned in Chapter 1, it is very easy to test a query that uses REST from your Web browser. To do so, you simply paste the URL into the browser and press Enter. The results are then displayed in XML format in the browser.

So, if you want to call the `ItemSearch` operation of the ECS Web API to retrieve a list of all the books that cover the Amazon and MapPoint APIs, you could paste the following code into the browser:

```
http://webservices.amazon.com/onca/xml?Service=AWSECommerceService
&SubscriptionId=[Your Subscription Id Goes Here]
&Operation=ItemSearch
&SearchIndex=Books
&Keywords=Amazon%20MapPoint%20API
```

Again, remember to remove the carriage returns (inserted to make for easier reading) that are shown in the previous example. Upon executing the previous search, you see results similar to those shown in Figure 4-9.

The capability to test REST queries in a Web browser is great, but to make meaningful use of the results in your programs, you have to programmatically send the HTTP-GET command and then parse the XML results in some fashion from your programming language of choice. For example, in .NET, you can use the `System.Net.WebRequest` object to perform the HTTP-GET, and then use the `System.Xml.XmlTextReader` object to parse the results.

Figure 4-9

Look at a very simple example in which you run the same search shown in Figure 4-9 from Visual Studio .NET. You see the unformatted results in a Web page. Create a new ASP.NET Web application. Add a command button and a label control to the Web form. Add the following code to the Click event of the command button:

```
Private Sub Button1_Click(ByVal sender As System.Object, ByVal e As _
        System.EventArgs) Handles Button1.Click

    Dim oReq As System.Net.HttpWebRequest
    Dim oResp As System.Net.HttpWebResponse
    oReq = _
System.Net.HttpWebRequest.Create("http://webservices.amazon.com/onca/xml?Service=AW
SECommerceService&SubscriptionId=[Your Subscription ID
Here]&Operation=ItemSearch&SearchIndex=Books&Keywords=Amazon%20MapPoint%20API")

    'use the StreamReader to get the response
    oResp = oReq.GetResponse
    Dim sr As New System.IO.StreamReader(oResp.GetResponseStream)
```

```
        Dim strResponse As String

        'read the entire stream to retrieve the results
        strResponse = sr.ReadToEnd

        'write the results to the web browser
        Response.Write(strResponse)

    End Sub
```

Save and execute the project, and you should see a screen similar to the one shown in Figure 4-10.

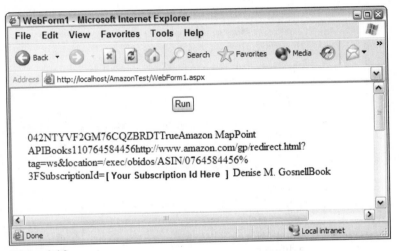

Figure 4-10

The results shown in Figure 4-10 are not the prettiest, but they give you an example of using the `StreamReader` object to get the raw text stream. You can use an XML parser to work with the results element by element as desired.

Executing a Query Using SOAP

As you learned in Chapter 1, when you call a Web API using SOAP, you need to know the location of the WSDL file that describes how the Web API functions. Before jumping into the code example, you should know where you can find the WSDL files for each of the Amazon APIs.

The WSDL file for ECS currently resides in four locations depending on which locale you wish to search.

The WSDL file for the US site is located at:

```
http://webservices.amazon.com/AWSECommerceService/AWSECommerceService.wsdl
```

The WSDL file for the UK site is located at:

```
http://webservices.amazon.com/AWSECommerceService/UK/AWSECommerceService.wsdl
```

The WSDL file for the DE site is located at:

```
http://webservices.amazon.com/AWSECommerceService/DE/AWSECommerceService.wsdl
```

The WSDL file for the JP site is located at:

```
http://webservices.amazon.com/AWSECommerceService/JP/AWSECommerceService.wsdl
```

With respect to the ACIS Web API, the WSDL file, in the current beta form, is currently located at:

```
http://aws-beta.amazon.com/AWSAlexa/AWSAlexa.wsdl
```

With respect to the Simple Queue Service API, the WSDL file, in the current beta form, is currently located at:

```
http://webservices.amazon.com/AWSSimpleQueueService/AWSSimpleQueueService.wsdl
```

These locations and links may change as Amazon offers new releases, but you can find the current links in the online documentation for the APIs. Now, let's look at an example.

Walkthrough Example — Calling the Amazon APIs Using SOAP from Visual Studio .NET

In this section, you walk through a step-by-step example of using SOAP and WSDL to call a Web service from Visual Studio .NET. In this example, you call the `ItemSearch` operation with the same search criteria that you saw in the REST examples earlier in this chapter. Because you are using SOAP and Visual Studio .Net, the steps are quite different from the former procedure to call that same Web service.

1. Open Visual Studio .NET and select File ➪ New ➪ Project.

2. Select Visual Basic Project as the Project Type, and select Windows Application as the Template. For the project name, specify `AmazonSearch` and, for the path, specify the location where you want the project to be created. Click OK to create the new project.

3. Add a reference to the Amazon ECS API by selecting Project ➪ Add Web Reference. For the URL field, specify the WSDL for the desired locale, such as `http://webservices.amazon.com/AWSECommerceService/AWSECommerceService.wsdl`.

4. Click the GO button so that Visual Studio will locate the ECS Web API.

5. Change the Web Reference Name to `Amazon` so that you can use a shorter name in your project.

6. Click the Add Reference button to add the reference to your project. Visual Studio .NET uses the WSDL file to identify the methods that are available for execution from your project.

7. Use the toolbox to drag and drop one command button onto the form.

8. Add the following imports statement to the top of the `Form1` code section of your project, prior to all other code:

```
Imports AmazonSearch.Amazon
```

9. Add the following procedure to `Form1`:

```
Private Sub Button1_Click(ByVal sender As System.Object, ByVal e As _
        System.EventArgs) Handles Button1.Click

        Dim AmazonProductData As New AWSECommerceService
        Dim AmazonSearch As New ItemSearch
        Dim AmazonResponse As New ItemSearchResponse
        Dim AmazonRequest(1) As ItemSearchRequest

        'Developer/Subscription ID
        AmazonSearch.SubscriptionId = "Insert your Subscription ID Here"

        'We are only making one request, not batching multiple requests
        'Thus element 0 of the array is all we need to assign and work with
        AmazonRequest(0) = New ItemSearchRequest
        AmazonRequest(0).SearchIndex = "Books"
        AmazonRequest(0).Keywords = "Amazon MapPoint API"

        'assign the search object to the request object with the assigned
        'parameters
        AmazonSearch.Request = AmazonRequest

        'run the search and populate the response
        AmazonResponse = AmazonProductData.ItemSearch(AmazonSearch)

        Dim item As New Item
        Dim strOutput As String

        strOutput = "Search results for keyword(s): " & _
            AmazonRequest(0).Keywords & " in " & _
            AmazonRequest(0).SearchIndex & ":" & vbCrLf & vbCrLf

        'loop through the results
        For Each item In AmazonResponse.Items(0).Item
            strOutput = strOutput & item.ItemAttributes.Title & vbCrLf & vbCrLf
        Next

        'display the results in a message box
        MsgBox(strOutput)

    End Sub
```

10. Input your Subscription ID on the line of code where indicated. As mentioned previously, these values are provided in the information e-mail you receive when you set up your account.

11. Select File ➪ Save All to save all changes to the project.

12. Select Debug ➪ Start (or press F5) to run the project.

13. You should see a window similar to Figure 4-11 that displays the search results.

Figure 4-11

At the time of this book's writing, the Amazon.com WSDL file has a problem that requires manual correction. If you receive an error message stating that CustomerReviews1 cannot be reflected, then here is how you can work around the bug:

1. From your Visual Studio .NET Solution, double-click Web References in the Solution Explorer.

2. Double-click the **WebReference** *object and the Object Browser window will open.*

3. In the left pane of the Object Browser, double-click the object with the name **AmazonSearch.Amazon** *to expand the list.*

4. Double-click the **WebReference** *object and it expands to a list of objects.*

5. Double-click **AWSECommerceService** *to open up the source code file that VS.NET generates from the WSDL.*

6. Search for public class CustomerReviews1. You should see the Public Class CustomerReviews1 declaration. Change the **TypeName** *value to* **CustomerReviews1***, as shown following.*

```
<System.Xml.Serialization.XmlTypeAttribute(TypeName:="CustomerReviews1",
[Namespace]:="http://webservices.amazon.com/AWSECommerceService/2004-11-10")> _
Public Class CustomerReviews1
```

7. You may also need to make one other correction to keep a separate error from occurring. Search for the following:

```
"public request()() as string" (Visual Basic) or "string[][] Request;" (C#).
```

8. If present, remove the extra parentheses or brackets. Also, remove the **GetType** *parameter, so the code looks similar to the following:*

```
<System.Xml.Serialization.XmlArrayItemAttribute("BrowseNodeId", IsNullable:=false)> _
Public Request() As String
```

9. Save this file. Rerun your application, and the errors should be eliminated.

Looping Through Results

Various types of Amazon API searches limit the number of results that can be returned. For example, each `ItemSearch` operation of the ECS Web API returns up to ten product listings. You can use the `ItemPage` parameter to retrieve additional pages of ten listings, up to 500 pages. If you do not specify the `ItemPage` property, the first page of ten is returned by default.

The `SellerLookup` method of the ECS Web API returns only the first five feedback records. You can use the `OfferPage` parameter to retrieve additional pages.

If you want to retrieve more results than are returned in a single operation, you have to write code that loops multiple times through calling the operation.

Five Creative Ways to Use the Amazon APIs

In this section, you learn five ways to use the Amazon APIs. The first four examples use the E-Commerce Service (ECS), and the last one uses the Alexa Web Information Service (AWIS). For the sake of simplicity, the examples illustrate the URL for a REST call, as opposed to SOAP. Let's jump right into the first example.

#1 — Retrieve Feedback about a Seller with ECS

The following example retrieves feedback about a particular seller using the `SellerLookup` method of the ECS Web API.

```
http://webservices.amazon.com/onca/xml?Service=AWSECommerceService
&SubscriptionId=[Your Subscription Id Here]
&Operation=SellerLookup&SellerId=A35O48Y1QVX6
```

#2 — Retrieve Product Pricing with ECS

The following example retrieves pricing of Sony's new LCD using the `ItemSearch` method of the ECS Web API.

```
http://webservices.amazon.com/onca/xml?Service=AWSECommerceService
&SubscriptionId=[Your Subscription Id Here]
&Operation=ItemSearch
&SearchIndex=Electronics
&Manufacturer=Sony
&Keywords=LCD
&Condition=New
&MerchantId=All
&ResponseGroup=Medium,OfferFull
```

#3 — Look Up a Friend or Family Member's Wish List with ECS

You can use the wish list feature in the ECS Web API to look up a friend or family member's wish list so that you can purchase an item from their list. The following example looks up and retrieves a wish list using the `ListSearch` and `ListLookup` methods of the ECS Web API.

The first step is to look up the wish list of a person by his name, e-mail address, and so on. The example that follows looks up a person by name.

```
http://webservices.amazon.com/onca/xml?Service=AWSECommerceService
&SubscriptionId=[Your Subscription Id Here]
&Operation=ListSearch
&ListType=WishList
&Name=Denise%20Gosnell
```

Next, you can use the list ID that is returned in the previous search to retrieve the list content, as shown in the following section.

```
http://webservices.amazon.com/onca/xml?Service=AWSECommerceService
&SubscriptionId=[Your Subscription Id Here]
&Operation=ListLookup
&ListType=WishList
&ListId= YQLZOK4N6RZ5
&ResponseGroup=Request,ListFull
```

#4 — Create an Amazon.com Shopping Cart with ECS

The following example illustrates how easy it is to create a remote shopping cart that contains a single item using the CartCreate method of the ECS Web API. Remote shopping carts allow visitors to add items to Amazon shopping carts from their own Web sites.

```
http://webservices.amazon.com/onca/xml?Service=AWSECommerceService
&SubscriptionId=[Your Subscription Id Here]
&Operation=CartCreate
&Item.1.ASIN=0764584456
&Item.1.Quantity=1
```

You should consider doing an **ItemLookup** *on the item to find price and availability before adding to cart. The following is an example:*
http://webservices.amazon.com/onca/xml?Service=AWSECommerceService&Subscr iptionId=[Your Subscription Id]&Operation=ItemLookup&IdType=ASIN&ItemId=0764584456 &ResponseGroup=Medium,OfferFull.

Upon executing this method, a Cart ID and HMAC shopping cart token are returned. These values must be used to work with that particular shopping cart in the future.

If the product was actually not available when you attempted to add it to the cart, it is added to the cart as a **<SavedForLaterItem>** *rather than a* **<CartItem>** *in the* **<Cart>** *element.*

After the shopping cart is finalized, you can just transfer the customer to the Amazon URL specified in the PurchaseURL value that was returned by the CreateCart operation. To test this for yourself, you can run the PurchaseURL from the Web browser. Because you probably do not want to complete this purchase, you may not want to run it at this time.

#5—Retrieve URL Information with Alexa Web Information Service

The following example uses the `UrlInfo` operation of the AWIS Web API to retrieve links of Web pages that are related to the `www.amazon.com` Web site.

```
http://aws-beta.amazon.com/onca/xml?Service=AlexaWebInfoService
&Operation=UrlInfo
&SubscriptionId=[Your Subscription ID]
&Url=www.amazon.com
&ResponseGroup=RelatedLinks
```

Other Ways to Use the Amazon APIs

In the previous sections, you looked at five examples to give you an idea of how you can use the Amazon APIs in your applications. Following are some additional examples of ways you might want to use the Amazon APIs. Additional examples of the Amazon APIs are also included in the later chapters and case studies at the end of this book.

Here are examples of other ways to use the Amazon ECS Web API:

❑   Retrieve cover art for albums

❑   Make recommendations for other products a customer should consider

❑   Retrieve additional data about a product based on a partial match (ISBN based on title, and so on)

❑   Analyze sales data from Amazon purchases for product development research

Here are examples of other ways to use the Alexa Web Information Service:

❑   Analyze your Web site's statistics

❑   Analyze the Web site statistics of your competitors to help point you to the companies you should be looking at

❑   Find out if someone is improperly linking and/or framing to your Web site. Such a feature might be useful for attorneys and companies trying to track down infringers of intellectual property.

Here are some creative examples of ways you might use the Simple Queue Service:

❑   Create an application that allows users to submit requests to the queue and then check the queue periodically to perform the requested action (for example: search Google with specified criteria contained in the message in the queue).

❑   Use the queue as a bulletin board of sorts with an application that reads the queue to allow multiple people to share information with each other (for example: a to-do list, project information, and so on).

❑ Use the queue to store a simple list of information you want to access from anywhere (for example: list of favorites, personal information that is not sensitive, and so on). You can then use HTTP/GET (REST) for the particular URL to retrieve the list from a Web browser from any computer in the world with an Internet connection.

Third-Party Amazon Extensions

Dozens of third parties have used the ECS Web API in creative ways. You can find an extensive list of what some of these third parties have done on the Amazon.com Web site. The list is currently located at `http://www.amazon.com/gp/aws/samples.html/102-8555922-5718568`.

As one example, SellerEngine (`http://www.sellerengine.com`) enables Amazon Marketplace sellers to load, price, and manage their Marketplace listings directly from their desktop. As another example, Amazon.pl XML uses the ECS Web API and allows Associates to add Amazon.com products easily to their Web sites. All you need to know to use the service is how to insert simple HTML links into Web pages.

Here are some more interesting ways third parties are using the Amazon APIs. Amazon Lite simulates a lite version of Amazon and can be found at `http://kokogiak.com/amazon/`, as illustrated in Figure 4-12.

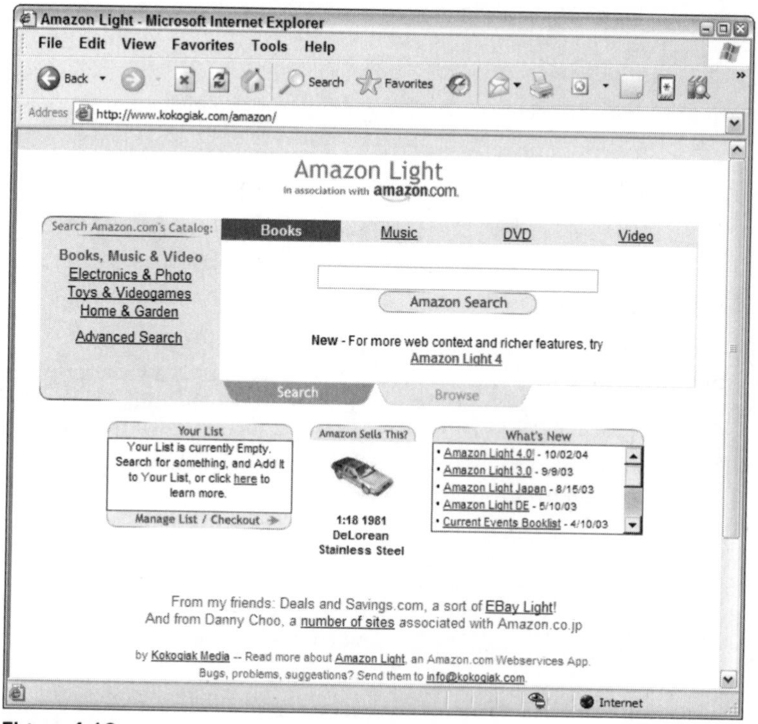

Figure 4-12

One of my favorites is a tool at `http://www.allconsuming.net` that combines results from the Amazon API, the Alexa API, a blogging API, and others in a creative way. It monitors blogs (Web logs) to see what books people are talking about, and then displays information about those books from Amazon. An example is shown in Figure 4-13.

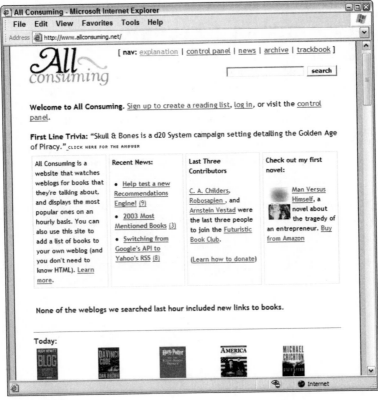

Figure 4-13

WWWinkazon (`http://www.naturallyopen.com/wwwinkazon`) is a browser plug-in that allows you to access Amazon.com products from any site on the Web. To use the plug-in, you highlight text on a Web page and click on the browser's WWWinkazon icon. A pane is then opened right in your browser that includes a list of Amazon.com products and images pertaining to the keywords you selected. You can click on the link to open an Amazon.com page.

Feedburner (`http://www.feedburner.com`) is a tool that allows you to earn Amazon Associates referral fees from RSS feeds by inserting relevant Amazon.com products into the feeds. You can match Amazon stores to your own content categories, and the tool uses the Amazon ECS API to match the specific content of the RSS feeds to relevant Amazon.com products.

Other parties are using the Amazon ECS API to offer complex Amazon.com searches, such as by using the tools available at `www.pluck.com` and `www.hivegroup.com/amazon4.html`.

Summary

In this chapter, you learned about various products and services offered by Amazon and its related companies. For example, you learned about the Alexa Web crawler and the A9.com search engine. You also learned how to make use of the Amazon e-Commerce Web Service and the Alexa Web Information Service in your own programs. These Amazon APIs have various features that are well beyond the scope of this chapter. Additional examples of using the Amazon APIs are included in some of the later chapters, such as in the chapters that illustrate using Web APIs from Microsoft Office, from mobile devices, and in the comprehensive case studies.

So far, you have explored APIs offered by Google, Microsoft (MapPoint), and Amazon.com. Let's turn to Chapter 5 where you will learn about the API offered by eBay.

5

Using the eBay API

Unless you have been living in a cave, you have heard about eBay, and you probably have used eBay yourself to purchase or sell items. eBay is known for inventing the online global marketplace that brings millions of people all over the world together to sell new and used items. eBay is making it easier than ever before for you to write your own software applications using the eBay API or the eBay SDK to interact with eBay features. You can obtain a free developer account that can be used for individual purposes in a test and production environment for a limited number of calls. You can also purchase commercial accounts if you want to write applications for others that interact with eBay. This chapter covers the following:

- ❑ Introduction to eBay as an online global marketplace

- ❑ How to set up a developer account and obtain all the necessary identifiers to use the eBay API

- ❑ The syntax of eBay API queries

- ❑ How to call the eBay API using HTTP-POST using Visual Studio .NET

- ❑ How to call the eBay API using SOAP from Visual Studio .NET

- ❑ Five examples of how to use the eBay APIs

- ❑ Additional ideas for how you might use the eBay API

As with the other APIs you have explored in this book so far, the eBay API is very comprehensive and would take numerous chapters or perhaps an entire book to cover in detail. This chapter will help you set up your eBay developer account and will walk you through some simple examples to illustrate the potential ways you can use the API. You can consult the eBay documentation online, as well as the case studies later in this book, for additional information.

eBay 101

eBay is an online auction house that started off as an online rummage sale of sorts. All those unwanted items in your closet could be auctioned off to someone out of state or out of the country, for that matter. eBay has evolved over the years to be a powerhouse online marketplace for new and used items. Many companies have their own online stores, but sell more from eBay listings than from their own private Web sites. One very powerful feature of eBay is the Search. You can, for example, search for all computers for sale in a certain price range whose auction listings expire within a specific period of time. Figure 5-1 shows an example of such a search.

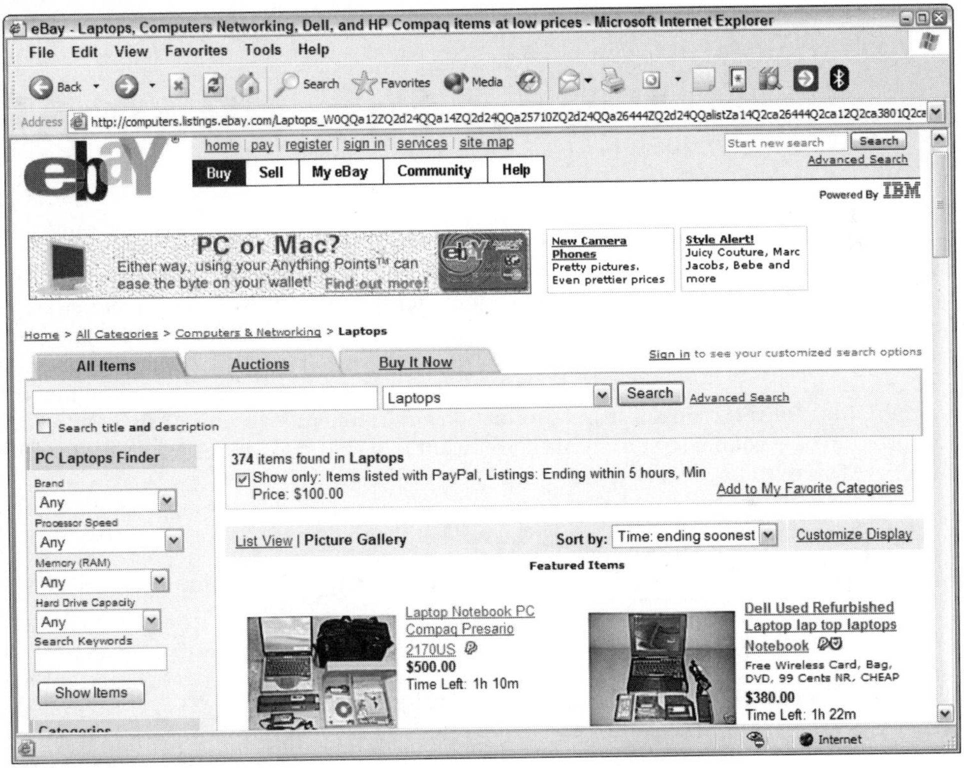

Figure 5-1

These materials have been reproduced with the permission of eBay Inc. Copyright © eBay Inc. All rights reserved.

You can select a particular item and then review additional details about the item, such as one or more photos, information about the seller, bid history, and so on.

Introduction to the eBay API

Now that you have a basic idea of the services offered by eBay, it's time to learn about the eBay Web API. The eBay API is an XML Web service that can be called in one of two ways. The first way is by using HTTP-POST to submit an XML document containing the request and to receive an XML document

response. The second way to call the eBay API is using the SOAP protocol. These concepts are discussed in Chapter 1.

Supported Features

The eBay API allows you to work with the most popular eBay features from your own programs, such as:

- ❑ Retrieving auction listings that match a specified criteria
- ❑ Retrieving customer reviews of a seller
- ❑ Retrieving the status of a particular auction listing
- ❑ Adding a new auction listing
- ❑ Revising an existing auction listing
- ❑ Retrieving details, such as the winning-bidder information for a particular auction listing

More details about the features supported by the eBay can be found later in this chapter, as well as from the eBay Web site.

Licensing Options

In order to use the eBay API, you must first sign up for a developer account. Various tiers of developer accounts exist. You can obtain a free individual license that allows you to use the eBay API to manage your own listings or to test the eBay API before deciding to buy a commercial license. The individual license allows you to make up to 5,000 calls per day in the Sandbox (test) environment and up to 50 calls per day in the live eBay environment for free. Commercial licenses are available for purchase as well, if you want to offer your solution to third parties or use the eBay API more than the individual license allows.

In addition to the limitations on the number of calls, eBay also has a series of requirements that must be met to have a test application certified so that it can run in the live environment. Please consult the eBay online documentation for more information on pricing, certification, and other related information.

Joining the Developer's Program and Establishing an Account

Signing up for a free individual account is not overly difficult, but it is a bit tedious. In this section, I walk you through these steps of signing up for an account to get you up and running quickly. First, you should visit the eBay Web site for the API, which is currently at http://developer.ebay.com. Click the link under Membership that says Join. Follow the prompts on the screen to fill in the requested information and request a developer account.

Upon completing the first part of the registration successfully, you receive a confirmation e-mail. You must click on the link in the e-mail to go to another page for completing the registration. Upon clicking the link in the confirmation e-mail, a screen like the one shown Figure 5-2 is then displayed.

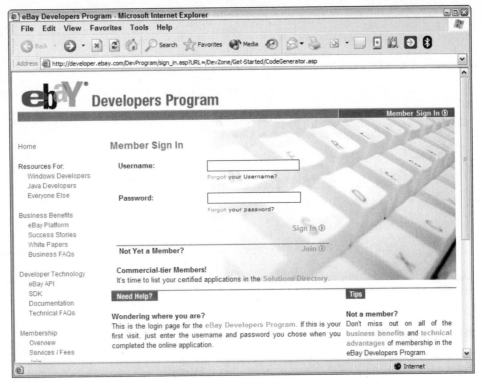

Figure 5-2

These materials have been reproduced with the permission of eBay Inc. Copyright © eBay Inc. All rights reserved.

On this screen, you should specify the developer account username and password that you just created. You are then prompted to specify your eBay user ID, password, and confirmation code as shown in Figure 5-3.

> *A developer account is not the same as an eBay account. You may already have an eBay account for buying and selling items online, but you need a separate account to use the Web API.*

After you fill in the required information and click the Submit button, your individual developer codes are generated, as shown in Figure 5-4.

Print the screen shown in Figure 5-4, which gives you your keys, and save them in an electronic format as well.

At this point, you have three of the four keys you need in order to use the eBay API. The remaining key you need is a token. eBay refers to the step of obtaining the token as the step of validating a test user — or obtaining a token specific to a particular user so you can use the Sandbox test environment.

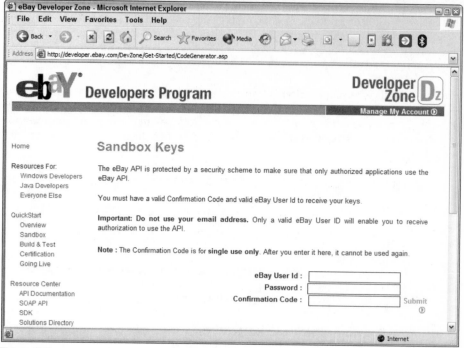

Figure 5-3

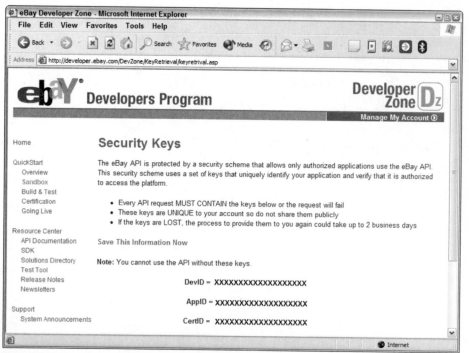

Figure 5-4

Before you can obtain a user token, you first must create a new user account in the Sandbox environment. To register a test user, go to the Sandbox eBay Web site at `http://sandbox.ebay.com`. The Sandbox site looks nearly identical to the live eBay site, and it provides a place for you to test your application to ensure it works before going live. Click the links to register for a new user account and submit the registration request.

You receive an e-mail confirmation after submitting the registration for a new user account on the Sandbox site. Follow the instructions in the e-mail you receive to complete the registration. For example, you will be taken to a screen that prompts you to enter your e-mail address and confirmation code from the e-mail. A confirmation screen, as shown in Figure 5-5, is then displayed to let you know the new user account has been created.

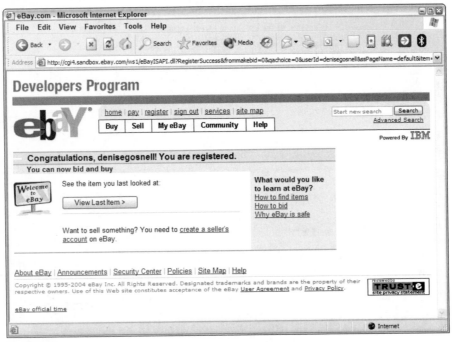

Figure 5-5

These materials have been reproduced with the permission of eBay Inc. Copyright © eBay Inc. All rights reserved.

Now that you have successfully established a new test user account, you are ready to obtain the user token — to validate the test user. Navigate to `http://developer.ebay.com/tokentool/Credentials.aspx`. An Authentication Token Tool like the one shown in Figure 5-6 is displayed.

Fill in the information on the screen and then click the Generate Token button. You are next prompted to log in to the eBay Sandbox environment. Specify the username and password for the test user account created previously, as shown in Figure 5-7.

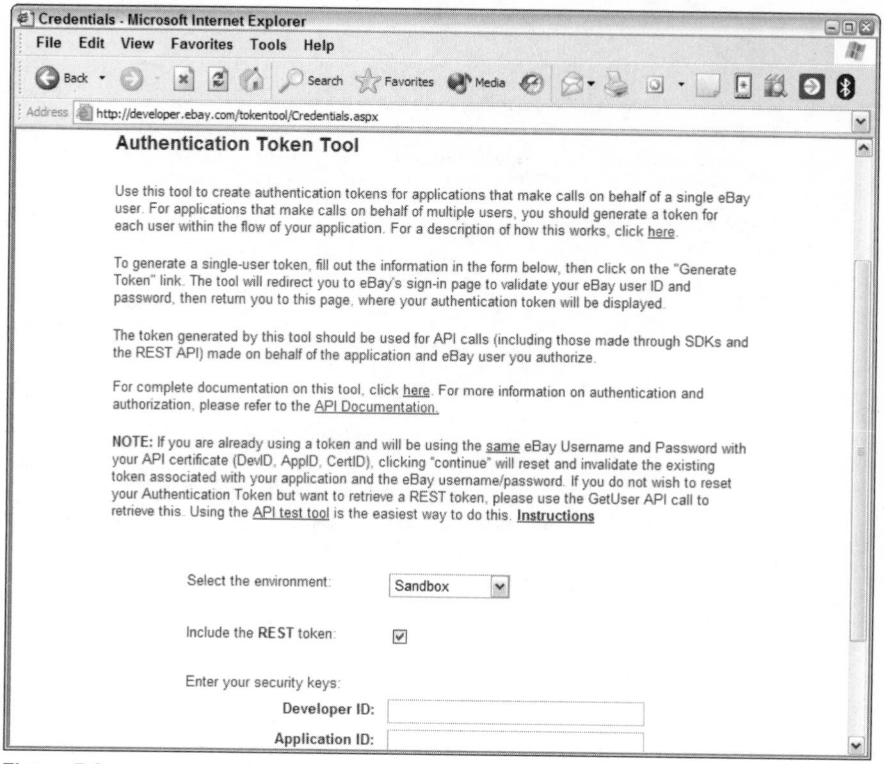

Figure 5-6

You are prompted to accept the terms. Click the Agree button on the screen and continue. You see a notice telling you that the tokens are being generated. Do not close or refresh the browser while the token generation is in progress. Finally, a Token Authentication Tool screen is displayed that gives you your token for the specified user. An example of this is illustrated in Figure 5-8.

Copy and paste your tokens from the screen to save them electronically for later use and print a copy for your file, too. It is very important that you save an electronic version of the token so you do not have to retype the long token later. Now you have all the keys you need to work with the eBay API.

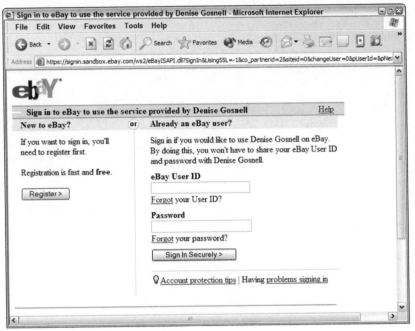

Figure 5-7

These materials have been reproduced with the permission of eBay Inc. Copyright © eBay Inc.
All rights reserved.

The eBay API Documentation

eBay has an extensive collection of online documentation that you should take advantage of. The online documentation includes code examples in various languages, as well as comprehensive whitepapers and other articles that illustrate how to use the API. With hundreds of pages of documentation online, it can be a bit hard to find what you need. As mentioned in a previous section, the documentation can be found at http://developer.ebay.com.

The eBay Software Developer's Kit (SDK)

In addition to the eBay API, eBay has also released a software development kit (SDK) for .NET that allows you to work with the API through another layer that does not require you to know as many details about the API. You can obtain the SDK from the online documentation, as well as whitepapers that can help you decide whether to use the API directly, or whether your application will benefit from your using the SDK instead. This chapter focuses on the API itself, and not the SDK.

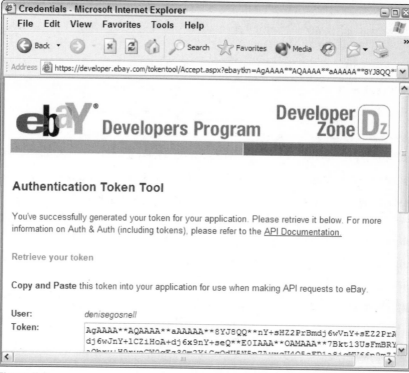

Figure 5-8

Anatomy of an eBay API Query

At this point, you're ready to explore how an eBay API query is structured. You then take a look at some simple examples of how to execute queries and work with the results.

Query Syntax

As you see in the code examples in the following sections, all calls to the eBay API require certain security information, such as the developer identifiers that you were provided.

Currently, you can call the following methods of the eBay API:

❑ **AddItem** — List an item.

❑ **AddToItemDescription** — Modify an existing item's description, or modify an existing item's hit counter.

- ❑ **EndItem** — End a listing for an item.

- ❑ **GetAccount** — Retrieve account information for the specified user. This can be requested only for your own account.

- ❑ **GetAdFormatLeads** — Retrieve sales leads for real estate listings.

- ❑ **GetAPIAccessRules** — Retrieve the access rules and usage statistics for each API call.

- ❑ **GetBidderList** — Retrieve a list of all items for a particular bidder.

- ❑ **GetCategories** — Retrieve a list of the categories that are children of a specified category.

- ❑ **GetCategory2DomainMap** — Retrieve a list of categories and their domains.

- ❑ **GetCategoryListings** — Retrieve the items listed in a particular category.

- ❑ **GetDescriptionTemplates** — Retrieve the theme and layout specifications for an item's description.

- ❑ **GetDomains** — Retrieve information about item specifics domains.

- ❑ **GeteBayOfficialTime** — Retrieve the eBay official time.

- ❑ **GetFeedback** — Retrieve feedback score information for a particular user.

- ❑ **GetHighBidders** — Retrieve the highest bidders for a Dutch auction.

- ❑ **GetItem** — Retrieve auction item information for one or more auction items.

- ❑ **GetItemTransactions** — Retrieve summary information about an item purchase.

- ❑ **GetLogoURL** — Retrieve the URL for small, medium, or large eBay Marketplace logo images.

- ❑ **GetSearchResults** — Retrieve items that match a specified search criteria.

- ❑ **GetSellerEvents** — Retrieve prices and other information related to a seller's listings.

- ❑ **GetSellerList** — Retrieve a list of items of a particular seller.

- ❑ **GetSellerTransactions** — Retrieve transactions for a seller.

- ❑ **GetStoreDetails** — Retrieve custom categories for a user's eBay stores.

- ❑ **GetUser** — Retrieve information about a specified user.

- ❑ **GetWatchList** — Retrieve a list of items for a user's watch list.

- ❑ **LeaveFeedback** — Leave feedback for a user after an auction ends.

- ❑ **RelistItem** — Relist an item that was not sold.

- ❑ **ReviseCheckoutStatus** — Update the status of an item after user has gone through checkout.

- ❑ **ReviseCheckoutTransactionDetails** — Update transaction before the payment or checkout process is complete.

❑   **ReviseItem**—Revise an item listed with the `AddItem` method.

❑   **SetSellerPaymentAddress**—Specify a seller's shipping address.

❑   **ValidateTestUserRegistration**—Activate a test user.

❑   **VerifyAddItem**—Validate the arguments for `AddItem`.

Executing a Query Using HTTP-POST

Now that you have a basic idea of the types of operations supported by the eBay, let's look at some simple code examples to see how they work. eBay API calls can be executed using HTTP-POST operations or SOAP operations. In this section, you walk through the basics of executing queries against the eBay API using HTTP-POST.

Just as with HTTP-GET (REST)–style operations, with HTTP-POST operations you have to build the command in your code and then submit the HTTP post operation to execute the command. The difference with HTTP-POST is that you actually submit an XML file with various parameters describing the operation to be performed and the values to use in the operation. As you may recall, with REST-style operations, the parameters are included as part of a URL and not submitted as a separate XML file.

In Visual Studio .NET, you can use the `System.Net.WebClient.UploadData` method to perform an HTTP-POST operation, as illustrated in the following example.

Walkthrough Example—Calling the eBay API Using HTTP-POST from Visual Studio .NET

This section contains a step-by-step example of using HTTP-POST to call the eBay Web service from Visual Studio .NET. In this example, you call the `GetSearchResults` operation to look up all eBay auction items in the Sandbox environment that have the word *computer* and are not priced higher than $1,000. You set up this example so that it can be used later in the chapter for the corresponding SOAP example as well.

    1.   Open Visual Studio .NET and select File ⇨ New ⇨ Project.

    2.   Select Visual Basic Project as the Project Type and Windows Application as the Template. For the project name, specify `eBaySample`, and for the path specify the location where you want the project to be created. Click OK to create the new project.

    3.   Use the toolbox to drag and drop two command buttons and one text box onto the form. Change the text property of the first text box to HTTP-POST Example, and change the text property of the second text box to SOAP Example. Change the multiline property of the text box to True and resize the text box so that it is large enough to display XML results. An example of how the form looks after these changes is shown in Figure 5-9.

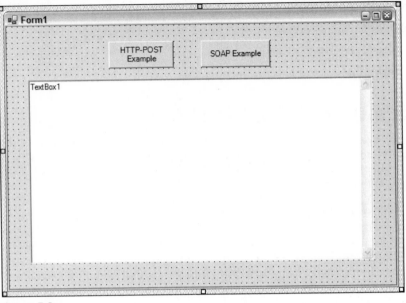

Figure 5-9

4. Add the following procedure to Form1 for the click event for the first button:

```
Private Sub Button1_Click(ByVal sender As System.Object, ByVal e As _
    System.EventArgs) Handles Button1.Click

    Dim web As New System.Net.WebClient

    Dim strDevId As String
    Dim strAppId As String
    Dim strCertId As String

    'specify credentials required to access API
    strDevId = "Your Dev Id Here"
    strAppId = "Your App Id Here"
    strCertId = "Your Cert Id Here"

    'specify the configuration headers
    web.Headers.Add("X-EBAY-API-CALL-NAME", "GetSearchResults")
    web.Headers.Add("X-EBAY-API-SITEID", "0")
    web.Headers.Add("X-EBAY-API-DETAIL-LEVEL", "0")
    web.Headers.Add("X-EBAY-API-COMPATIBILITY-LEVEL", "311")
    web.Headers.Add("Content-Type", "text/xml")

    'add required security headers for all API calls
    web.Headers.Add("X-EBAY-API-SESSION-CERTIFICATE", strDevId + ";" + _
```

```
                        strAppId + ";" + strCertId)
          web.Headers.Add("X-EBAY-API-DEV-NAME", strDevId)
          web.Headers.Add("X-EBAY-API-APP-NAME", strAppId)
          web.Headers.Add("X-EBAY-API-CERT-NAME", strCertId)

          Dim strXML As String

          'list of items for sale that match search criteria

          strXML = "<?xml version=""1.0"" encoding=""utf-8"" ?>" & _
          "<request>" & _
          "<RequestToken>Your Token Here</RequestToken>" & _
          "<ErrorLevel>1</ErrorLevel>" & _
          "<Verb>GetSearchResults</Verb>" & _
          "<Query>computer</Query>" & _
          "<HighestPrice>1000.00</HighestPrice>" & _
          "<MaxResults>5</MaxResults>" & _
          "<SiteId>0</SiteId>" & _
          "</request>"

          'add the xml string to the byte array
          Dim d As Byte() = System.Text.Encoding.ASCII.GetBytes(strXML)

          'call the ebay api and pass the byte array containing the XML string
          Dim res As Byte() = _
            web.UploadData("https://api.sandbox.ebay.com/ws/api.dll", "POST", d)

          TextBox1.Multiline = True

          'display the results of the call in a text box on the form
          TextBox1.Text = System.Text.Encoding.ASCII.GetString(res)

      End Sub
```

5. Input your Dev ID, App ID, Cert ID, and Token on the lines of code where indicated. As I mentioned previously, these values are provided on the information screens you received when you set up your account.

6. Select File ➪ Save All to save all changes to the project.

7. Select Debug ➪ Start (or press F5) to run the project. Click the button that says HTTP-POST Example to run the HTTP-POST Example.

8. You should see a window similar to Figure 5-10 that displays the XML results returned from the eBay API. They begin with the first item that matched the search criteria.

You must use an XML parser to parse the values you use in your application in order to work with this in meaningful ways. eBay has recently announced a SOAP enhancement for many API operations that gives you the option of calling the API without having to parse XML in your underlying programs. Let's see how this works.

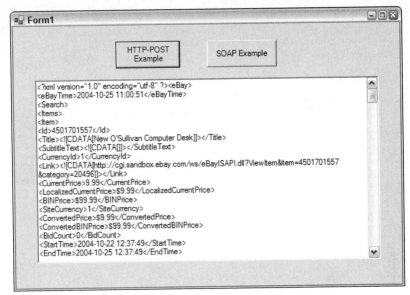

Figure 5-10

Executing a Query Using SOAP

As you learned in Chapter 1, when you call a Web API over SOAP, you specify the location of the WSDL file so your application knows how the Web API functions. The WSDL file for the eBay API is currently located at:

```
http://developer.ebay.com/webservices/latest/eBaySvc.wsdl
```

The WSDL file is then interpreted by your programming language, such as Visual Studio .NET, to allow you to refer to the API in a more object-oriented fashion in your code. In other words, by using the SOAP protocol to execute eBay calls, you can work with the results without having to parse XML. Let's look at an example of how this works.

Walkthrough Example — Calling the eBay API Using SOAP from Visual Studio .NET

You can extend the prior example to add the functionality to call the eBay API using SOAP. Because you are using SOAP instead of HTTP-POST, the steps to call that same Web service are quite different.

1. Reopen the eBaySample application you created in the prior example if it is not already open.

2. Add a reference to the eBay API by selecting Project ➪ Add Web Reference. For the URL field, specify the location of the WSDL file, for example with this URL: http://developer.ebay.com/webservices/latest/eBaySvc.wsdl.

3. Click the GO button so that Visual Studio locates the eBay Web API.

4. Change the Web Reference Name to eBay so that you can use a shorter name in your project.

5. Click the Add Reference button to add the reference to your project. Visual Studio .NET uses the WSDL file to identify the methods that are available for execution from your project.

6. Add the following procedure to Form1 to the click event of the second button:

```
Private Sub Button2_Click(ByVal sender As System.Object, ByVal e As _
        System.EventArgs) Handles Button2.Click


    'SOAP example

    Dim strToken As String
    Dim strDevId As String
    Dim strAppId As String
    Dim strCertId As String

    'specify credentials required to access API
     strToken = "Your Token Here"
    strDevId = "Your Dev Id Here"
    strAppId = "Your App Id Here"
    strCertId = "Your Cert Id Here"


    Dim SOAPService As New ebay.eBayAPIInterfaceService
    SOAPService.Url = _
"https://api.sandbox.ebay.com/wsapi?callname=GetSearchResults&siteid=0&appid=" & _
strAppId & "version=383"

    SOAPService.RequesterCredentials = New ebay.CustomSecurityHeaderType
    SOAPService.RequesterCredentials.eBayAuthToken = strToken
    SOAPService.RequesterCredentials.Credentials = New ebay.UserIdPasswordType
    SOAPService.RequesterCredentials.Credentials.AppId = strAppId
    SOAPService.RequesterCredentials.Credentials.DevId = strDevId
    SOAPService.RequesterCredentials.Credentials.AuthCert = strCertId

    Dim Request As New ebay.GetSearchResultsRequestType
    Dim Response As New ebay.GetSearchResultsResponseType

    'specify the search criteria
    Request.Query = "computer"
    Request.Version = "383"

    'call the GetSearchResults method to run the search
    Response = SOAPService.GetSearchResults(Request)

    Dim items As ebay.SearchResultItemType

    TextBox1.Multiline = True

    'loop through the results and display the results
    For Each items In Response.SearchResultItemArray
        TextBox1.Text = TextBox1.Text & "Title:" & items.Item.Title & vbCrLf
        TextBox1.Text = TextBox1.Text & "Description: " & _
                items.Item.Description & vbCrLf
        TextBox1.Text = TextBox1.Text & "Item Id:" & items.Item.ItemID & _
                vbCrLf & vbCrLf
```

```
        Next

    End Sub
```

7. Input your Token, Dev ID, App ID, and Cert ID on the lines of code where indicated. As mentioned previously, these values are provided in the information screens provided when you set up your account.

8. Select File ⇨ Save All to save all changes to the project.

9. Select Debug ⇨ Start (or press F5) to run the project. Click the button that says SOAP Example to run the SOAP Example.

10. You should see a window similar to that shown in Figure 5-11 that displays the search results. Notice that you were able to refer to the data elements of the API call within your code without having to parse any XML.

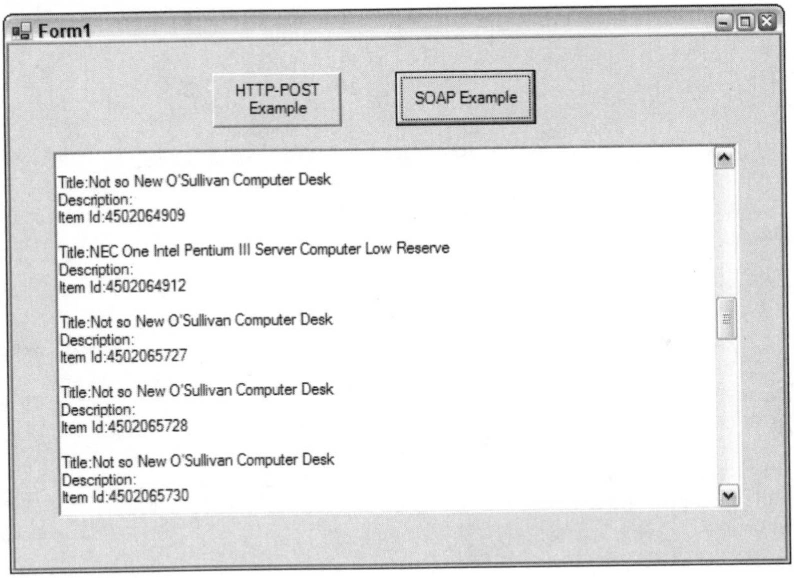

Figure 5-11

As new versions of the eBay API are released, some of the code in this chapter may no longer function in exactly the same way as it did in prior versions. This is certainly true of the other APIs as well, but eBay seems to release new versions more frequently than some of the others.

Five Creative Ways to Use the eBay API

Now look at five ways to use the eBay API. You see both SOAP and XML code examples. The complete code listing is provided for the SOAP example, as that is probably what you will use from within Visual Studio .NET.

The account credentials are duplicated in each of these SOAP examples so each can stand alone. You should specify the credentials in a single place to avoid duplication of code in your own eBay solutions.

The XML examples are also provided for your convenience. However, if you want to run the XML examples from Visual Studio .NET, modify the strXML value in `Button1_Click` event of `Form1` to include the XML code shown in the respective example. You also will need to modify the `"X-EBAY-API-CALL-NAME"` parameter to specify the verb (procedure to call) as shown in the respective example, instead of the `"GetSearchResults"` procedure.

#1 — List an Item for Sale

This example illustrates how to use the `AddItem` method to list an item for sale. You must first create an eBay Seller's Account on the Sandbox text environment for this example to work. Visit sandbox.ebay.com, select the Sellers option, and follow the links to create a new account.

SOAP Example

You must set up a few details in your existing Visual Studio .NET project so these five examples run easily. You then add the code specific to this first example.

1. Open the project you created earlier in this chapter. Add another command button to the form and change the Text property to Examples 1 to 5, as shown in Figure 5-12.

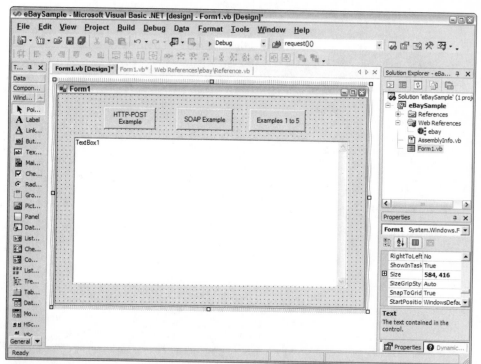

Figure 5-12

2. Add the following procedure to the Click event of the new button. This procedure will prompt you to specify which example you want to run.

```
Private Sub Button3_Click(ByVal sender As System.Object, ByVal e As _
     System.EventArgs) Handles Button3.Click

    Dim intExample As Integer

    'run the example specified by the user
    intExample = InputBox("Please enter example number (1-5):")

    Select Case intExample
        Case 1
            Call Example1()
        Case 2
            Call Example2()
        Case 3
            Call Example3()
        Case 4
            Call Example4()
        Case 5
            Call Example5()
        Case Else
            MsgBox("Please enter a number from 1-5")
    End Select

End Sub
```

3. Add the Example1 procedure that calls the AddItem method to list a new item on eBay. Replace the variables in the following code with your account information.

```
Sub Example1()

    On Error GoTo handleerror

    Dim strToken As String
    Dim strDevId As String
    Dim strAppId As String
    Dim strCertId As String

    'specify credentials required to access API
    strToken = "Your Token Here"
    strDevId = "Your Dev Id Here"
    strAppId = "Your App Id Here"
    strCertId = "Your Cert Id Here"

    Dim SOAPService As New ebay.eBayAPIInterfaceService
    SOAPService.Url = _
"https://api.sandbox.ebay.com/wsapi?callname=AddItem&siteid=0&appid=" & _
strAppId & "version=383"

    SOAPService.RequesterCredentials = New ebay.CustomSecurityHeaderType
    SOAPService.RequesterCredentials.eBayAuthToken = strToken
    SOAPService.RequesterCredentials.Credentials = New ebay.UserIdPasswordType
    SOAPService.RequesterCredentials.Credentials.AppId = strAppId
```

```
SOAPService.RequesterCredentials.Credentials.DevId = strDevId
SOAPService.RequesterCredentials.Credentials.AuthCert = strCertId

Dim Request As New ebay.AddItemRequestType
Dim Response As New ebay.AddItemResponseType
Dim Item As New ebay.ItemType

'specify the API version
Request.Version = "383"

Item.Title = "Johnny Horton Greatest Hits CD"
Item.Description = "A forgotten classic!"

'specify the listing details
Item.QuantitySpecified = True
Item.Quantity = 1
Item.CurrencySpecified = True
Item.Currency = New ebay.CurrencyCodeType
Item.Currency = ebay.CurrencyCodeType.USD
Item.CountrySpecified = True
Item.Country = New ebay.CountryCodeType
Item.Country = ebay.CountryCodeType.US
Item.ListingDurationSpecified = True
Item.ListingDuration = New ebay.ListingDurationCodeType
Item.ListingDuration = ebay.ListingDurationCodeType.Days_7
Item.Location = "Indianapolis, IN"
Item.ListingDetails = New ebay.ListingDetailsType
Item.ListingDetails.ConvertedBuyItNowPrice = New ebay.AmountType
Item.ListingDetails.ConvertedBuyItNowPrice.currencyID = New _
    ebay.CurrencyCodeType
Item.ListingDetails.ConvertedBuyItNowPrice.currencyID = _
    ebay.CurrencyCodeType.USD
Item.ListingDetails.ConvertedBuyItNowPrice.Value = 5.0
Item.StartPrice = New ebay.AmountType
Item.StartPrice.currencyID = New ebay.CurrencyCodeType
Item.StartPrice.currencyID = ebay.CurrencyCodeType.USD
Item.StartPrice.Value = 1.0
Item.RegionID = 60
Item.ShippingTerms = ebay.ShippingTermsCodeType.BuyerPays
Item.PrimaryCategory = New ebay.CategoryType
Item.PrimaryCategory.CategoryID = 1573
Item.ListingTypeSpecified = True
Item.ListingType = ebay.ListingTypeCodeType.FixedPriceItem
Item.ShippingOption = ebay.ShippingOptionCodeType.WorldWide

'assign the item object to the request object
Request.Item = Item

'call the AddItem method to list the item
Response = SOAPService.AddItem(Request)

Dim intCount As Integer

If IsNothing(Response.Errors) Then
    'display the new item ID returned from
```

```
                    'eBay after the listing was successful
                    TextBox1.Text = "Item Listed" & vbCrLf & "Item ID: " & Response.ItemID
            Else
                    'display the errors that were returned
                    TextBox1.Text = ""
                    For intCount = 0 To Response.Errors.Length - 1
                        TextBox1.Text = TextBox1.Text & "Error: " & _
                                Response.Errors(intCount).ErrorCode
                        TextBox1.Text = TextBox1.Text & vbCrLf & "Message: " & _
                                Response.Errors(intCount).LongMessage
                    Next intCount
            End If

            Exit Sub

handleerror:
            MsgBox("An error occurred: " & Err.Number & " - " & Err.Description)
            Exit Sub

End Sub
```

4.   Run the program, and specify 1 when prompted to run this example.

XML Example

The following code is an example of XML that lists an item using the AddItem method. Follow the instructions described in the beginning of this section if you want to run this example from the existing project. Also, replace the values with the information for the item you wish to list.

```
<?xml version="1.0" encoding="utf-8" ?>
<request>
<RequestToken>Your Token Here</RequestToken>
<DetailLevel>0</DetailLevel>
<ErrorLevel>1</ErrorLevel>
<ErrorLanguage>0</ErrorLanguage>
<SiteId>0</SiteId>
<Category>1573</Category>
<CheckoutDetailsSpecified>0</CheckoutDetailsSpecified>
<Country>US</Country>
<Currency>1</Currency>
<Description><![CDATA[ A forgotten classic! ]]></Description>
<Duration>7</Duration>
<Location>Indianapolis, IN</Location>
<LotSize>6</LotSize>
<MinimumBid>1.00</MinimumBid>
<PaymentSeeDescription>1</PaymentSeeDescription>
<Quantity>1</Quantity>
<Region>60</Region>
<SellerPays>0</SellerPays>
<Title>Johnny Horton Greatest Hits CD</Title>
<Version>2</Version>
<VisaMaster>1</VisaMaster>
<Verb>AddItem</Verb>
</request>
```

#2 — Retrieve a List of Categories

In this example, you use the `GetCategories` method to retrieve all of the categories for a particular eBay site.

SOAP Example

1. Add the following `Example2` procedure to the code section of the existing project. Replace the values where specified with your own eBay credentials.

```
Sub Example2()

        On Error GoTo handleerror

        Dim strToken As String
        Dim strDevId As String
        Dim strAppId As String
        Dim strCertId As String

        'specify credentials required to access API
        strToken = "Your Token Here"
        strDevId = "Your Dev Id Here"
        strAppId = "Your App Id Here"
        strCertId = "Your Cert Id Here"

        Dim SOAPService As New ebay.eBayAPIInterfaceService
        SOAPService.Url = _
    "https://api.sandbox.ebay.com/wsapi?callname=GetCategories&siteid=0&appid=" & _
    strAppId & "version=383"

        SOAPService.RequesterCredentials = New ebay.CustomSecurityHeaderType
        SOAPService.RequesterCredentials.eBayAuthToken = strToken
        SOAPService.RequesterCredentials.Credentials = New ebay.UserIdPasswordType
        SOAPService.RequesterCredentials.Credentials.AppId = strAppId
        SOAPService.RequesterCredentials.Credentials.DevId = strDevId
        SOAPService.RequesterCredentials.Credentials.AuthCert = strCertId

        Dim Request As New ebay.GetCategoriesRequestType
        Dim Response As New ebay.GetCategoriesResponseType

        'specify the API version
        Request.Version = "383"

        'get the categories for the U.S.
        Request.CategorySiteID = "0"

        'call the GetCategories method
        Response = SOAPService.GetCategories(Request)

        Dim intCount As Integer

        'display the list of eBay categories
        If IsNothing(Response.Errors) Then
            Dim items As ebay.CategoryType
```

137

```
                    'if no categories, then exit
                    If IsNothing(Response.CategoryArray) Then
                        TextBox1.Text = "No categories returned for this site id."
                        Exit Sub
                    End If

                    'display the categories
                    For Each items In Response.CategoryArray
                        TextBox1.Text = TextBox1.Text & vbCrLf & "Category ID:" & _
                                items.CategoryID & vbCrLf
                        TextBox1.Text = TextBox1.Text & "Category Name:" & _
                                items.CategoryName & vbCrLf
                    Next
                Else
                    'display any errors that occurred
                    TextBox1.Text = ""
                    For intCount = 0 To Response.Errors.Length - 1
                        TextBox1.Text = TextBox1.Text & "Error: " & _
                                Response.Errors(intCount).ErrorCode
                        TextBox1.Text = TextBox1.Text & vbCrLf & "Message: " & _
                                Response.Errors(intCount).LongMessage
                    Next intCount
                End If

                Exit Sub

        handleerror:
                MsgBox("An error occurred: " & Err.Number & " - " & Err.Description)
                Exit Sub

        End Sub
```

2.   Run the project and specify 2 when prompted to run this example.

XML Example

The following XML code retrieves categories for the specified site using the GetCategories method. To run this example from the existing project, see the earlier instructions. Also, replace the CategorySiteId value with the identifier corresponding to the eBay site you wish to use in your search.

```xml
<?xml version="1.0" encoding="utf-8" ?>
<request>
<RequestToken>Your Token Here</RequestToken>
<ErrorLevel>1</ErrorLevel>
<CategorySiteId>0</CategorySiteId>
<Verb>GetCategories</Verb>
<DetailLevel>4</DetailLevel>
</request>
```

#3 — Retrieve List of Pending Auctions for Seller

This example calls the GetSellerList method to retrieve all pending auctions for a specified seller.

SOAP Example

1. Add the following `Example3` procedure to the code section of the existing project. Replace the values where specified with your own eBay credentials. Also replace the User ID value with a valid User ID of a seller for whom you wish to retrieve a list of items.

```
Sub Example3()

    On Error GoTo handleerror

    Dim strToken As String
    Dim strDevId As String
    Dim strAppId As String
    Dim strCertId As String

    'specify credentials required to access API
    strToken = "Your Token Here"
    strDevId = "Your Dev Id Here"
    strAppId = "Your App Id Here"
    strCertId = "Your Cert Id Here"

    Dim SOAPService As New ebay.eBayAPIInterfaceService
    SOAPService.Url = _
"https://api.sandbox.ebay.com/wsapi?callname=GetSellerList&siteid=0&appid=" & _
strAppId & "version=383"

    SOAPService.RequesterCredentials = New ebay.CustomSecurityHeaderType
    SOAPService.RequesterCredentials.eBayAuthToken = strToken
    SOAPService.RequesterCredentials.Credentials = New ebay.UserIdPasswordType
    SOAPService.RequesterCredentials.Credentials.AppId = strAppId
    SOAPService.RequesterCredentials.Credentials.DevId = strDevId
    SOAPService.RequesterCredentials.Credentials.AuthCert = strCertId

    Dim Request As New ebay.GetSellerListRequestType
    Dim Response As New ebay.GetSellerListResponseType

    'specify the API version
    Request.Version = "383"

    'specify user id for seller you wish to retrieve list for
    Request.UserID = "Specify User Id Here"

    'call the GetSellerList method to get the list
    Response = SOAPService.GetSellerList(Request)

    Dim intCount As Integer

    'display the list of items for this seller
    If IsNothing(Response.Errors) Then
        Dim items As New ebay.ItemType
        TextBox1.Text = "Number of items for seller:" & _
                Response.ReturnedItemCountActual & vbCrLf

        'if no items, then exit
        If IsNothing(Response.ItemArray) Then
```

```
                    TextBox1.Text = "No items for this seller"
                    Exit Sub
              End If

              'display the items
              For Each items In Response.ItemArray
                    TextBox1.Text = TextBox1.Text & vbCrLf & "Title:" & _
                            items.Title & vbCrLf
                    TextBox1.Text = TextBox1.Text & "Description:" & _
                            items.Description & vbCrLf
              Next
        Else
              'display any errors that occurred
              TextBox1.Text = ""
              For intCount = 0 To Response.Errors.Length - 1
                    TextBox1.Text = TextBox1.Text & "Error: " & _
                          Response.Errors(intCount).ErrorCode
                    TextBox1.Text = TextBox1.Text & vbCrLf & "Message: " & _
                          Response.Errors(intCount).LongMessage
              Next intCount

        End If

        Exit Sub

handleerror:
        MsgBox("An error occurred: " & Err.Number & " - " & Err.Description)
        Exit Sub

End Sub
```

2. Run this program and specify 3 when prompted to run this example.

XML Example

The following code is an example of XML code that retrieves all pending auctions for a specified seller using the GetSellerList method. Follow the instructions described in the beginning of this section if you want to run this example from the existing project. Also, replace the User ID with the ID of someone for whom you want to retrieve pending auctions.

```
<?xml version="1.0" encoding="utf-8" ?>
<request>
<RequestToken>Your Token Here</RequestToken>
<ErrorLevel>1</ErrorLevel>
<UserId>Valid User Id Goes Here</UserId>
<Verb>GetSellerList</Verb>
<DetailLevel>32</DetailLevel>
<ItemsPerPage>10</ItemsPerPage>
<PageNumber>1</PageNumber>
<EndTimeFrom>2004-10-20 00:00:01</EndTimeFrom>
<EndTimeTo>2004-10-20 23:59:59</EndTimeTo>
</request>
```

#4 — *Retrieve Winning Bidders of Dutch Auction*

This example calls the `GetHighBidders` method to retrieve the winning bidders for a Dutch auction.

SOAP Example

1. Add the following `Example4` procedure to the code section of the existing project. Replace the values where specified with your own eBay credentials. Also specify a valid Dutch auction item ID on the Sandbox test eBay site where indicated.

```
Sub Example4()

        On Error GoTo handleerror

        Dim strToken As String
        Dim strDevId As String
        Dim strAppId As String
        Dim strCertId As String

        'specify credentials required to access API
        strToken = "Your Token Here"
        strDevId = "Your Dev Id Here"
        strAppId = "Your App Id Here"
        strCertId = "Your Cert Id Here"

        Dim SOAPService As New ebay.eBayAPIInterfaceService
        SOAPService.Url = _
    "https://api.sandbox.ebay.com/wsapi?callname=GetHighBidders&siteid=0&appid=" & _
    strAppId & "version=383"

        SOAPService.RequesterCredentials = New ebay.CustomSecurityHeaderType
        SOAPService.RequesterCredentials.eBayAuthToken = strToken
        SOAPService.RequesterCredentials.Credentials = New ebay.UserIdPasswordType
        SOAPService.RequesterCredentials.Credentials.AppId = strAppId
        SOAPService.RequesterCredentials.Credentials.DevId = strDevId
        SOAPService.RequesterCredentials.Credentials.AuthCert = strCertId

        Dim Request As New ebay.GetHighBiddersRequestType
        Dim Response As New ebay.GetHighBiddersResponseType

        'specify the API version
        Request.Version = "383"

        'specify the item id for the dutch auction
        Request.ItemID = "Put Item Id Here"

        'call the AddItem method to list the item
        Response = SOAPService.GetHighBidders(Request)

        Dim intCount As Integer

        'display the successful list of users who purchased
        'this item under the dutch auction
        If IsNothing(Response.Errors) Then
```

```
                Dim items As ebay.OfferType

                'if no users, then exit
                If IsNothing(Response.BidArray) Then
                    TextBox1.Text = "No users were returned."
                    Exit Sub
                End If

                For Each items In Response.BidArray
                    TextBox1.Text = TextBox1.Text & vbCrLf & "User Id:" & _
                            items.User.UserID & vbCrLf
                    TextBox1.Text = TextBox1.Text & "Quantity:" & items.Quantity & _
                            vbCrLf
                Next
            Else
                'display any errors that occurred
                TextBox1.Text = ""
                For intCount = 0 To Response.Errors.Length - 1
                    TextBox1.Text = TextBox1.Text & "Error: " & _
                        Response.Errors(intCount).ErrorCode
                    TextBox1.Text = TextBox1.Text & vbCrLf & "Message: " & _
                        Response.Errors(intCount).LongMessage
                Next intCount
            End If

            Exit Sub

handleerror:
            MsgBox("An error occurred: " & Err.Number & " - " & Err.Description)
            Exit Sub

        End Sub
```

2. Run the project and specify 4 when prompted to run this example.

XML Example

This example shows the XML code for retrieving the winning bidders of a Dutch auction using the GetHighBidders method. See the earlier instructions for using this in the existing project. Replace the ItemId value with the Item ID of a listing for which you wish to retrieve winning bidders.

```xml
<?xml version="1.0" encoding="utf-8" ?>
<request>
<RequestToken>Your Token Here</RequestToken>
<ErrorLevel>1</ErrorLevel>
<ItemId>4501701557</ItemId>
<Verb>GetHighBidders</Verb>
</request>
```

#5 — Retrieve Feedback about a Seller

This final example calls the GetFeedback method to retrieve feedback about a particular seller.

SOAP Example

1. Add the following `Example5` procedure to the code section of the existing project. Replace the values where specified with your own eBay credentials.

```
Sub Example5()

        On Error GoTo handleerror

        Dim strToken As String
        Dim strDevId As String
        Dim strAppId As String
        Dim strCertId As String

        'specify credentials required to access API
        strToken = "Your Token Here"
        strDevId = "Your Dev Id Here"
        strAppId = "Your App Id Here"
        strCertId = "Your Cert Id Here"

        Dim SOAPService As New ebay.eBayAPIInterfaceService
        SOAPService.Url = _
    "https://api.sandbox.ebay.com/wsapi?callname=GetFeedback&siteid=0&appid=" & _
    strAppId & "version=383"

        SOAPService.RequesterCredentials = New ebay.CustomSecurityHeaderType
        SOAPService.RequesterCredentials.eBayAuthToken = strToken
        SOAPService.RequesterCredentials.Credentials = New ebay.UserIdPasswordType
        SOAPService.RequesterCredentials.Credentials.AppId = strAppId
        SOAPService.RequesterCredentials.Credentials.DevId = strDevId
        SOAPService.RequesterCredentials.Credentials.AuthCert = strCertId

        Dim Request As New ebay.GetFeedbackRequestType
        Dim Response As New ebay.GetFeedbackResponseType

        'specify the API version
        Request.Version = "383"

        'specify the seller's user id to retrieve feedback for
        Request.UserID = "Specify a Valid Seller User Id"

        'call the GetFeedback method to retrieve the feedback
        Response = SOAPService.GetFeedback(Request)

        Dim intCount As Integer

        'display the feedback about the seller
        If IsNothing(Response.Errors) Then
            Dim items As New ebay.FeedbackDetailType

            'if no feedback, then exit
            If IsNothing(Response.FeedbackDetailArray) Then
                TextBox1.Text = "No feedback for this seller"
                Exit Sub
            End If
```

```
                         'loop through and display the feedback
                         For Each items In Response.FeedbackDetailArray
                              TextBox1.Text = TextBox1.Text & vbCrLf & "Commenting User:" & _
                                   items.CommentingUser & vbCrLf
                              TextBox1.Text = TextBox1.Text & "Comment:" & items.CommentText & _
                                   vbCrLf
                         Next
                    Else
                         'display any errors that occurred
                         TextBox1.Text = ""
                         For intCount = 0 To Response.Errors.Length - 1
                              TextBox1.Text = TextBox1.Text & "Error: " & _
                                   Response.Errors(intCount).ErrorCode
                              TextBox1.Text = TextBox1.Text & vbCrLf & "Message: " & _
                                   Response.Errors(intCount).LongMessage
                         Next intCount
                    End If

                    Exit Sub

          handleerror:
                    MsgBox("An error occurred: " & Err.Number & " - " & Err.Description)
                    Exit Sub

          End Sub
```

2. Run the project, and specify 5 when prompted to run this example.

XML Example

The following XML code retrieves feedback about a particular seller using the `GetFeedback` method. See the earlier instructions for running this example from the existing project. Replace the `UserId` value with the User ID of the person for whom you want to retrieve feedback.

```
<?xml version="1.0" encoding="utf-8" ?>
<request>
<RequestToken>Your Token Here</RequestToken>
<ErrorLevel>1</ErrorLevel>
<DetailLevel>1</DetailLevel>
<Verb>GetFeedback</Verb>
<UserId>Specify User Id Here</UserId>
</request>
```

Other Ways to Use the eBay API

In the previous sections, you looked at five examples to give you an idea of how you can use the eBay API in your applications. Following are some additional examples of ways you might want to use the eBay API. Additional examples of the eBay API are also included in the later chapters and case studies at the end of this book.

Here are examples of other ways to use the eBay Web API:

❑ Send an automatic e-mail to the winning bidder after you determine the auction has closed and a winner has been established.

❑ Sign up for platform notifications (commercial-tier members only) where an HTTP post is made to a URL you specify when certain events occur, such as a buyer leaving feedback or an auction ending.

❑ Retrieve a daily or other periodic status report of your listings on eBay.

❑ Create a third-party listing tool that enables your customers to more easily manage their listings from within their existing inventory management applications.

Third-Party eBay Extensions

As with the other APIs discussed so far, dozens of third parties have used the eBay Web API in creative ways. On the eBay Web site, you can find an extensive list of what some of these third parties have done. The list is currently located at `http://developer.ebay.com/DevProgram/business/stories.asp`.

For example, Bonfire Media (`www.bonfiremedia.com`) currently offers a product called Pocket Auctions, which is an application that uses the eBay API to allow users to shop, compare prices, bid, and so on from their mobile phones. An example of a screen from the Bonfire Media Web site discussing Pocket Auctions is illustrated in Figure 5-13.

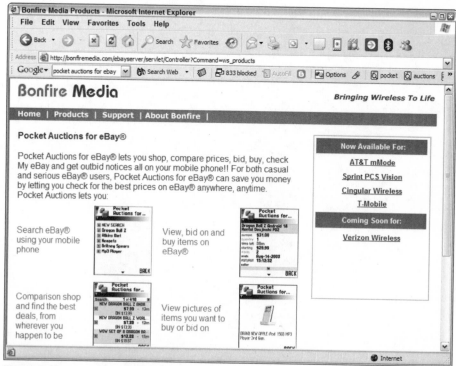

Figure 5-13

Another example is a company called MarketWorks (www.marketworks.com) that has used the eBay API to streamline the listing of over 2 million listings per month. Other companies have used the API to integrate eBay features into existing applications or have created listing tools to make management of listings easier.

Summary

You learned about eBay as a leading online auction house, and how eBay is helping assure its future success by making it easy for you to include eBay functionality in your own programs. You learned about the two different ways you can call an eBay API, and you looked at some examples of how you can use the API in your own programs. If you want more information about the eBay API, additional examples are included in some of the later chapters or in the comprehensive online documentation.

Now, turn to Chapter 6 where you learn about the eBay's sister API: PayPal.

Using the PayPal API

If you are familiar with eBay, you are probably also familiar with PayPal. PayPal became famous for allowing individuals and businesses alike to easily accept credit cards and other electronic payments for their eBay auction sales. PayPal is also accepted as a payment service by companies other than just eBay. Companies all over the world have established PayPal merchant accounts to allow payment for their goods and services online by customers who have a PayPal account. Given that eBay currently owns PayPal, it is not surprising that an API has also been released to allow developers to more easily integrate PayPal payment transactions into their custom applications.

This chapter gets you up and running with the PayPal API, and more specifically, covers the following:

❑   An introduction to PayPal as an online payment service

❑   How to set up a developer account and a security certificate required to use the PayPal API

❑   How to convert the security certificate to the required format

❑   The syntax of PayPal API queries

❑   How to call the PayPal API using SOAP from Visual Studio .NET

❑   Additional ideas for how you might use the PayPal API

Although the setup process to use the PayPal API is a bit tedious, the PayPal API itself is less detailed than the others you have looked at so far because you have only a few different ways to process payments. Additional information, including code examples and API documentation, is available on the PayPal developer site. This chapter spends the majority of time helping you get set up to use the PayPal API and also providing a simple example to illustrate how to call the API to process payments from your programs.

PayPal 101

PayPal offers secure online payment options. Buyers can set up a PayPal account and fund the account with a credit card, a bank account, or by sending in money to PayPal. Merchants can use PayPal to accept various types of payments and pays PayPal a commission for handling the transaction. To set up a PayPal buyer or merchant account for use online, visit www.paypal.com, as shown in Figure 6-1.

Figure 6-1

PayPal was made famous because of eBay, but numerous other companies use PayPal to facilitate payment transactions on their own Web sites.

Introduction to the PayPal API

Now that you know the basics of the services that PayPal offers, let's turn to the PayPal API. The PayPal API is an XML Web service that can be called using the SOAP protocol. This concept was introduced in Chapter 1.

Supported Features

The PayPal API supports four services in the current form, which is the beta version of the PayPal API at the time of this book's writing:

- ❑ **GetTransactionDetails** — Retrieve details about a particular transaction
- ❑ **TransactionSearch** — Search for transactions that meet a specified criteria
- ❑ **RefundTransaction** — Refund a prior transaction in full or in part
- ❑ **MassPay** — Send one or more payments at a time

Each of these services is examined in more detail later in this chapter.

Getting Set Up to Use the PayPal API

Like eBay, PayPal has a test environment called the *Sandbox* where you can test the workings of your program without hitting a live server. With PayPal, because money is involved, additional steps must be taken to ensure the communications are highly secure.

In this section, I will navigate you through the tedious process of getting a developer account set up, creating some test accounts, adding some money to those test accounts, manually creating transactions, and getting a security certificate. All these setup steps are necessary before you can take advantage of the PayPal API in the test environment. Of course, because money is involved and you are presumably new to the PayPal API, this chapter focuses on the Sandbox test environment. If you want to work with the live PayPal API later on, you must change the URL to point to the live site instead.

Setting Up a Developer's Account

In order to access the Sandbox test environment and to access the online documentation for the PayPal API, you need a developer's account. First, go to `http://developer.paypal.com`, as shown in Figure 6-2.

Click the link that says "Sign Up Now" and a signup screen, as shown in Figure 6-3, will be displayed.

Fill in the requested information and follow the online instructions for completing the account registration. After you have a developer account, you can revisit developer.paypal.com and log in with your new account. A screen like the one shown in Figure 6-4 is then displayed.

After you log into PayPal Developer Central, you have access to the various resources that enable you to work with the API. The Sandbox option allows you to manage test accounts and log into the Sandbox using one of the test accounts. The Test Certificates option allows you to view test certificates for your accounts. The Email option allows you to view a virtual e-mail inbox of the test accounts you have created. All e-mails that would normally be sent to an actual e-mail are instead placed in the virtual e-mail account online when you work with the Sandbox test environment. Forums are available where you can collaborate with others regarding the PayPal API. Finally, the Help Center option allows you to download code examples and documentation.

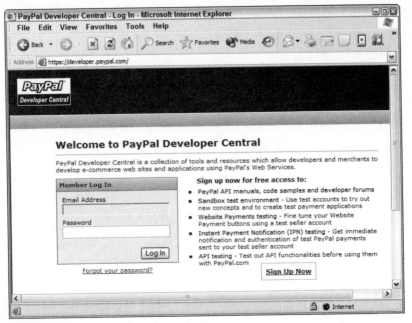

Figure 6-2

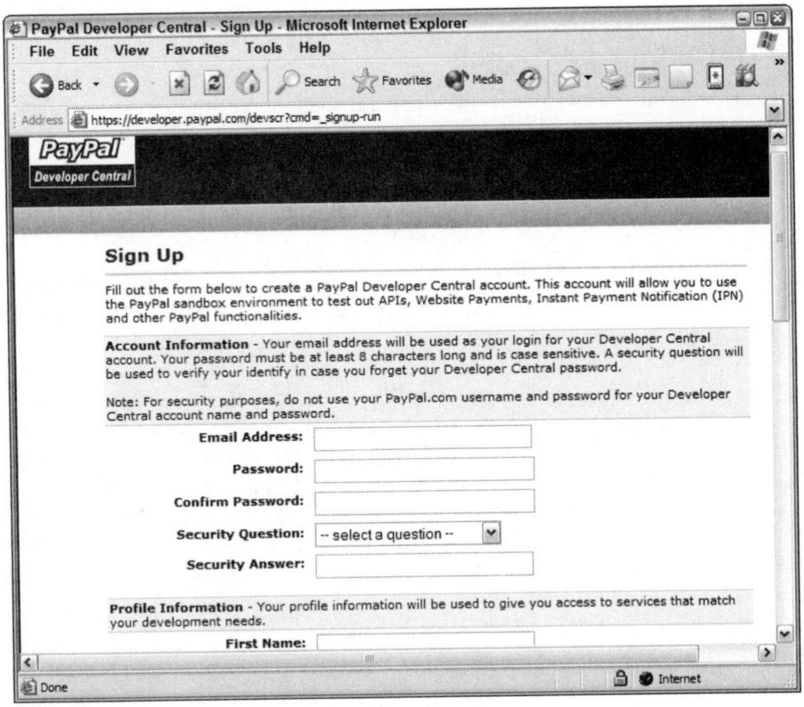

Figure 6-3

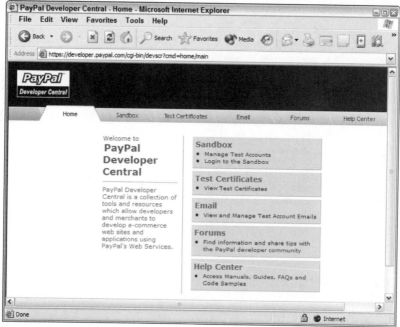

Figure 6-4

Setting Up Test Accounts

After you have created a developer account, you can create test accounts. While logged in to your developer account, click the Sandbox option. You need to set up a test Buyer and a test Seller account to use in the example later in this chapter. To do so, click the Create a Test Account link. A screen like the one shown in Figure 6-5 is displayed.

Choose the type of account you want to set up — personal or business — and click the Continue button, as shown in Figure 6-6. Select Personal Account and click Continue. You will repeat these steps later to create a business account.

An Account Sign Up form, as shown in Figure 6-7, is then displayed.

Fill in the address information and other information requested on the screen. You do not need to provide real data because this is just a test account. For security reasons, please do not use your actual PayPal password for this test account. You can provide totally fictitious data; you just need to remember the username and password that is specified so you can log into that account later. Do not worry about e-mails being sent to that e-mail address. As mentioned earlier, all e-mails go to your virtual inbox when you are working in the Sandbox test environment.

You can tell you are in the Sandbox by the Sandbox logo on the Web page, or from the URL itself.

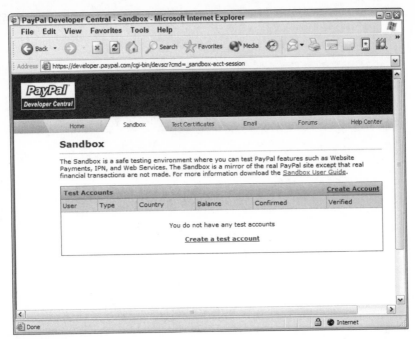

Figure 6-5

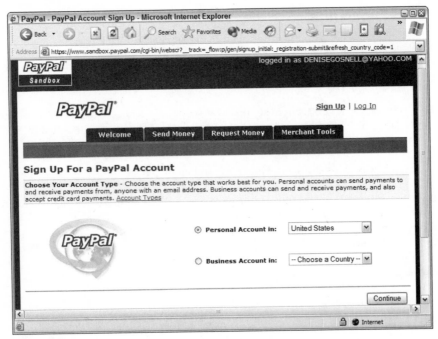

Figure 6-6

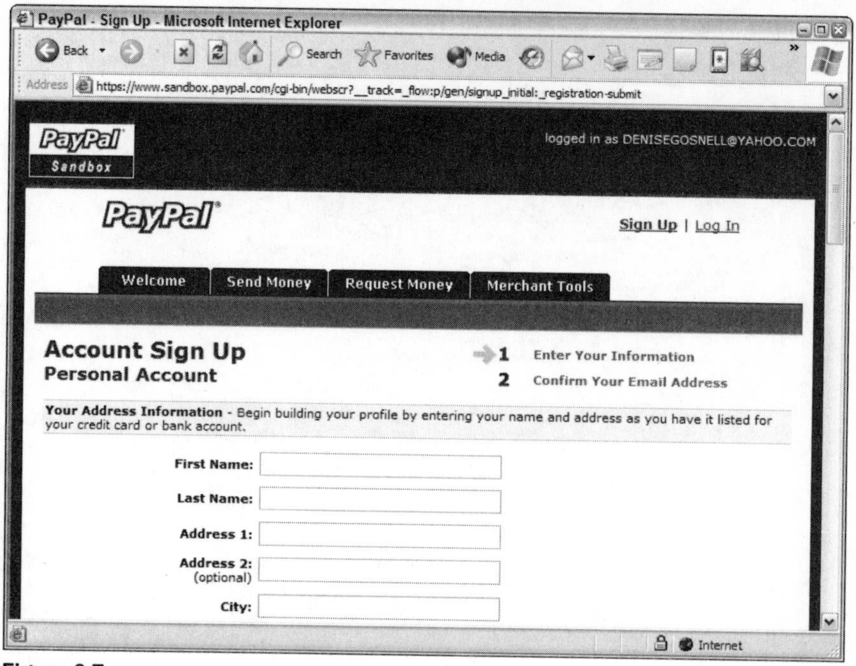

Figure 6-7

After you submit the new user registration, a screen similar to Figure 6-8 is displayed.

You are instructed to go to your e-mail to confirm the e-mail address. Again, because no e-mail is actually sent, it is really talking about your online virtual inbox. To access the message to confirm your e-mail address, simply visit developer.paypal.com, log in with your developer account, and then click the Email tab, as shown in Figure 6-9.

From the virtual e-mail inbox, open the confirmation e-mail. Follow the instructions in the message to confirm your account. You are prompted to enter the password associated with that test account. A confirmation screen is then displayed to indicate your account was activated. You are given the option to set up a bank account from that point. If you select Skip, you can add test bank account and/or credit card information later. Go ahead and click Continue, where you are taken to a screen that automatically fills in some test bank account information. You just fill in a test account name and click the option to create the test account.

> To log into the test user account at any time, log in to the developer.paypal.com site, select the Sandbox option, and then select the test account you want to log in to. You are then prompted to provide the login credentials for that account and redirected to the Sandbox environment for that account.

You should make sure to set up a test bank account and a test credit card for this new test user by selecting Add Credit Card or Add Bank Account option from the main screen after logging in to the Sandbox environment with that test user.

Repeat the process described previously to create a test business account for a seller.

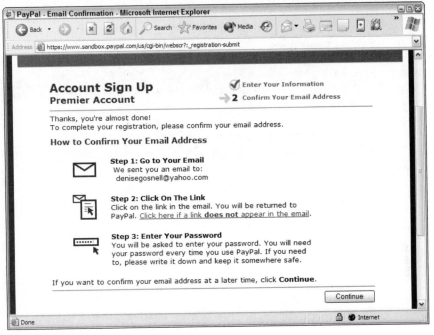

Figure 6-8
These materials have been reproduced with the permission of PayPal, Inc. Copyright © 2003 PayPal, Inc. All rights reserved.

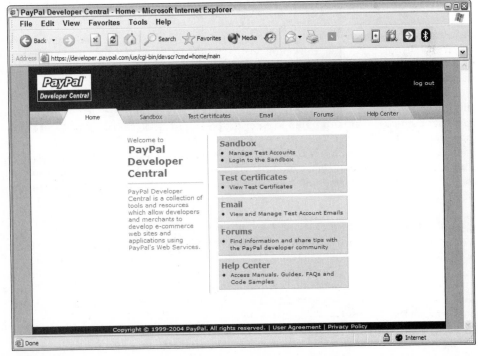

Figure 6-9
These materials have been reproduced with the permission of PayPal, Inc. Copyright © 2003 PayPal, Inc. All rights reserved.

Setting Up Test Transactions

Now that you have created a test personal account and a test business account, the next step is to fund the accounts and create some test transactions. The API cannot be used to add funds to an account or to create a transaction, but simply to work with existing transactions. Thus, you need to use the online tools to add some money to the test personal account and then send some money from that account to the test business account. To do so, log into developer.paypal.com (PayPal Developer Central), click the Sandbox tab, click the Launch Sandbox button, and log in with your test personal account.

Begin by manually adding some money to the test personal account you want to use for the purchase. While logged in to the Sandbox account for that user, select Add Funds. Under options, select Transfer Funds. Select the account and the dollar amount and click Continue.

Because this is a test account, you also have to manually clear the transaction. From the Overviews tab, the transaction should be listed as pending. If you click the Details link, an option to clear the transaction appears. Select the Clear Transaction link and the status of the transaction changes to Completed.

Next, you need to set up one or more test transactions so you can work with those transactions using the API. While still logged in to the test personal account, click the Send Money tab. Fill in the information for the test business account, including the e-mail address you assigned to that account and the amount you want to pay it. Follow the online instructions to complete the transaction.

Verify that the transaction was successful by logging out of the test personal account and by logging into the test business account. The payment should be shown on the Overview page, as shown in the example in Figure 6-10. Notice that the available balance has been reduced by the PayPal service fee.

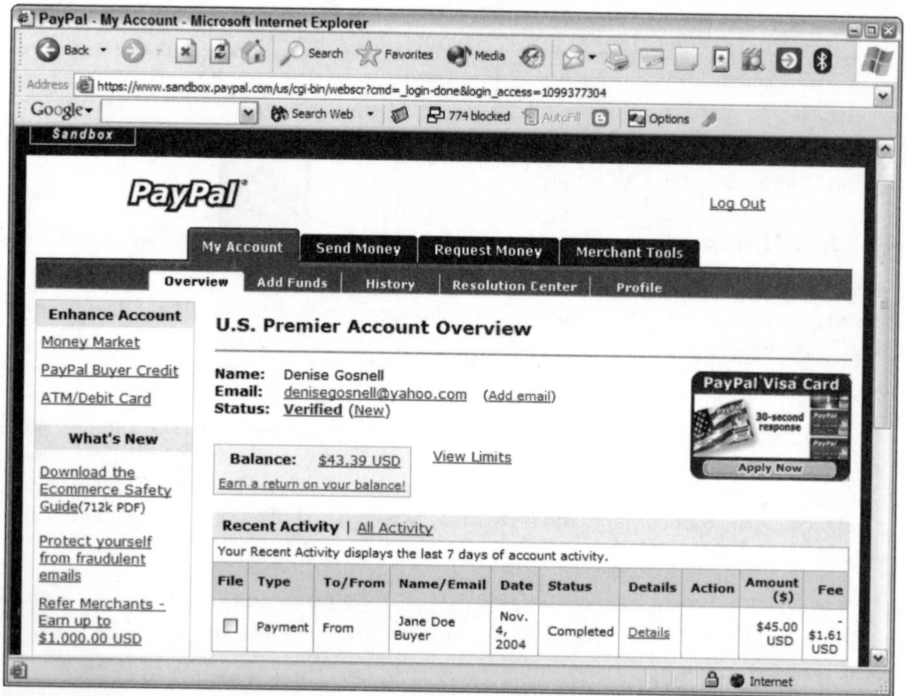

Figure 6-10

Click the Details link, and a screen similar to Figure 6-11 is displayed.

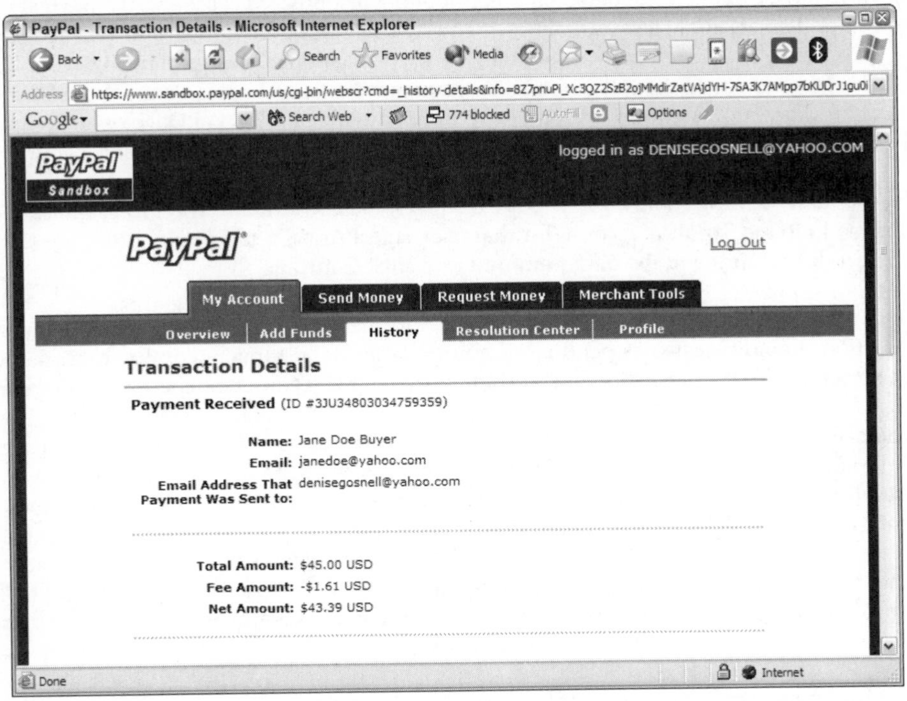

Figure 6-11

Write down or electronically copy the Transaction ID value so you can use that transaction for testing the API in the code example later in this chapter.

Obtaining and Converting a Security Certificate

You are now ready to perform the last setup step to enable you to use the API — obtaining and converting the security certificate. As mentioned previously, because the PayPal API deals with monetary transactions, you must use a higher level of security than you do with many other Web APIs discussed in this book.

To obtain a certificate, log into PayPal Sandbox with your test business (seller) account. Click on the Profile tab, and then click the API Access link. Then, click the API Certificate Request link. Fill in the information requested to set up a certificate, and then click the Generate Certificate button. Click the Download button to download the text file that contains the certificate. Save the text file to a location on your hard drive where you can find it later.

As another option, an e-mail is also sent that contains a link for downloading your certificate. Again, for the test Sandbox environment, the e-mail is placed in your online inbox as opposed to being sent to your actual e-mail address.

Open the text file in a text editor such as Notepad and separate the private key and the certificate into two separate files. The private key is indicated with the Begin and End RSA Private Key comment, and the certificate portion is indicated with the Begin and End Certificate comment. Save the private key in a file called `privatekey.pem` and save the certificate in a file called `certificate.pem`. Other names can also be used.

> *It is important that each file contains the comment in the correct syntax, with five dashes surrounding each comment. Otherwise, you will receive an error later when trying to create the P12 certificate. For example, the privatekey.pem file should contain the following:*
>
> *-----BEGIN RSA PRIVATE KEY-----Your key is here-----END RSA PRIVATE KEY-----*

At this point, you have to use a cryptographic tool to convert the certificates to a PKCS12 (.p12) certificate file. One example of such a tool is described in the PayPal documentation is OpenSSL, which is offered in an easy installation version for Windows at `www.slproweb.com`. More information about OpenSSL can also be found at `www.openssl.org`. Follow the instructions to download and install OpenSSL.

Open a command window and navigate to the path where OpenSSL.exe is located (based on where you installed the program). Copy your two .pem files to that same path to make this process easier. Type openssl.exe to run the program, and at the OpenSSL prompt, type the following command to convert the certificate files created previously:

```
pkcs12 -export -inkey privatekey.pem -in certificate.pem -out my_paypal_cert.p12
```

You are prompted to enter a password associated with the certificate. Make sure to write down this password for future use. Upon successful creation of the p12 certificate, a screen like the one shown in Figure 6-12 is displayed.

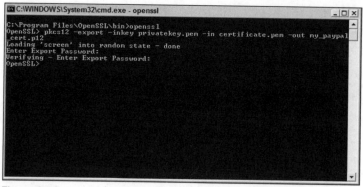

Figure 6-12

Type Exit to exit the OpenSSL tool. Verify that your .p12 certificate, called my_paypal_cert.p12, was created in that same directory. You need this file later, so copy it to a location where you can find it.

At this point, you must convert the .p12 certificate into the type of certificate required by your programming language. For example, to use the PayPal API from Visual Studio .NET, you convert the .p12 certificate to a .CER certificate. To do so, you first should double-click the previously created my_paypal_cert.p12 file. The Certificate Import Wizard appears. Follow the prompts to import the certificate, specifying your certificate password when prompted. Accept the defaults, and a message should appear indicating that the import was successful.

Next, after the wizard completes, you export the .p12 certificate from Internet Explorer to a .CER file. To do so, open Internet Explorer, and then select Tools ⇨ Internet Options and select the Content tab. Click the Certificates button and select the .p12 certificate that you use to access the Sandbox. It should appear on the Personal tab. Click the Export button, and a Certificate Export Wizard appears. Follow the wizard to accept the defaults, and on the File to Export screen, select Browse and specify the path and filename for the new certificate. Click Save to save the file and follow the prompts to finish the wizard. It is important that you keep track of the name and location where you saved the .CER file because you will need it in calls to the API later on.

Anatomy of a PayPal API Query

Now that you have all the messy setup out of the way, let's take a look at how a PayPal API query is structured. You then see a simple example of how to execute queries using the API.

Query Syntax

Currently, you can call one of four methods of the PayPal API: `RefundTransaction`, `TransactionSearch`, `GetTransactionDetails`, and `MassPay`. Each of these is covered detail.

RefundTransaction

The `RefundTransaction` method is used to request a payment refund. A `RefundTransactionRequest` is an object that is passed to the `RefundTransaction` method and supports the following properties:

❑ **TransactionId** — Required. Unique identifier for a transaction.

❑ **RefundType** — Type of refund. Currently `Full` or `Partial`.

❑ **Amount** — Amount of refund. Required if partial refund.

❑ **Memo** — Custom comment about the refund.

The `RefundTransaction` method responds by returning a `RefundTransactionResponse` object.

TransactionSearch

The `TransactionSearch` method requests a historical transaction search. Up to 100 exact matches can be retrieved. Various criteria can be specified to limit the search results. The following properties are supported by the `TransactionSearchRequest` object that is passed to the `TransactionSearch` method:

❑ **StartDate** — Required. Starting date range to use for search.

❑ **End Date** — Ending date range to use for search.

❑ **Payer** — E-mail address of buyer.

❑ **Receiver** — E-mail address of receiver.

❑ **ReceiptId** — PayPal Account Optional Receipt ID. If specified, other search values ignored.

❑ **TransactionId** — Transaction ID of the buyer or seller. If specified, other search values ignored.

❑ **InvoiceId** — Invoice identification key as set by merchant for original transaction.

❑ **PayerName** — Various name combinations.

❑ **AuctionItemNumber** — Auction Item Number. If specified, other search values ignored.

❑ **TransactionClass** — Classification (examples include "All", "Payments", "Sent", "Received", and so on).

❑ **Amount** — Transaction amount that was charged to the buyer.

❑ **CurrencyCode** — Currency code to search for (examples include "USD", "GBP", "EUR", and so on).

❑ **Status** — Status of transaction (examples include "None", "Completed", "Failed", "Pending", "Denied", and so on).

The `TransactionSearch` method responds by returning a `TransactionSearchResponse` object with details about the transactions meeting the specified criteria.

GetTransactionDetails

The `GetTransactionDetails` method requests details about a payment. Currently, the `GetTransactionDetailsRequest` object that is passed to the `GetTransactionDetails` object supports the following properties:

❑ **TransactionId** — Required. Unique identifier for a transaction.

❑ **Version** — Required. String that represents the version of the response schema (currently "1.0").

The `GetTransactionDetails` method responds by returning a `GetTransactionDetailsResponse` object with details about the particular transaction.

MassPay

The `MassPay` method allows a merchant to make payment distribution requests. The `MassPayRequest` object that is passed to the `MassPay` method currently supports the following properties:

❑ **EmailSubject** — E-mail subject to use in e-mail to recipients.

❑ **ReceiverEmail** — Required. E-mail address of recipients.

❑ **Amount** — Required. Amount to send to each recipient.

❑ **UniqueId** — Unique ID for each recipient to be used for tracking purposes.

❑ **Note** — Customized note for each recipient.

The `MassPay` method responds by returning a `MassPayResponse` object with details about the success or failure of the request.

Executing a Query

Now that you have a basic idea of the types of operations supported by the PayPal API, let's look at some simple code examples to see how they work. PayPal API calls can be executed using SOAP operations. As you recall, with SOAP operations, you have to specify the location of the WSDL file that describes the Web API and then create a proxy so that your program knows how to communicate with the Web API. Visual Studio .NET handles the creation of the proxy for you when you add a Web reference.

Walkthrough Example — Calling the PayPal API Using SOAP from Visual Studio .NET

Let's walk through a step-by-step example of using SOAP to call the PayPal Web service from Visual Studio .NET. In this example, you call the `RefundTransaction` operation to fully refund a prior transaction that you manually created earlier in this chapter.

1. Open Visual Studio .NET and select File ⇨ New ⇨ Project.

2. Select Visual Basic Project as the Project Type, and select Windows Application as the Template. For the project name, specify `PayPalSample`, and for the path, specify the location where you want the project to be created. Click OK to create the new project.

3. Drag and drop one command button from the Toolbox onto the form.

4. Add a reference to the PayPal API by selecting Project ⇨ Add Web Reference. For the URL field, specify the location of the WSDL file, such as:

   `www.sandbox.paypal.com/wsdl/PayPalSvc.wsdl`

5. Click the GO button so that Visual Studio can locate the PayPal Web API.

6. Change the Web Reference Name to `PayPal` so that you can use a shorter name in your project.

7. Click the Add Reference button to add the reference to your project. Visual Studio .NET uses the WSDL file to identify the methods that are available for execution from your project.

8. Add the following procedure to `Form1` to the `Click` event of the second button:

```
Private Sub Button1_Click(ByVal sender As System.Object, ByVal e As _
    System.EventArgs) Handles Button1.Click

    On Error GoTo handle_error

    'create a reference to the paypal service
    Dim pp As New PayPal.PayPalAPIInterfaceService

    'set the required credentials for using the service
    pp.RequesterCredentials = New PayPal.CustomSecurityHeaderType
    pp.RequesterCredentials.Credentials = New PayPal.UserIdPasswordType
    pp.RequesterCredentials.Credentials.Username = "Your PayPal DevZone userid"
    pp.RequesterCredentials.Credentials.Password = "Your PayPal DevZone pwd"
    pp.RequesterCredentials.Credentials.AuthCert = "my_paypal_certificate.cer"
    pp.Url = "https://api.sandbox.paypal.com/2.0/"

    Dim request As New PayPal.RefundTransactionReq
    request.RefundTransactionRequest = New PayPal.RefundTransactionRequestType
```

```
        request.RefundTransactionRequest.Version = "1.0"
        request.RefundTransactionRequest.TransactionID = "ID of your transaction"

        Dim response As New PayPal.RefundTransactionResponseType

        response = pp.RefundTransaction(request)

        Exit Sub
handle_error:
        MsgBox(Err.Description)
        Exit Sub

    End Sub
```

9. Input your specific User Name, Password, .CER Certificate location/name, and Transaction ID on the lines of code where indicated.

10. Select File ⇨ Save All to save all changes to the project.

11. Select Debug ⇨ Start (or press F5) to run the project. Click the button to run the example.

12. After the operation finishes successfully, log in to the test personal account that you used earlier to perform the transaction. That is the account that should receive the refund.

13. Upon logging in to that account, you should see a window similar to Figure 6-13 that displays a refund entry from the test business account.

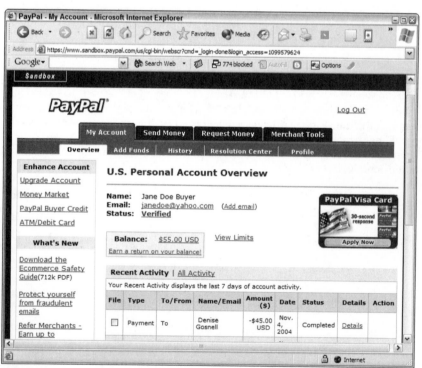

Figure 6-13

Because PayPal has provided a test client called API Client that illustrates how to use each of the available methods, they are not covered in this chapter. Please visit the Help Center in the PayPal Developer Zone for more information on downloading the API Client project.

Other Ways to Use the PayPal API

In the previous section, you looked at an example of how to use the PayPal API in your applications. Here are a couple of other ideas of how you might use the PayPal API:

❑ Perform a search for transactions that were denied so you can follow-up with those customers to make alternate payment arrangements.

❑ Perform a search for transactions that were processed over a particular time period to calculate your total sales revenue.

Third-Party PayPal Extensions

Various third parties offer solutions that work with PayPal, including some that use the API. You can find a list of what some of these third parties have done on the PayPal Web site. The list is currently located at:

```
https://www.paypal.com/us/cgi-bin/webscr?cmd=p/pdn/3p-solutions
```

Summary

PayPal is a leading online payment provider that allows buyers and sellers to exchange funds in various ways. Buyers can securely provide credit card and other payment methods to PayPal and then PayPal handles disbursement to the specified merchant. PayPal has made various features available in an API to merchants so that the transactions can be managed from custom programs. You learned the various features supported by the PayPal API, as well as how to call the API using SOAP. Additional examples are provided in the API Client project in the Help Center of the PayPal developer site, as well as in the other documentation contained on that site.

With PayPal under your belts, let's turn to Chapter 7 where you learn about several additional APIs, including InterFax, UPS, FedEx, and Bloglines.

7
Other Web APIs

So far in this book, you have explored several leading APIs in detail. This chapter provides a very brief introduction to some additional Web APIs. You will also learn how to locate additional APIs for use in your programs. This chapter specifically covers the following:

❑   An introduction to InterFax faxing Web API

❑   An example of sending a fax programmatically from Visual Studio .NET

❑   An introduction to the UPS API

❑   An example of submitting a request to the UPS API

❑   An introduction to the FedEx API

❑   An example of submitting a transaction using FedEx Ship Manager Direct

❑   An introduction to the Bloglines API

❑   Information on how to locate additional Web service APIs

If you want more information about any of the Web APIs covered in this chapter, visit the respective Web sites. Comprehensive documentation and code examples are available for each of them.

Faxing APIs

If you are like me, I'm sure that at times you have wanted to send a fax from your computer without using a phone line. Luckily for us, fax Web APIs are available today that enable us to send faxes from our own programs with just an Internet connection. For example, a company called InterFax Inc. (www.interfax.net) offers an XML Web service that allows faxes to be sent with and without file attachments to one or more fax numbers worldwide.

InterFax charges per page to use the service, and you purchase a prepaid number of pages before using the service. More information about pricing is available online at `http://www.interfax.net/scripts/prices.asp?lang=en`. For example, at the time of this book's writing, faxes can be sent using the service for a charge of approximately 7 cents to 11 cents per page depending on volume.

InterFax offers a free developer program that allows you to send unlimited faxes to a single fax number, such as to your own fax number, for testing your programs. I'll quickly walk you through the steps for obtaining a developer registration and sending a test fax using the service.

Setting Up a Free Developer Account

To set up a free developer account, go to `http://www.interfax.net/en/dev/index.html`, as shown in Figure 7-1.

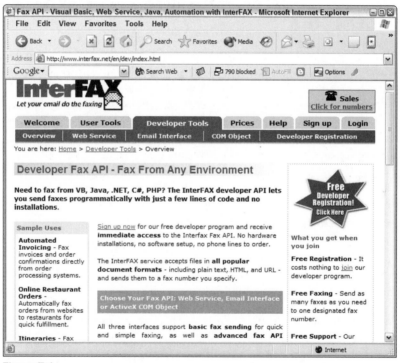

Figure 7-1

Click the Sign Up Now link and fill in the information requested on the registration form shown in Figure 7-2.

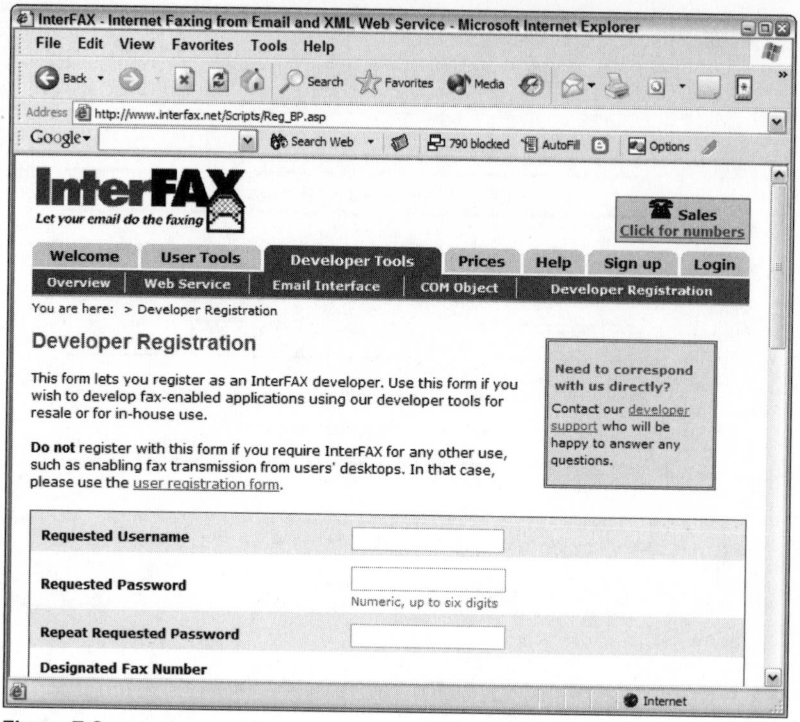

Figure 7-2

You must specify a username, a numeric password, the fax number to use in your testing, and so on. The fax number you specify is the only one to which you can send faxes for free with your developer account. After you have completed filling in all the information on the registration form, click the Submit button. A confirmation screen is then displayed that provides your Partner Code. You should print this page for your records. An e-mail confirmation is also sent to the address you specified in the registration. Now that you have a developer account, try sending a sample fax.

Sending a Test Fax

In this section, you use the InterFax API to send a fax to the fax number associated with your developer account. The code is written using Visual Studio .NET for illustration purposes. You should first decide which file you want to fax to yourself. You can create a test fax in a Word processor. Alternatively, you can select an existing file that you wish to send and just use that one in the example. An example of a test fax is shown in Figure 7-3.

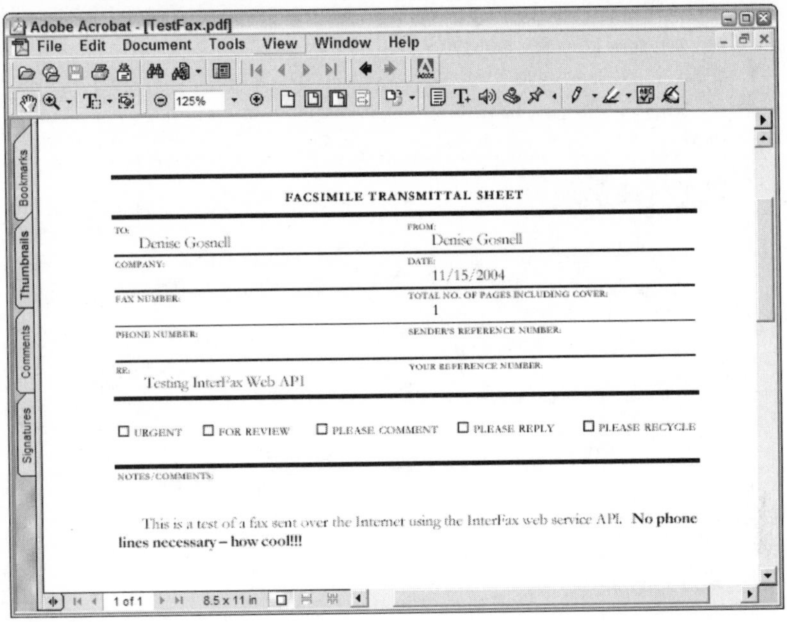

Figure 7-3

At this point, let's get started writing the code.

1. Open Visual Studio .NET and select File ⇨ New ⇨ Project.

2. Select Visual Basic Project as the Project Type, and select Windows Application as the Template. For the project name, specify `InterFaxSample`, and for the path, specify the location where you want the project to be created. Click OK to create the new project.

3. Drag and drop one command button from the Toolbox onto the form.

4. Add a reference to the InterFax API by selecting Project ⇨ Add Web Reference. For the URL field, specify the location of the WSDL file, such as `http://ws.interfax.net/dfs.asmx?wsdl`.

5. Click the GO button so that Visual Studio locates the InterFax Web API.

6. Change the Web Reference Name to `InterFax` so that you can use a shorter name in your project.

7. Click the Add Reference button to add the reference to your project. Visual Studio .NET uses the WSDL file to identify the methods that are available for execution from your project.

8. Add the following procedure to `Form1` to the `Click` event of the button:

```
Private Sub Button1_Click(ByVal sender As System.Object, ByVal e As _
        System.EventArgs) Handles Button1.Click

    Dim wsFax As New InterFax.InterFax
    Dim f As System.IO.File
    Dim fs As System.IO.FileStream
```

```
Dim lngResult As Long
Dim strType As String
Dim strFileName As String
Dim strUsername As String
Dim strPassword As String
Dim strFaxNumber As String

'specify the user credentials and fax settings
strUsername = "Your User Name"
strPassword = "Your Numeric Password"
strFaxnumber = "Your Developer Fax Number"
strFileName = "Path/FileName ex: c:\testfax.pdf"

'Read the file into a byte array
fs = f.Open(strFileName, IO.FileMode.Open, IO.FileAccess.Read)
Dim b(fs.Length - 1) As Byte
fs.Read(b, 0, fs.Length)
f = Nothing
fs.Close()

'Retrieve the file type extension
strType = Mid(strFileName, InStrRev(strFileName, ".") + 1)

'Call the Sendfax method to send the fax
lngResult = wsFax.Sendfax(strUsername, strPassword, strFaxNumber, b, _
    strType)

'See if submission to the fax queue was successful
If lngResult > 0 Then
    MsgBox("Your fax was submitted to the fax queue for transmission.")
Else
    MsgBox("An error occurred in submitting the fax.")
End If

wsFax = Nothing

End Sub
```

9. Input your specific username, password, fax number, and filename on the lines of code where indicated.

10. Select File ➪ Save All to save all changes to the project.

11. Select Debug ➪ Start (or press F5) to run the project. Click the button to run the example.

12. You should see a message such as that shown in Figure 7-4 that indicates the success or failure of the fax submission.

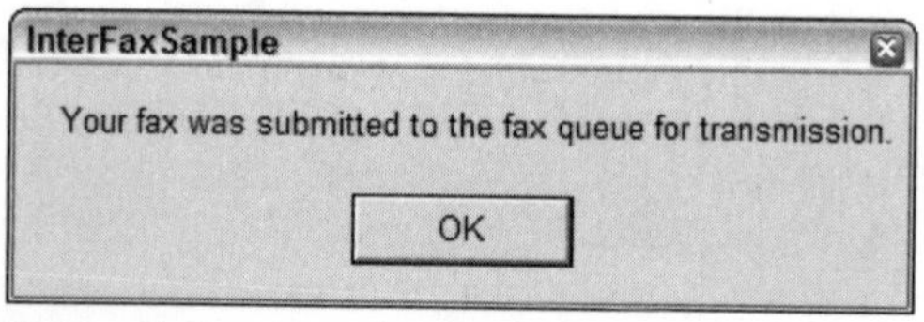

InterFaxSample

Your fax was submitted to the fax queue for transmission.

OK

Figure 7-4

13. If the submission was successful, you receive the fax at the specified fax number within a short time period.

See how easy it is to send a fax using the InterFax Web service! On your own, you can modify the previous example to implement features that allow the user to browse for and specify the file to send and the fax number to send the fax to (which should be your developer fax number if you're using the developer account).

For more information about the methods available from the InterFax Web service, please visit the InterFax Web site at `www.interfax.net`.

Another example of a free faxing Web service can be found at `http://www.webservicex.net/WS/WSDetails.aspx?CATID=4&WSID=7`. *WebserviceX.Net* offers a variety of Web services. The SendFax method is free to use, but currently appears to allow you to send only text faxes and not file attachments.

The UPS API

UPS has several tools available for integration. TheUPS OnLine Tools available at `ups.ec.com` are for use by an end user. An end user incorporates the tools into their business's e-commerce-enabled applications that are not available for commercial sale. Third-party developers such as web developers, system integrators, or IT consultants that integrate UPS OnLine Tools for end users must register as a third party. The same holds true for an independent software vendor or application service provider that integrates the tools into their software application(s) for direct or indirect sale to the public. UPS requires a separate third party developer license agreement and product certification by an outside test lab for those applications for sale to the public. If you are interested in licensing UPS OnLine(r) Tools as an Third Party, you need to submit your request to UPS using the Third Party Product Provider License Request (`http://www.ec.ups.com/ecommerce/gettools/prodcompanies.html`).

Before you can use the UPS API, you must set up a developer account and obtain access keys. Let's walk through the registration steps, and then you can use the API to track a package programmatically.

Setting Up a UPS Developer Account

The first step in setting up a developer account involves navigating to `http://www.ec.ups.com/ecommerce/gettools/gtools_intro.html`. A screen similar to the one shown in Figure 7-5 is displayed.

Click the Register link. You are prompted to accept the terms of the UPS license agreement. You then need to fill in the registration information, including a username and password. Upon successful registration, you are directed to the online documentation.

At this point, you still have not completed creation of a developer account. Select Get Tools from the navigation pane, and on the page that says "Choose your UPS online tool," select the type of tool you want to use (rate tracking, and so on). You are prompted to accept the Developer agreement. You are also prompted to specify and/or verify your information. Upon completion of the registration, a confirmation screen like the one shown in Figure 7-6 is displayed.

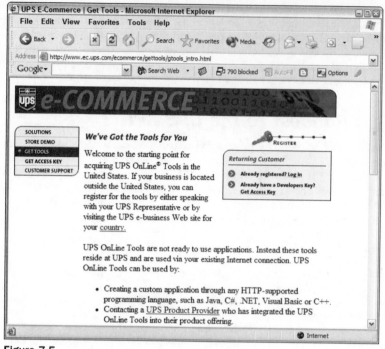

Figure 7-5

Copyright © 2005, United Parcel Service of America, Inc.

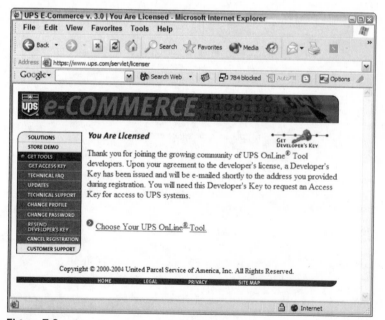

Figure 7-6

Copyright © 2005, United Parcel Service of America, Inc.

A developer key will be e-mailed to you whichyou should save for later use. The developer key enables you to access the online documentation. To access the APIs you need an access key. Next, select the Get Access Key link in the left-hand navigation page, and then specify the type of access key you want to obtain (HTML or XML Access Key). Select XML Access Key in order to work with the XML examples in the following section. You are prompted to enter your developer key and provided with an access key that can be used in your calls to the Web API.

Submitting a Request to the UPS API

The UPS Web API can be accessed by posting HTML or XML documents to the specified UPS Web address, such as `https://www.ups.com/ups.app/xml/Track`. You learned in prior chapters, such as Chapter 5, how to use HTTP-POST to submit an XML document for processing to a Web service. The same techniques can be applied to working with the XML version of the UPS API. One difference in the UPS API is that you must submit two different XML documents for each call to the API. The first XML document contains the credentials for accessing the service, such as:

```
<?xml version="1.0"?>
<AccessRequest xml:lang="en-U">
   <AccessLicenseNumber>YourLicenseNumber</AccessLicenseNumber>
   <UserId>YourUserId</UserId>
   <Password>YourPassword</Password>
</AccessRequest>
```

The second XML document contains details about the service to call, such as the following example that performs a Track request.

```
<?xml version="1.0"?>
<TrackRequest xml:lang="en-US">
<Request>
  <TransactionReference>
    <CustomerContext>UPS Example</CustomerContext>
    <XpciVersion>1.0001</XpciVersion>
  </TransactionReference>
  <RequestAction>Track</RequestAction>
  <RequestOption>activity</RequestOption>
</Request>
<TrackingNumber>YourTrackingNumber</TrackingNumber>
</TrackRequest>
```

Because XML is simply text, you can post both XML documents together as part of the same text string. Here is another example showing both XML documents listed together. This example illustrates how to locate shipment activity by a reference number.

```
<?xml version="1.0"?>
<AccessRequest xml:lang="en-US">
<AccessLicenseNumber>YourLicenseNumber</AccessLicenseNumber>
<UserId>YourUserId</UserId>
<Password>YourPassword</Password>
</AccessRequest>
<?xml version="1.0"?>
<TrackRequest xml:lang="en-US">
```

```
<Request>
<TransactionReference>
<CustomerContext>UPS Example 2</CustomerContext>
<XpciVersion>1.0001</XpciVersion>
</TransactionReference>
<RequestAction>Track</RequestAction>
<RequestOption>none</RequestOption>
</Request>
<ReferenceNumber><Value>YourReferenceNumber</Value></ReferenceNumber>
</TrackRequest>
```

Let's look at a Visual Basic .NET example to see how this works. This example tracks a particular package. Create a new Windows Application and paste the code that follows in the `Form1_Load` event procedure.

```
Dim web As New System.Net.WebClient

Dim strXML As String

strXML = "<?xml version=""1.0""?>" & _
    "<AccessRequest xml:lang=""en-U"">" & _
    "<AccessLicenseNumber>YourLicenseNumber</AccessLicenseNumber>" & _
    "<UserId>YourUserId</UserId>" & _
    "<Password>YourPassword</Password>" & _
    "</AccessRequest>" & _
    "<?xml version=""1.0""?>" & _
    "<TrackRequest xml:lang=""en-US"">" & _
    "<Request>" & _
    "<TransactionReference>" & _
    "<CustomerContext>UPS Example</CustomerContext>" & _
    "<XpciVersion>1.0001</XpciVersion>" & _
    "</TransactionReference>" & _
    "<RequestAction>Track</RequestAction>" & _
    "<RequestOption>activity</RequestOption>" & _
    "</Request>" & _
    "<TrackingNumber>YourTrackingNumber</TrackingNumber>" & _
    "</TrackRequest>"


'add the xml string to the byte array
Dim d As Byte() = System.Text.Encoding.ASCII.GetBytes(strXML)

'call the UPS api and pass the byte array containing the XML string
Dim res As Byte() = _
    web.UploadData("https://www.ups.com/ups.app/xml/Track", "POST", d)

'display the results in a message box
MsgBox(System.Text.Encoding.ASCII.GetString(res))
```

You must specify your own login credentials and your own tracking number on the lines of code where specified.

171

Run the program from Visual Studio .NET, and you see XML results similar to the following in a message box.

```xml
<?xml version="1.0"?>
<TrackResponse>
<Response>
<TransactionReference>
<CustomerContext>UPS Example</CustomerContext>
<XpciVersion>1.0001</XpciVersion>
</TransactionReference>
<ResponseStatusCode>1</ResponseStatusCode>
<ResponseStatusDescription>Success</ResponseStatusDescription>
</Response>
<Shipment>
<Shipper>
<ShipperNumber>596R6V</ShipperNumber>
<Address><AddressLine1>927 SW 22ND ST</AddressLine1>
<City>FORT LAUDERDALE</City>
<StateProvinceCode>FL</StateProvinceCode>
<PostalCode>33315</PostalCode>
<CountryCode>US</CountryCode></Address>
</Shipper>
<ShipTo>
<Address><AddressLine1>10368 Steeplebush Court</AddressLine1>
<City>NOBLESVILLE</City>
<StateProvinceCode>IN</StateProvinceCode>
<PostalCode>46060</PostalCode>
<CountryCode>US</CountryCode></Address>
</ShipTo>
<Service>
<Code>002</Code><Description>2ND DAY AIR</Description>
</Service>
...portions omitted...
</Shipment>
</TrackResponse>
```

See how easy it is to interact with the UPS API. To call different methods of the UPS API, you simply vary the XML code accordingly, and then use code similar to the previous to post the XML document to UPS and process the response.

The FedEx APIs

FedEx offers a number of solutions for incorporating FedEx functionality into your programs. FedEx currently offers a Ship Manager API and a Return Manager API. The *FedEx Ship Manager API* allows you to integrate FedEx shipping, tracking, and rate estimation into your programs. The *FedEx Return Manager API* allows you to automate the returns process and integrate with your internal systems.

These FedEx APIs require that a software program with the necessary DLLs be loaded onto your computer before the features can be used. This is not the same as the Web service APIs that you have been exploring throughout this book so far. Recently, FedEx has released what it calls *Ship Manager Direct*

which allows you to interact with the FedEx functions by submitting XML documents. Unlike the APIs, Ship Manager Direct does not require that you install any software before using it. Please note that in some cases, both Ship Manager API and Ship Manager Direct are referred to generically as the Ship Manager API.

Setting Up a FedEx Developer Account

Before you can use the FedEx APIs or the Ship Manager Direct service, you must first set up a developer account. The process is a bit confusing, so I'll walk you through it here to save you a lot of time. For starters, you must have a FedEx account before you can register for a developer account. You can use the one for your company or take out a personal one in your own name.

Assuming you already have a FedEx account, you can sign up for a developer account by visiting `http://www.fedex.com/us/solutions/wis/index.html/`, as shown in Figure 7-7.

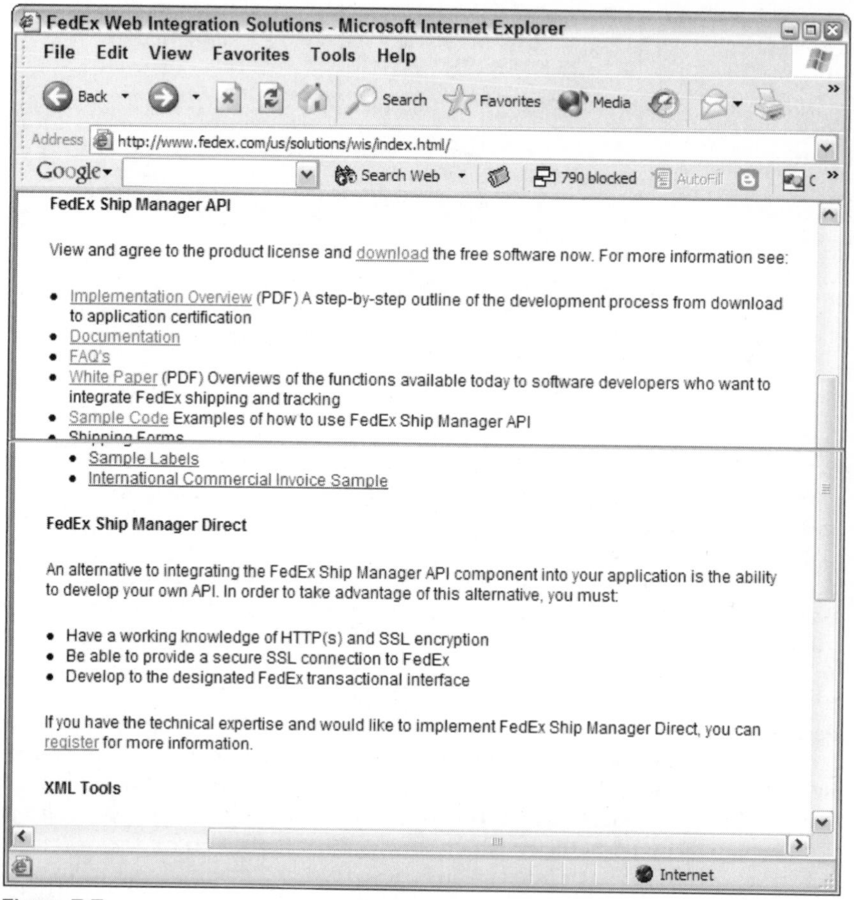

Figure 7-7

If you prefer to use the Ship Manager Direct service so you do not have to install any software on your computer, you should click the Register link under the FedEx Ship Manager Direct section. A registration form similar to the one shown in Figure 7-8 is then displayed.

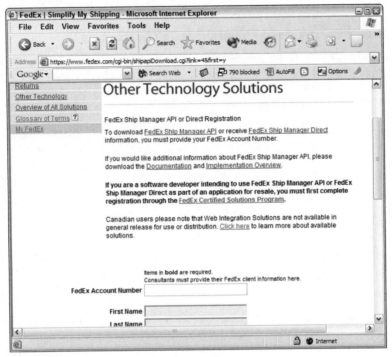

Figure 7-8

Scroll down to the data input fields and fill in the information. If you are performing work for a customer, you are prompted to specify your customer's FedEx account number. After completing the registration process, you have access to the online documentation for the service that you want to use.

Before you can use any of the Web API services, you must send an e-mail to the FedEx e-mail address specified in the documentation with a sample portion of your code. The code does not have to be working, but FedEx just wants to see that you are serious. They then set you up with access to the test environment within 24–48 hours.

Unfortunately, at this point, you still do not have everything you need in order to submit transactions to FedEx. You must also send a Subscribe request transaction containing your account number and contact information to obtain a meter number that is used in later transactions. The response transaction contains your assigned FedEx Meter Number. The exact syntax of the Subscribe request transaction and all other transactions can be found in the FedEx online document called *FedEx Tagged Transaction Listing*. One way in which you can submit a transaction is described in the section that follows.

The next section walks you through the steps of sending a transaction to FedEx using the Ship Manager Direct tool. Unlike the Ship Manager API, Ship Manager Direct does not require that any particular software be installed on your computer. However, Ship Manager Direct is very complicated to work with compared to the XML Web services you have learned about in earlier chapters, and it takes significantly more time to implement in your programs.

If you prefer to use the Ship Manager API instead, you must first download the Ship Manager API software to install on your computer. FedEx offers sample code in a variety of programming languages to illustrate how to use the Ship Manager API. Please consult the FedEx Web site for more details.

Submitting Transactions Using FedEx Ship Manager Direct

In general, you must take the following steps to submit a transaction using the FedEx Ship Manager Direct tool:

1. Format a transaction in the manner described in the FedEx Ship Manager API User's Guide.

2. Put the transaction into an HTTP POST request containing the following:

```
POST /GatewayDC HTTP/1.0
Referer: YourCompanyName
Host: FedExSSLHostURL
Accept: image/gif, image/jpeg, image/pjpeg, text/plain, text/html, */*
Content-Type: image/gif
Content-length: LengthOfYourFedExTransaction

YourFedExTransaction
```

3. Each line should be followed by one new line character except for the Content-length line and the FedEx transaction line. Two new line characters should follow the Content-length line, and no new line characters should follow the YourFedExTransaction line.

4. The FedExSSLHostURL is provided to you by FedEx when you contact Web support to request test setup.

5. Open an SSL connection to FedEx.

6. Send the transaction to FedEx using a SSL connection.

7. Receive and process the response to see any errors.

The following Visual Basic .NET code segment illustrates submitting a track request (a 402 transaction) to FedEx.

```
Dim APITrans As String

'specify the Fed Ex Transaction details to track a particular package
'Consult the Fed Ex documentation for exact syntax
APITrans = "0," + Chr(34) + "402" + Chr(34) + "29," + Chr(34) +
"YourFedExTrackingNumber" + Chr(34) + "99," + Chr(34) + Chr(34)
```

```
'Create an HTTP Web Request object
Dim req As System.Net.HttpWebRequest =
CType(System.Net.WebRequest.Create("FedExSSLHostURLGoesHere"),
System.Net.HttpWebRequest)

req.Method = "POST"
req.Referer = "YourCompanyName"
req.Accept = "image/gif, image/jpeg, image/pjpeg, text/plain, text/html, */*"
req.ContentType = "image/gif"
req.ContentLength = Len(APITrans)

Dim reqstream As System.IO.StreamWriter = New
System.IO.StreamWriter(req.GetRequestStream())

'write the transaction to the stream - i.e. submit to server
reqstream.Write(APITrans)
reqstream.Close()

'get the response from the server
Dim resp As System.net.HttpWebResponse = CType(req.GetResponse(),
System.Net.HttpWebResponse)

'declare a stream to read the results
Dim sr As New System.IO.StreamReader(resp.GetResponseStream)
Dim strResponse As String

'read the entire stream to retrieve the results
strResponse = sr.ReadToEnd
'display the results
MsgBox(strResponse)
```

For more information about the FedEx Ship Manager Direct tool, please consult the documentation available on the FedEx Web site, including the FedEx Ship Manager Direct Programmer's Guide.

Bloglines Web API

Bloglines is a company that offers free online news feed and blogging services, including searching, sub-scribing, publishing, and sharing (www.bloglines.com) news feeds and blogs. At the time of this book's writing, Bloglines just released new Web services in beta version that are called the Bloglines Web Services (BWS). The Bloglines Web Services (BWS) enable you to access subscription and feed data from within your own programs. BWS is a Web service that can be called using HTTP-GET/REST. As you learned in the earlier chapters, including Chapter 1, REST APIs are invoked by sending URLs that contain the parameters.

To find out more information about the Bloglines Web services, go to http://www.bloglines.com/services/. A screen similar to that shown in Figure 7-9 is displayed.

You can then learn more about the methods available in the APIs by visiting http://www.bloglines.com/services/api/ or clicking the Documentation link shown on the screen in Figure 7-9. A screen similar to that shown in Figure 7-10 is displayed that describes the methods available in the Web services and the third-party implementations that are also available.

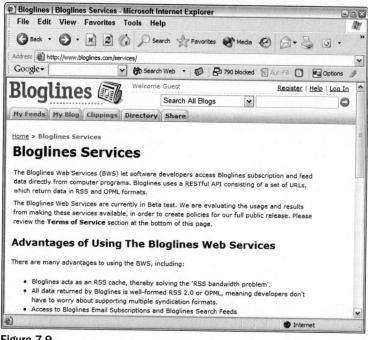

Figure 7-9

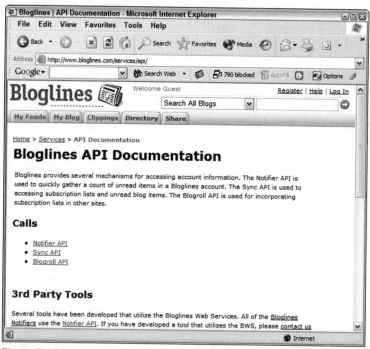

Figure 7-10

Locating Additional Web APIs

You can find which Web service APIs are available in various ways, such as searching the Internet for various Web services listings. Unfortunately, no one-stop shop lists them all. Microsoft and IBM started the effort some years ago of creating a directory of Web services called *Universal Description, Discovery, and Integration (UDDI)*. The idea behind UDDI is to provide a central directory, like a phone book, for locating available Web services.

UDDI has not caught on as quickly as expected, mostly because Web services were not adopted by the industry as quickly as everyone expected. At this point, now that there are several leading vendors releasing Web APIs, the UDDI directory is gaining popularity. Thus, if you are searching for available Web services, one place to visit is `http://uddi.microsoft.com`. You then can click the search option on the navigation pane to perform a search.

Figure 7-11 is an example that illustrates the Web services that Amazon has listed with the UDDI service at the time of this book's writing.

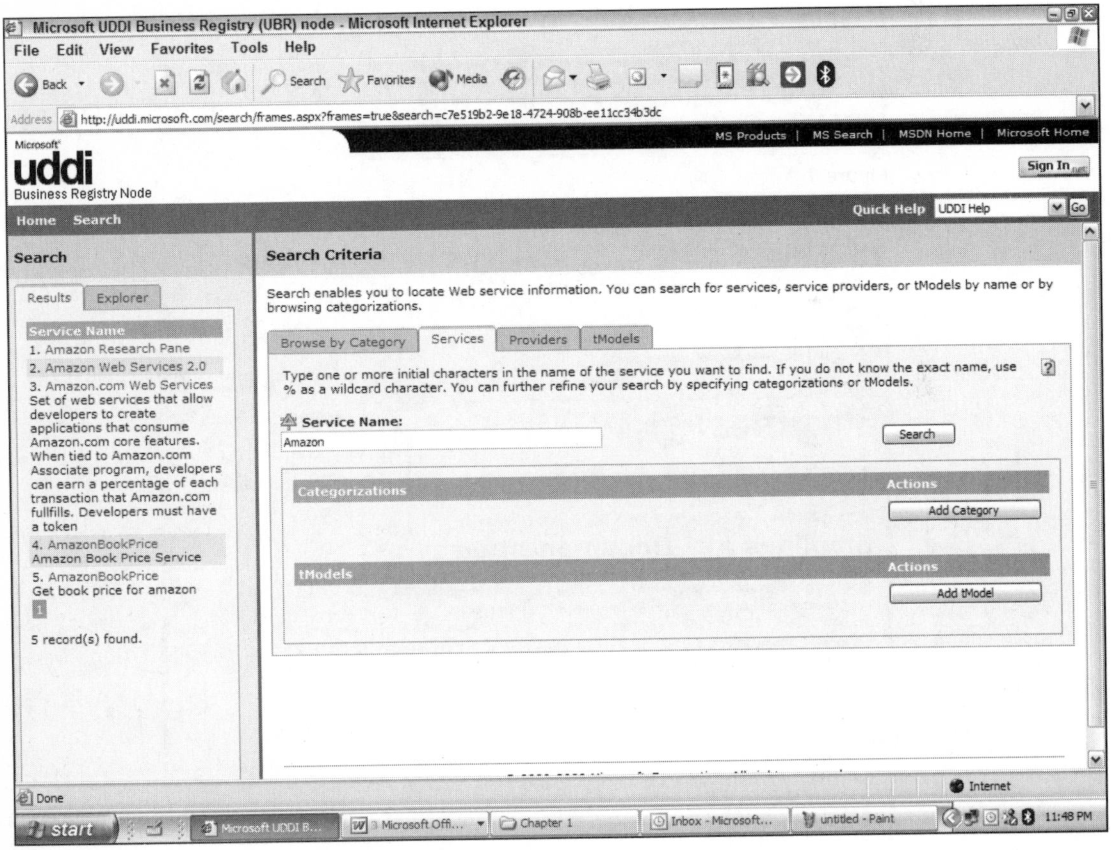

Figure 7-11

Although the UDDI directory does not contain every Web service available, it is a good place to start when you want to find out what companies are offering.

Another directory I like to use can be found at `http://www.bindingpoint.com`. As shown in Figure 7-12, the site allows you to browse Web services by categories or search the database based on keywords.

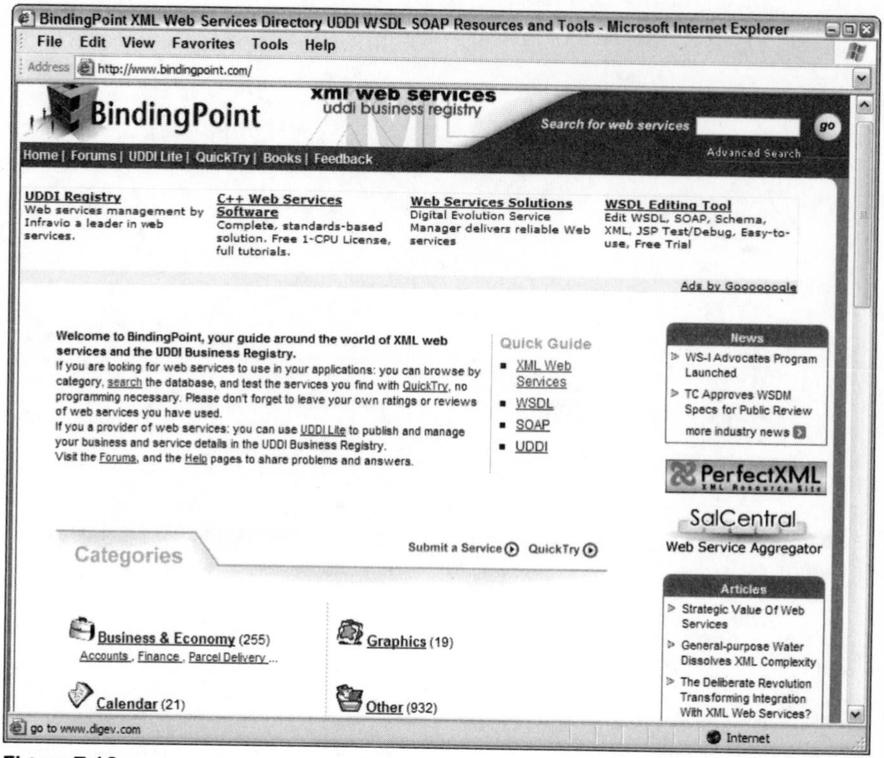

Figure 7-12

This page feels more like an on-line portal. Bindingpoint.com includes links to top-rated Web services, new services, and more, as shown in Figure 7-13.

As you can see, Bindingpoint.com is a very useful site that you should bookmark for later use, although it does not contain all Web services available. You may still need to use other sources to locate available Web services, such as a search engine like good ol' Google!

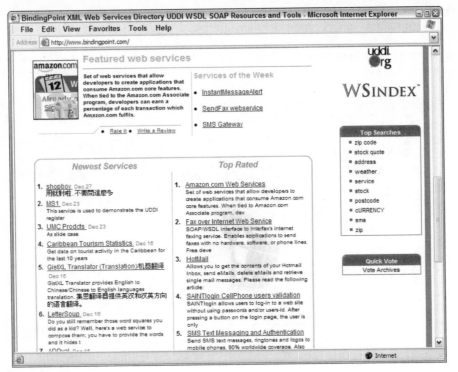

Figure 7-13

Summary

In this chapter, you learned about some additional Web APIs that are available. You learned some basic information about the InterFax faxing service, the UPS and FedEx services, and the Bloglines service. More information about each of these services can be found at their respective Web sites and documentation. Finally, you learned about how to locate additional Web APIs that you might wish to use in your programs.

At this point, you should have a good feeling for how powerful Web service APIs can be, and how easy it can be to enhance your own applications to use features from other services. It's time to move on to Chapter 8, where you will explore how to call Web service APIs from mobile devices.

Calling Web APIs from Mobile Devices

With today's focus on a mobile lifestyle, it is becoming increasingly popular to have access to the same tools on a personal digital assistant (PDA) as you do on a desktop computer. So far in this book, you have explored several leading XML Web APIs and have looked at how to call those APIs from desktop applications. In this chapter, you learn how to call these Web APIs from a mobile or embedded device, such as a Windows Mobile Pocket PC or a Palm device.

This chapter specifically covers the following:

❑ Calling an XML Web service from a Windows device

❑ Calling an XML Web service from a Palm device

❑ Creating a sample .NET pocket PC application that calls a Web API using the SOAP protocol

❑ Creating a sample .NET pocket PC application that calls a Web API using HTTP/GET (REST)

❑ Using an emulator to test the application

What Devices Support XML Web APIs?

Hundreds of mobile and embedded devices are in circulation today, ranging from personal digital assistants that are handheld, palm size, or even the size of a watch. Many mobile devices have phone and PDA functionality integrated in one device. Devices can also be embedded into other devices, such as a computer integrated within an appliance or automobile, to name a few examples. Many of these mobile or embedded devices are capable of calling the XML Web APIs you have explored throughout this book.

In order for these devices to take advantage of XML Web APIs, the following criteria must be met:

❑ The device must be updateable so that developers can write applications that run on the device.

❑ The device must be able to access the Internet because Web APIs are called over the Internet.

❑ The device must support the capability to communicate using SOAP, HTTP/POST, and/or HTTP/GET (REST), depending on the type of Web API you want to use.

In most cases, if the device is capable of connecting to the Internet, it can communicate using SOAP, HTTP/POST, and/or HTTP/GET. However, on some devices, the only way to implement such communications is to write a lot of code yourself to implement the communication protocols. On newer devices, such as those running Windows Mobile 2002 or 2003 for Pocket PCs or Smartphones, software development tools make this process easy. Let's look at Pocket PCs and Palm devices in more detail.

Windows Pocket PCs and Smartphones

There seems to be a lot of confusion of terminology when it comes to personal digital assistants. For example, many people use the terms Pocket PC and Smartphone to mean the same thing. There are distinct differences between these terms.

A *Pocket PC* runs a smaller version of Microsoft Windows, such as Windows Mobile 2002 or 2003 for Pocket PCs. These operating systems are often called Pocket PC 2002 or Pocket PC 2003. Pocket PCs typically have a larger screen and focus on the PDA functionality, although they may also have an integrated phone. Pocket PCs enable you to manage your contacts, calendar, and tasks; surf the Internet; plus run mini versions of programs such as Microsoft Word and Microsoft Excel.

A *Smartphone*, on the other hand, runs Windows Mobile 2002 or 2003 for Smartphones, also called Smartphone 2002 or 2003. Smartphones typically have a smaller screen and focus on the phone functionality, although they also have integrated PDA features. Smartphones allow you to access your contacts, calendar, and tasks, and surf the Internet, but they cannot run programs such as Microsoft Word or Microsoft Excel.

You can find more general information about the Windows Mobile operating system for both Pocket PCs and Smartphones at www.microsoft.com/windowsmobile.

With the latest version of the Microsoft development tools, such as Visual Studio .NET 2002 and 2003, you can easily write programs that will run on newer Pocket PCs or Smartphones that can run the .NET Compact Framework, such as those running Windows Mobile 2002 or 2003. Furthermore, you can also enable those mobile device applications to call Web APIs, as long as they have an Internet connection. The .NET Compact Framework provides rich support for XML, SOAP, and other Web services concepts. As you have already learned in earlier chapters, calling a SOAP Web service can be as easy as adding a Web reference to the Web service WSDL location and then working with the service in your code. The .NET Compact Framework works the same way.

The .NET Compact Framework enables you to write programs in Visual Basic .NET or C# using the same tools and techniques as you do for desktop programs that use the .NET Framework. What is great about using Visual Studio .NET is that you can write the application one time for the desktop, and then use a large portion of that same code to write one or more mobile versions of the program to run on a Pocket PC and/or Smartphone. Because of the memory, database, and screen-size limitations imposed by mobile devices, you usually have to rework some of the code. After a mobile version of a program

has been designed, it is pretty easy to use that same code for both Pocket PCs and Smartphones. As a general rule, approximately 85 percent of the code is the same between a Pocket PC version of a program and the Smartphone version of the program; and in most cases, the differences occur because of changes to accommodate the user interface.

Visual Studio .NET 2003 and later versions have what is referred to as *Smart Device Programmability (SDP)* features. What this really means is that the .NET Compact Framework has been integrated with VS .NET 2003 and comes preinstalled. For Visual Studio .NET 2002, you have to download the .NET Compact Framework separately and install it. Later in this chapter, you create two sample mobile device applications using Visual Studio .NET so you can see how this works.

When you want to write native applications that are optimized in memory and speed, you may choose to use a language such as C++ or Visual Basic. At other times, you may want to write a mobile device program without using Visual Studio .NET. Microsoft offers *eMbedded Visual Tools* to allow you to create applications in a separate environment from VS .NET. The eMbedded Visual Tools come with the necessary compilers, debugging tools, and documentation, and they can be downloaded for free from the Microsoft Web site.

For more information about the .NET Compact Framework and eMbedded Visual Tools, visit the following Microsoft Web site: `http://msdn.microsoft.com/mobility/windowsmobile/default.aspx`.

Palm and Other Devices

Palm devices are those that run the Palm operating system, as opposed to a Microsoft Windows operating system. According to some statistics, Windows Pocket PCs have surpassed Palm devices in popularity. One reason is probably because Microsoft has made it easy to develop applications on Pocket PCs and Smartphones, a task that is typically much more difficult on a Palm device. This trend is changing. As mobility and Web services have become more important, substantial improvements have recently made it easier to develop Web-enabled programs that run on a Palm device.

As one example, Palm Solutions Group has released a *Web Services for Palm (WSP) program* that allows you to write Java or C programs for a Palm device that calls Web services. The WSP program provides support for SOAP, XML, HTTP, and other Web services concepts. WSP reads the WSDL file of the Web service and generates the necessary code to enable your application to communicate using SOAP. This tool performs a function similar to adding a Web reference from within Visual Studio .NET.

More information about the Web services for Palm programs can be found at `http://pluggedin.palmone.com/regac/pluggedin/WebServices.jsp`.

IBM has introduced a *Web Services Tool Kit for Mobile Devices* that enables you to develop mobile applications that use Web services. The toolkit includes a Java Web service runtime environment that is supported on any device that supports the Java 2 Micro Edition (J2ME), WCE, and SMF environments. The toolkit also includes a C Web service runtime environment that is supported on any *Palm* or *Symbian* device. You can download the toolkit at `http://www.alphaworks.ibm.com/tech/wstkmd`.

Developers can use IBM's WebSphere Studio Device Developer (WSDD) as a graphical development environment for J2ME mobile applications. More information on WSDD can be found at `http://www-306.ibm.com/software/wireless/wsdd/?Open&ca=daw-prod-wstkmd`.

Now that you have an idea of the various options available for calling Web APIs from mobile devices, let's walk through a couple of examples to see this in action.

Calling Web APIs from Pocket PC Applications

In this section, you create two sample mobile device applications using Visual Studio .NET 2003. These examples illustrate how easy it is to use the APIs covered earlier in this book in mobile applications. The first example uses the MapPoint API and the SOAP Protocol to retrieve specified driving directions. The second example uses the Amazon.com API to retrieve a list of books matching specified search criteria. You don't need a Pocket PC in order to run these examples because VS .NET has emulators that allow you to test the application without an actual device. Before actual deployment, however, you should test on an actual device.

Example 1 — Call MapPoint API Using SOAP Protocol to Retrieve Driving Directions

In this example, you use the MapPoint API to get driving directions. MapPoint is covered in detail in Chapter 3. Let's get started by creating the application to run on a Pocket PC.

1. Open Visual Studio .NET and select File ⇨ New ⇨ Project.

2. Select Visual Basic Project as the Project Type, and select Smart Device Application as the Template. For the project name, specify `PocketPCTest`, and for the path specify the location where you want the project to be created. This is illustrated in Figure 8-1. Click OK to create the new project.

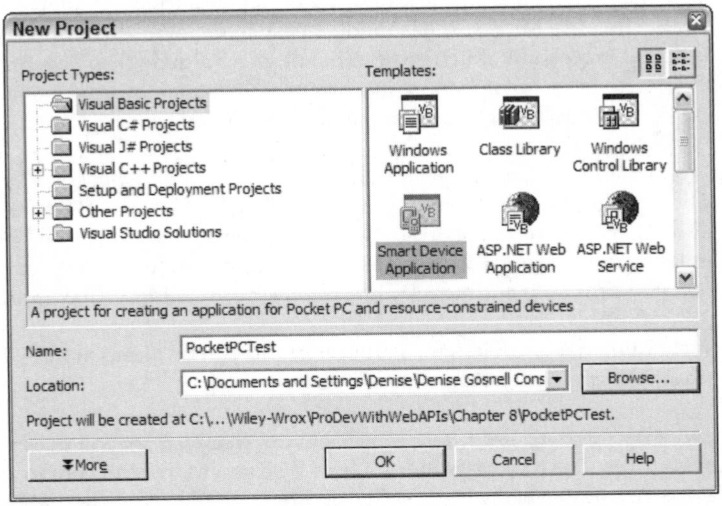

Figure 8-1

3. The Smart Device Application Wizard appears, as shown in Figure 8-2. Select Pocket PC and Windows Application and click OK.

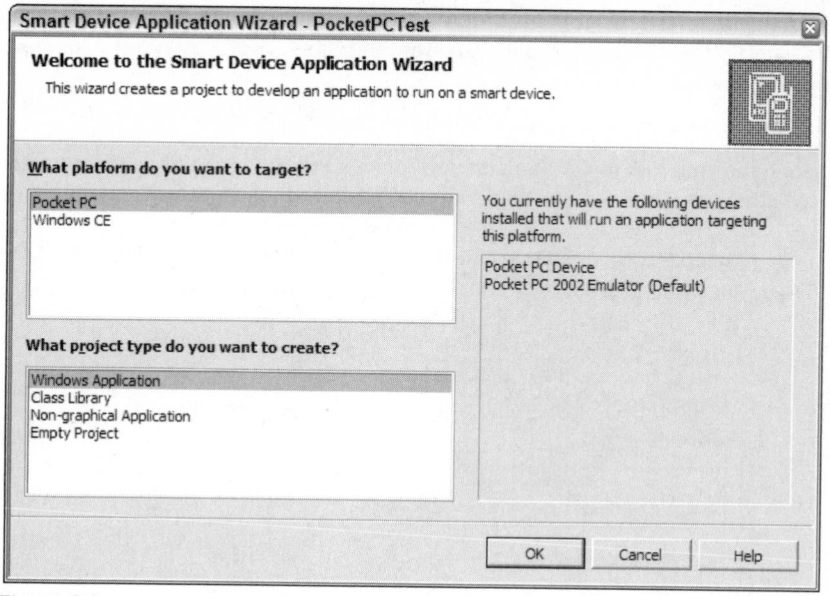

Figure 8-2

4.   A new Pocket PC project is created, with the default form sized according to the standard size of the device.

5.   Use the toolbox to drag and drop two labels, three text boxes, and a button control onto the Form.

6.   Using the Properties window, change the Name property of the first text box to `txtStartingAddress`, the Name of the second text box to `txtEndingAddress`, the Name property of the third text box to `txtResults`, and the Name property of the button to `btnRetrieve`. Modify the `MultiLine` property of `txtResults` to `True`. Rename the `Text` property of the labels as shown in Figure 8-3.

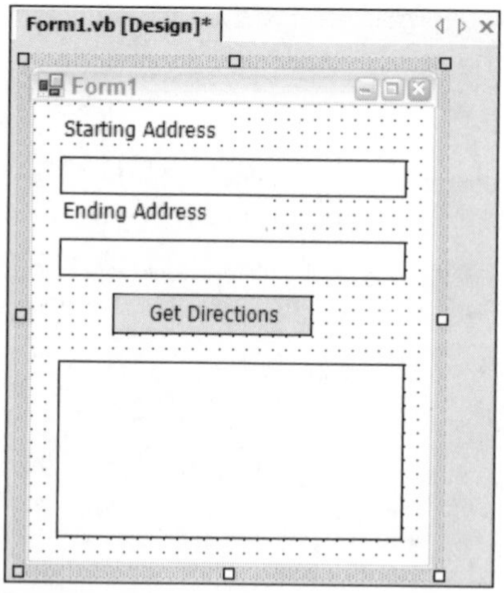

Figure 8-3

7. Add a reference to the MapPoint API by selecting Project ⇨ Add Web Reference. For the URL field, specify the WSDL file location, such as `http://staging.mappoint.net/standard-30/mappoint.wsdl`.

8. Click the GO button so that Visual Studio locates the MapPoint Web API.

9. Change the Web Reference Name to `MapPoint` so that you can use a shorter name in your project. At this point, the screen should appear similar to the one shown in Figure 8-4.

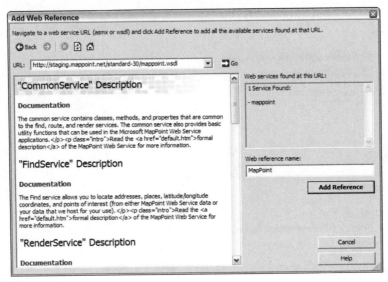

Figure 8-4

10. Click the `Add Reference` button to add the reference to your project. Visual Studio .NET uses the WSDL file to identify the methods that are available for execution from your project.

11. Add the following imports statement to the top of the code segment (before the `Public Class Form1` statement) so that you can refer to the MapPoint service in the project in shorthand mode.

```
Imports PocketPCTest.MapPoint
```

12. Add the following `btnRetrieve_Click` event to the form, inserting your customer ID and password in two places in the applicable lines of code:

```
Private Sub btnRetrieve_Click(ByVal sender As System.Object, ByVal e As _
        System.EventArgs) Handles btnRetrieve.Click

    'Purpose: Obtain Driving Directions from one address to
    'another

    'Specify the credentials for the find service
    'Use the customer id and password you were provided
    Dim findService As New FindServiceSoap
    findService.Credentials = New _
        System.Net.NetworkCredential("YOUR CUSTOMER ID", "YOUR PASSWORD")
```

```
        findService.PreAuthenticate = True

        Dim findSpec As New FindSpecification
        findSpec.DataSourceName = "MapPoint.NA"
        'specify and obtain details for the starting address
        findSpec.InputPlace = txtStartingAddress.Text
        Dim StartingAddress As FindResults = findService.Find(findSpec)

        'specify and obtain details for the ending address
        findSpec.InputPlace = txtEndingAddress.Text
        Dim EndingAddress As FindResults = findService.Find(findSpec)

        'specify the route segment details
        Dim rteSegmentSpec(1) As SegmentSpecification
        rteSegmentSpec(0) = New SegmentSpecification
        rteSegmentSpec(0).Waypoint = New Waypoint
        rteSegmentSpec(0).Waypoint.Name = _
        StartingAddress.Results(0).FoundLocation.Entity.Name
        rteSegmentSpec(0).Waypoint.Location = _
            StartingAddress.Results(0).FoundLocation
        rteSegmentSpec(1) = New SegmentSpecification
        rteSegmentSpec(1).Waypoint = New Waypoint
        rteSegmentSpec(1).Waypoint.Name = _
            EndingAddress.Results(0).FoundLocation.Entity.Name
        rteSegmentSpec(1).Waypoint.Location = _
            EndingAddress.Results(0).FoundLocation

        'specify the route specification details
        Dim routeSpec As New RouteSpecification
        routeSpec.DataSourceName = "MapPoint.NA"
        routeSpec.Segments = rteSegmentSpec

        'Specify the credentials for the route service
        'Use the customer id and password you were provided
        Dim routeService As New RouteServiceSoap
        routeService.Credentials = New _
            System.Net.NetworkCredential("YOUR CUSTOMER ID", "YOUR PASSWORD")
        routeService.PreAuthenticate = True

        'call the calculate route method to retrieve the route
        Dim Route As Route
        Route = routeService.CalculateRoute(routeSpec)

        Dim intCount As Integer
        Dim strResults As String

        'loop through the results returned
        For intCount = 0 To Route.Itinerary.Segments(0).Directions.Length - 1
            strResults = strResults & _
                Route.Itinerary.Segments(0).Directions(intCount).Instruction & vbCrLf
        Next intCount

        'display the results
        txtResults.Text = strResults

    End Sub
```

---

13. Save and run the program. As shown in Figure 8-5, you are prompted to specify whether to use an emulator or whether to test on an actual Pocket PC device.

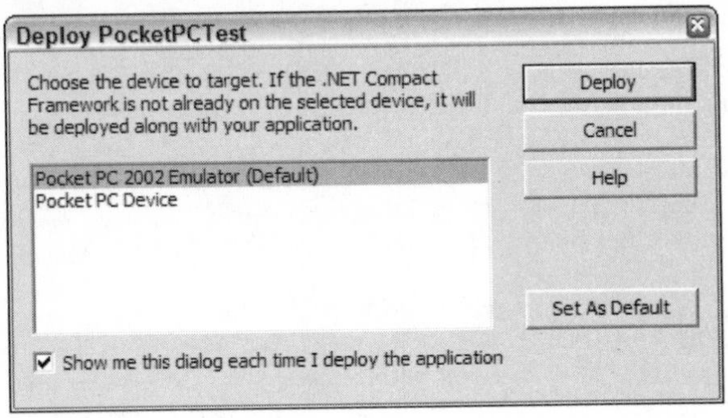

Figure 8-5

14. If you want to deploy the application directly to the Pocket PC device, you select Pocket PC Device. For this example, select Pocket PC 2002 Emulator and click Deploy. Visual Studio .NET takes a minute or two to set up the emulator environment. A screen that emulates a Pocket PC is displayed, and shortly thereafter the program opens on the emulated screen. The emulated screen that appears is similar to the one shown in Figure 8-6.

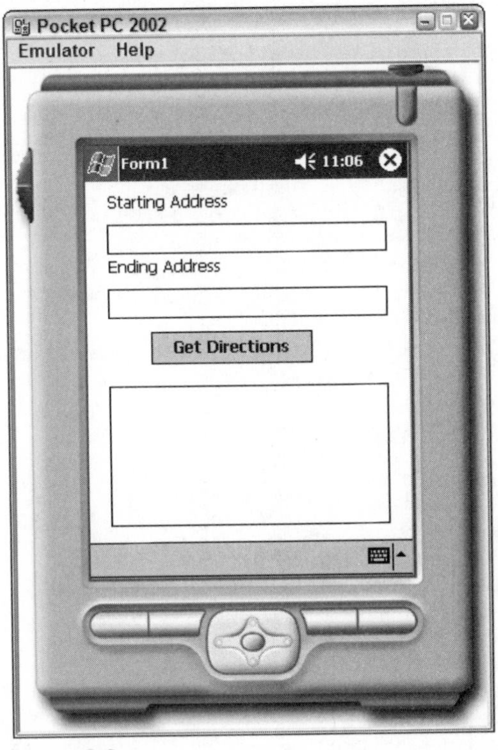

Figure 8-6

15. Type in a starting address and an ending address in the text boxes on the device. Then click the Get Directions button. You should see driving directions based on the address you entered, such as those shown in Figure 8-7.

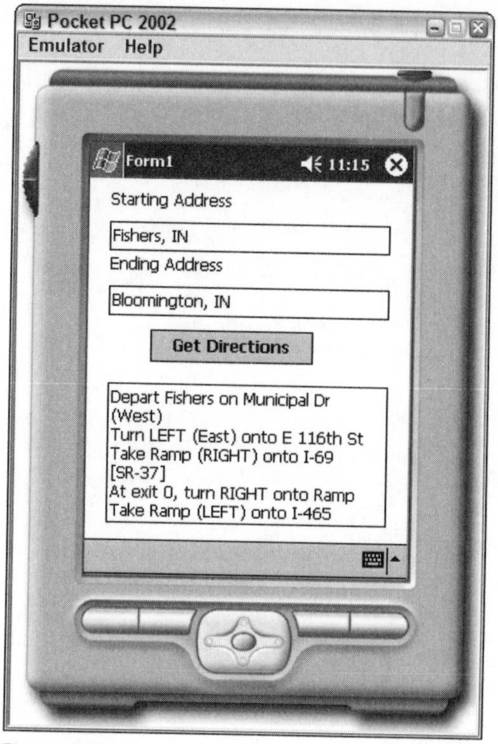

Figure 8-7

Example 2 — Call Amazon.com API Using HTTP/GET (REST) Protocol

In this example, you call the Amazon.com API to look up a list of books that match the specified criteria. The Amazon.com API was covered in greater detail in Chapter 4. You will use the HTTP/GET (REST) protocol in this example. You already learned that REST uses a series of parameters included in the URL to communicate with the Web API. You also learned that REST returns the results in an XML document. For the sake of simplicity, our program displays the XML document returned as a result of the call. In your own programs, you can use an XML parser to parse the results and work with them in any way you wish.

Let's get started with creating the mobile devices example to use the Amazon.com API.

1. Open Visual Studio .NET and select File ⇨ New ⇨ Project.

2. Select Visual Basic Project as the Project Type, and select Smart Device Application as the Template. For the project name, specify `PocketPCTest2`; for the path, specify the location where you want the project to be created. Click OK to create the new project.

3. The Smart Device Application Wizard appears. Select Pocket PC and Windows Application and click OK.

4. A new Pocket PC project is created, again with the default form sized according to the standard size of the device.

5. Use the toolbox to drag and drop one label, two text boxes, and a button control onto the Form.

6. Using the Properties window, change the Name property of the first text box to txtCriteria, the Name of the second text box to txtResults, and the Name property of the button to btnRetrieve. Modify the MultiLine property of txtResults to True. Rename the Text property of the labels as shown in Figure 8-8.

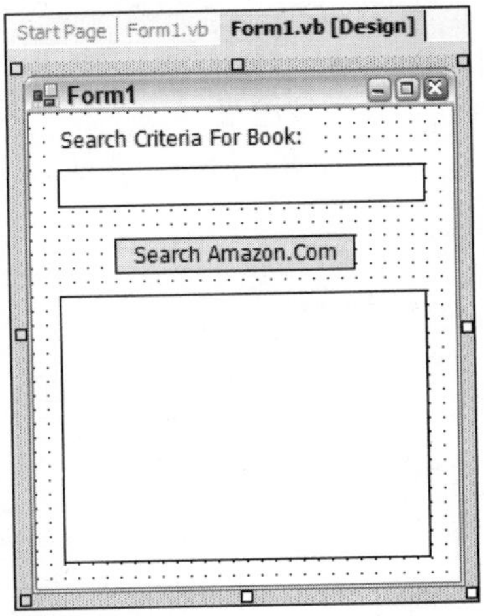

Figure 8-8

7. Add the following code to btnRetrieve_Click of Form1, modifying the code to replace [Your Subscription ID Here] with your Subscription ID for the Amazon.COM API:

```
Private Sub btnRetrieve_Click(ByVal sender As System.Object, ByVal e As _
        System.EventArgs) Handles btnRetrieve.Click

        Dim oReq As System.Net.HttpWebRequest
        Dim oResp As System.Net.HttpWebResponse
        oReq =
System.Net.HttpWebRequest.Create("http://webservices.amazon.com/onca/xml?Service=AW
SECommerceService&SubscriptionId=[Your Subscription Id
Here]&Operation=ItemSearch&SearchIndex=Books&Keywords=" & txtCriteria.Text)

        'use the StreamReader to get the response
        oResp = oReq.GetResponse
        Dim sr As New System.IO.StreamReader(oResp.GetResponseStream)
        Dim strResponse As String

        'read the entire stream to retrieve the results
```

```
        strResponse = sr.ReadToEnd

        'For simplicity, display XML response on Form
        'Would use XML parser to work
        'with results in desired fashion.
        txtResults.Text = strResponse

End Sub
```

8. Save and run the program. You are prompted to specify whether to use an emulator or whether to test on an actual Pocket PC device.

9. Select Pocket PC 2002 Emulator and click Deploy. As before, Visual Studio .NET takes a minute or two to set up the emulator environment. A screen that emulates a Pocket PC is then displayed, and shortly thereafter the program opens on the emulated screen. The emulated screen containing your program should be similar to the one shown in Figure 8-9.

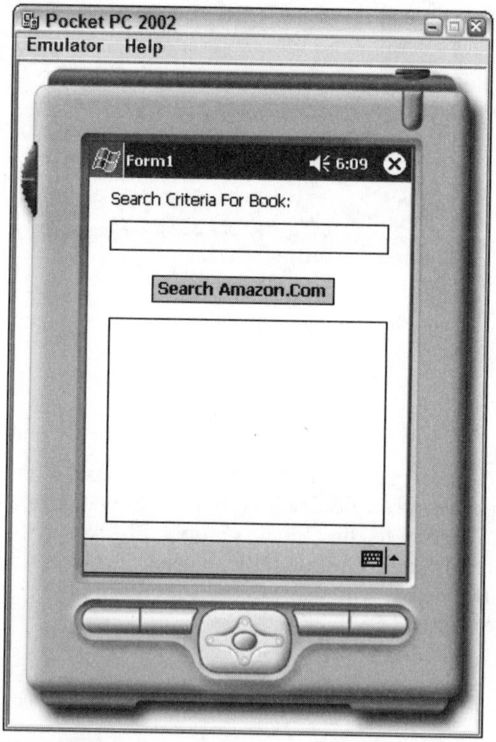

Figure 8-9

10. Type search criteria in the designated text box on the device. Then click the Search Amazon.com button. You should see an XML document containing the results of the search, such as that shown in Figure 8-10.

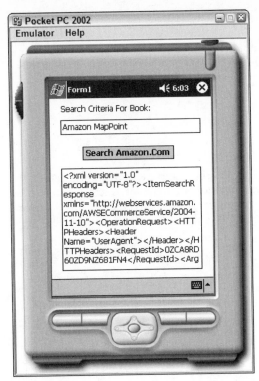

Figure 8-10

Summary

In this chapter, you learned how easy it can be to create applications for mobile devices that use XML Web APIs. You learned about some of the development tools available, depending on the type of device on which you want the application to run. Today's mobile lifestyle demands that developers spend more time writing applications for devices. The capability to communicate with external Web services using programs such as Microsoft Word or Microsoft Excel is increasingly important. Chapter 9 focuses on calling Web APIs from Microsoft Office.

Calling Web APIs from Microsoft Office

In Chapter 8, you explored various ways that you can call XML Web APIs from mobile devices. You can also use XML Web APIs to expand the features offered in your solutions written in Microsoft Office. This chapter covers various ways you can integrate Web APIs into Microsoft Office programs. Some of these methods require an additional software program or toolkit, whereas others can be done with just Microsoft Office and VBA. More specifically, this chapter covers the following:

- ❑ Calling a Web API using VBA and HTTP from Microsoft Excel
- ❑ Installing the SOAP Web services toolkit for VBA
- ❑ Calling a Web API using VBA and SOAP from Microsoft Excel
- ❑ Installing Visual Studio Tools for the Microsoft Office System
- ❑ Calling a Web API using the Visual Studio Tools program and SOAP from Microsoft Word

Calling Web APIs from VBA Code

VBA is an acronym that stands for *Visual Basic for Applications*. VBA is a programming language that is included as part of several Microsoft products, including Access, Word, and Excel. For example, Access 2003 VBA uses VBA version 6.0, which is the same version of VBA used by Word 2003 VBA and Excel 2003 VBA. VBA is a programming language that can be used to incorporate additional features into your applications. VBA should not be confused with the Microsoft Visual Basic or Visual Basic .NET programming products. VB and VB.NET each has its own syntax of the Visual Basic programming language. The VB syntax, the VB.NET syntax, and the VBA syntax are very similar, but there are also differences between them.

You can use VBA to call a Web API from a Microsoft Office program. Depending on the type of Web service you want to call, you may need to download one or more additional toolkits in order for your call to work. For example, if you want to call a Web service from VBA using SOAP, you

must install a free SOAP Web services toolkit so that Microsoft Office can generate the SOAP and other files for you. You also need to download the latest version of MSXML, Microsoft's XML parser. If you just want to call a Web API using HTTP/GET (REST) or HTTP/POST, then you install MSXML if it is not already installed. You learned in Chapter 1 that the party offering the Web API specifies which of these protocols the Web API will support. Let's look at an example of how each of these works.

Calling Web APIs Using VBA with HTTP/POST and HTTP/GET (REST)

You do not need to install the Web Services Toolkit for Office if you are not calling a Web API using SOAP. You can use VBA code to communicate using HTTP POST and/or GET (REST). Let's look at a basic example of how this works from Microsoft Excel.

Example — Calling Amazon.com from Excel Using VBA and HTTP/GET (REST)

In this example, you call the Amazon.com API discussed in Chapter 4 from Microsoft Excel. Open Excel and create a new workbook called VBATestFromExcel. On Sheet1 of the workbook, arrange the fields as shown in Figure 9-1. It is important that the cells be laid out exactly as shown in the figure if you want the results to be displayed in the correct cells. Use the Visual Basic toolbar to add a button in cell B2 as shown. To view the Visual Basic toolbar, select View ⇨ Toolbars ⇨ Visual Basic.

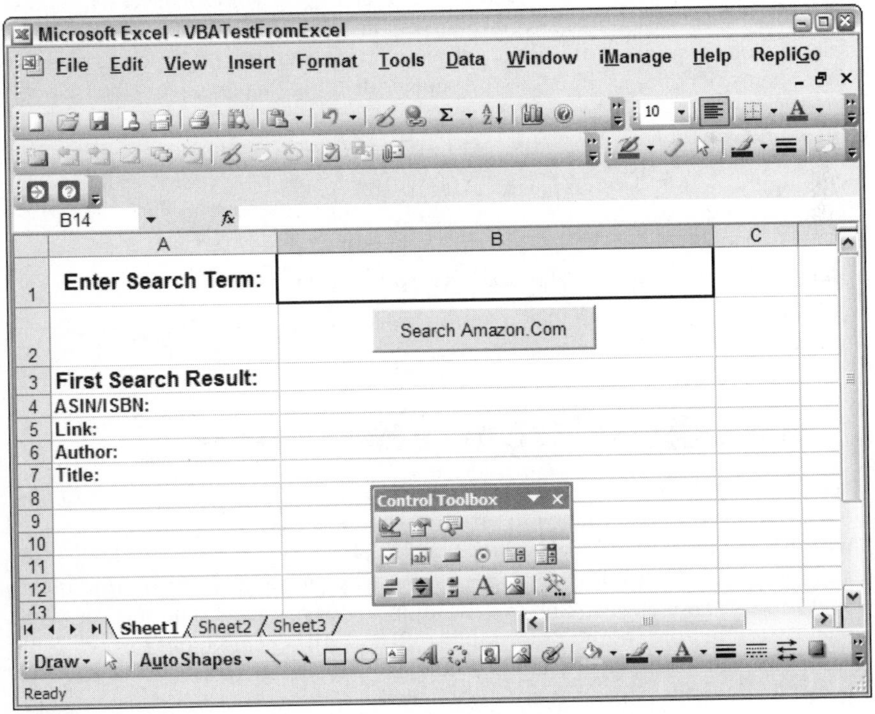

Figure 9-1

You can modify the name displayed on the Command button by viewing the Properties dialog box from the Toolbox and then changing the `Caption` property.

After adding the Command button, make sure you are still in design mode. If you are in design mode, you see that a Design Mode button on the toolbox in the upper-left corner is selected. If you are not in design mode, the code behind the button executes if you click or double-click the button. In order to add that code, you double-click the button when you are in design mode. You should see a Visual Basic Editor window open within the currently empty `CommandButton1_Click` event.

Add the following code to the `CommandButton1_Click` event, replacing `[YourIdGoesHere]` with your Amazon.com Subscription ID where indicated:

```
Private Sub CommandButton1_Click()

    Dim oXML As Object
    Dim oDom As Object
    Dim strXML As String
    Dim strResponse As String
    Dim strURL As String

    On Error GoTo Handler
    Set oXML = CreateObject("Microsoft.XMLHTTP")

    'set the parameters to be passed to the Amazon.com web API
    'including retrieving the search criteria entered in cell B1
    strURL =
"http://webservices.amazon.com/onca/xml?Service=AWSECommerceService&SubscriptionId=
[YourIdGoesHere]&Operation=ItemSearch&SearchIndex=Books&Keywords=" &
Worksheets("Sheet1").Range("B1").Value

    'Clear any prior results
    Worksheets("Sheet1").Range("B4").Value = ""
    Worksheets("Sheet1").Range("B5").Value = ""
    Worksheets("Sheet1").Range("B6").Value = ""
    Worksheets("Sheet1").Range("B7").Value = ""

    'Call the Amazon.com service
    With oXML
        .Open "GET", strURL, False
        'Needed to web service will recognize get/post
        .setRequestHeader "Content-Type", "application/x-www-form-urlencoded"
        .send
    End With

    'get the results
    strResponse = oXML.responseText

    'load the results into a new XML document
    Set oDom = CreateObject("MSXML.DOMDocument")
    oDom.loadXML (strResponse)

    'display the results on the spreadsheet
    If oDom.hasChildNodes Then
```

```
            Worksheets("Sheet1").Range("B4").Value = _
        oDom.documentelement.selectSingleNode("Items/Item/ASIN").Text
            Worksheets("Sheet1").Range("B5").Value = _
        oDom.documentelement.selectSingleNode("Items/Item/ItemAttributes/Title").Text
            Worksheets("Sheet1").Range("B6").Value = _
        oDom.documentelement.selectSingleNode("Items/Item/ItemAttributes/Author").Text
            Worksheets("Sheet1").Range("B7").Value = _
        oDom.documentelement.selectSingleNode("Items/Item/DetailPageURL").Text
    Else
    'No items matched search
        Worksheets("Sheet1").Range("B4").Value = ""
        Worksheets("Sheet1").Range("B5").Value = ""
        Worksheets("Sheet1").Range("B6").Value = ""
        Worksheets("Sheet1").Range("B7").Value = ""
        MsgBox ("No results were returned.")
    End If
    Set oXML = Nothing
    Set oDom = Nothing
    Exit Sub
Handler:
    MsgBox Err.Description
    Set oXML = Nothing
    Set oDom = Nothing
End Sub
```

The previous code calls the Amazon.com Web service using HTTP/GET and passes the URL with the search parameters. Then, the XML results are parsed by field to populate the cells with the returned values.

Save the code from the Visual Basic Editor and then return to Sheet1. Turn off design mode if you are still in it. Enter your search terms in cell B1 and click the Search button. A screen similar to the one shown in Figure 9-2 is then displayed.

As you can see, the first book matching the criteria specified is displayed in the cells on Sheet1. This is just a simple example of how you can use VBA with Microsoft Office to call Web APIs using HTTP.

Calling Web APIs Using SOAP Protocol

Before you can call a Web API from Microsoft Office, you must download and install the free SOAP Web services toolkit from Microsoft. If you go to the Microsoft download center at www.microsoft.com/downloads, you can search for the Office 2003 Web Services Toolkit, as shown in Figure 9-3. You also need to have an XML Parser installed as described on that Web site.

If you do not have MSXML installed to parse XML documents, you should also follow the links to download and install it from the Microsoft downloads site. Follow the instructions provided in the setup programs to complete the installation process. Now take a look at how to use the Toolkit from Microsoft Office.

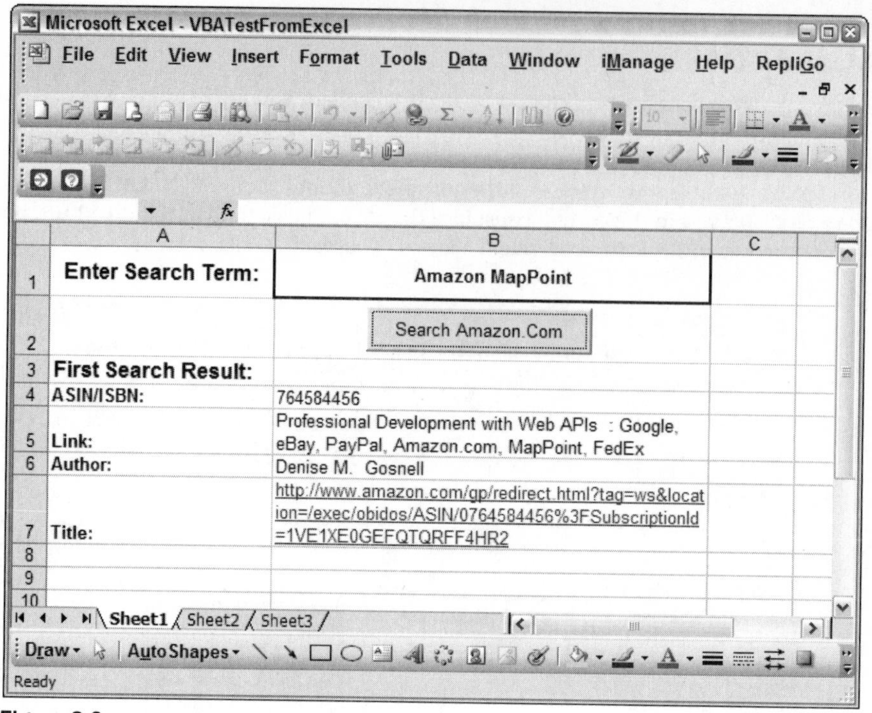

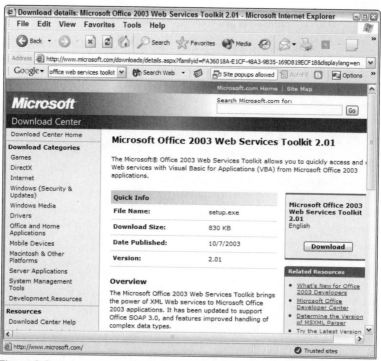

Figure 9-2

Figure 9-3

Example — Calling TerraServer Web Service from Excel Using VBA and SOAP

After you have the Web services toolkit and MSXML installed, you are ready to work with the toolkit. In this example, you call a Web service called Microsoft TerraServer from Microsoft Excel. Open Excel, and create a new workbook called VBATestFromExcelSOAP. On Sheet1 of the workbook, arrange the fields as shown in Figure 9-4. It is important that the cells be laid out exactly as shown in the figure if you want the results to be displayed in the correct cells. Use the Visual Basic toolbar to add a button as shown. Again, to view the Visual Basic toolbar, select View ➪ Toolbars ➪ Visual Basic.

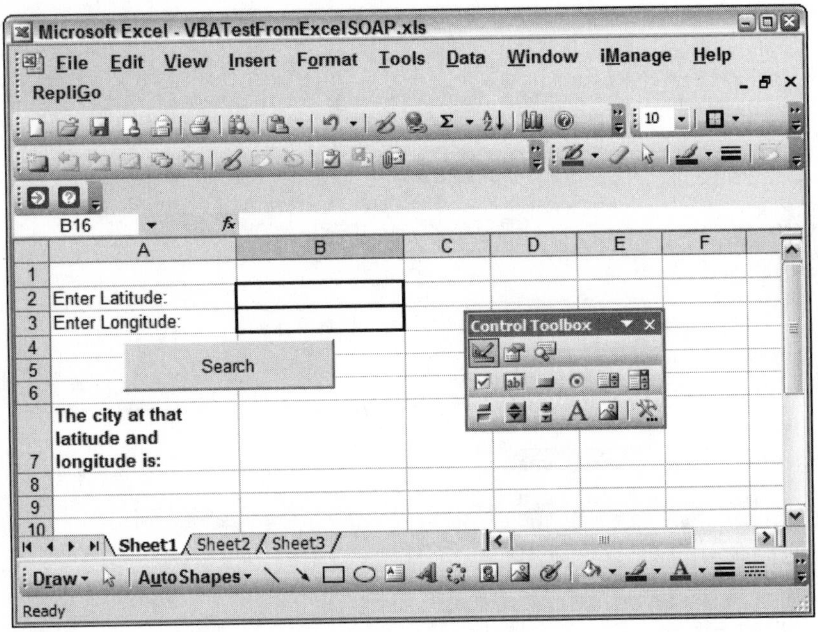

Figure 9-4

Next, from design mode, open the Visual Basic Editor by double-clicking the Command button you just added. A screen similar to Figure 9-5 should then de displayed.

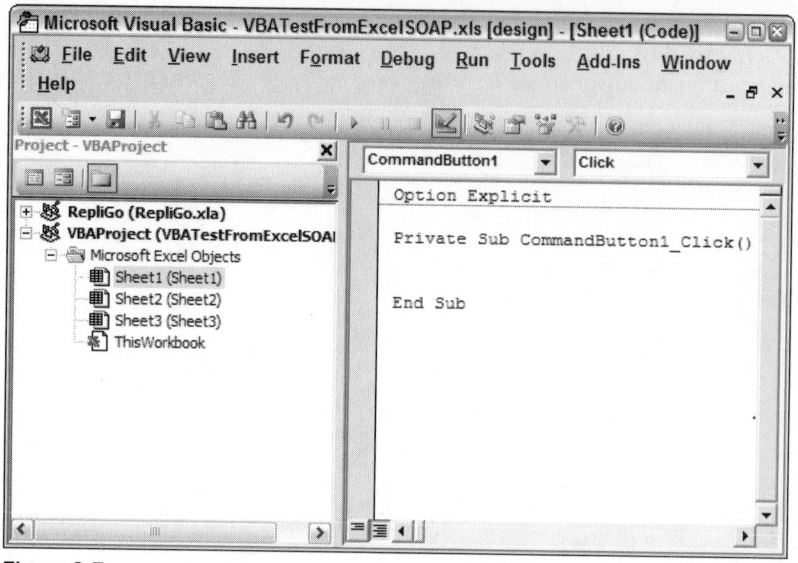

Figure 9-5

At this point, you are ready to add a Web reference. This is very similar to the steps you take to add a Web reference from Visual Studio .NET. Select Tools ⇨ Web Services References, as shown in Figure 9-6.

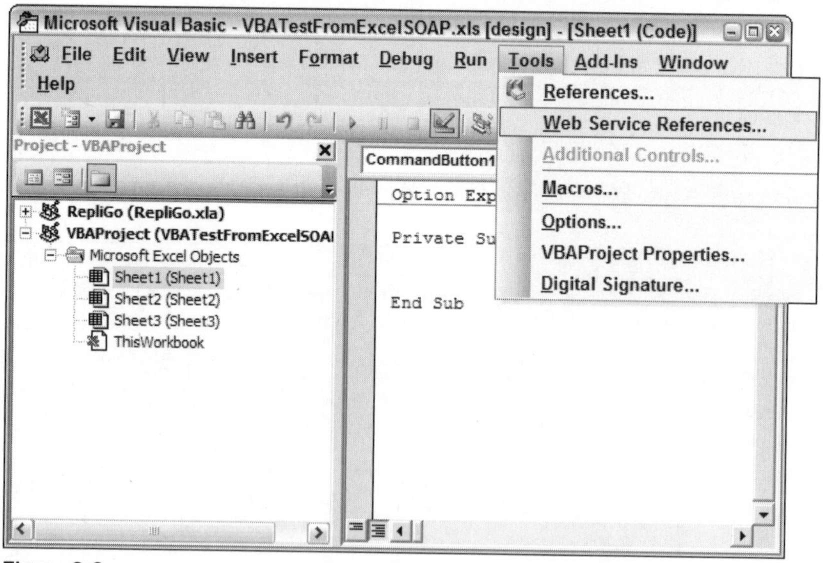

Figure 9-6

On the screen that appears, select the Web Service URL option and paste the following WSDL location for the TerraServer service:

```
http://terraserver-usa.com/TerraService2.asmx
```

Click the Search button, and then select TerraService from the search results pane, as shown in Figure 9-7.

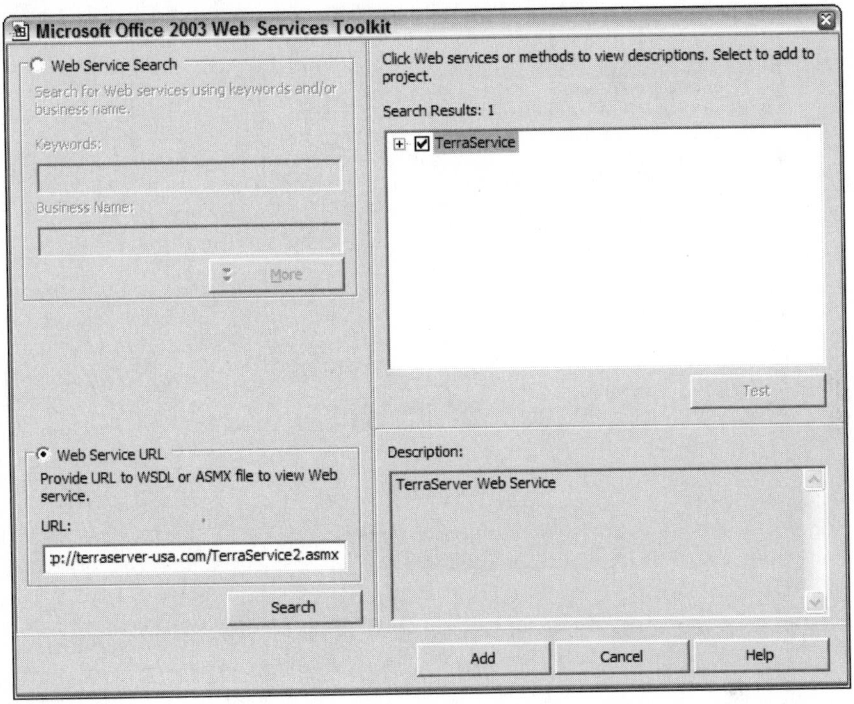

Figure 9-7

Click the Add button. A group of class modules are generated from the WSDL file, as shown in Figure 9-8.

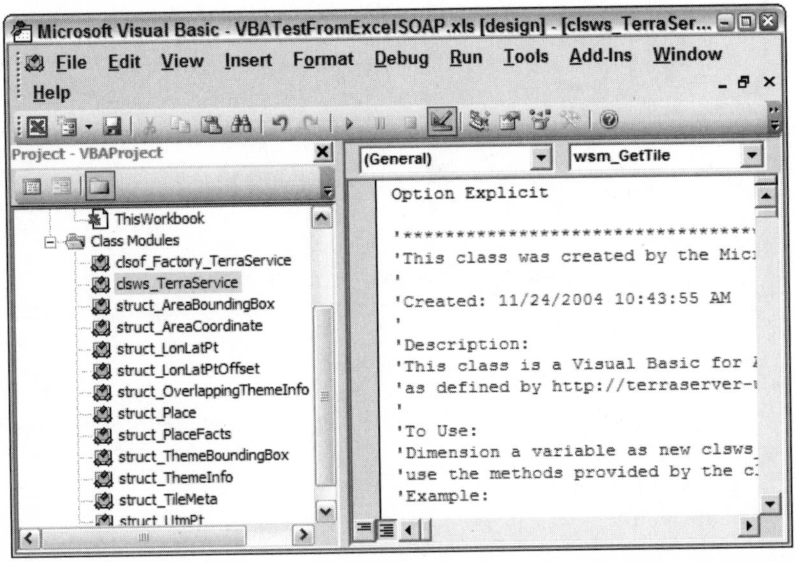

Figure 9-8

Now that you have added a Web reference to the Web service, you are ready to add code that will execute when the user clicks the Command button on Sheet1. Paste the following code in the CommandButton1_Click event. You can get to this event code section by double-clicking the command button from design mode in Sheet1, or from the Visual Basic Editor by selecting Sheet1 and then the name of the button.

Add the following code to the CommandButton1_Click event:

```
Private Sub CommandButton1_Click()
On Error GoTo Handler

    'declare a new instance of the web service
    Dim ts As clsws_TerraService
    Set ts = New clsws_TerraService

    'declare a structure to hold the latitude and longitude values
    Dim objLonLatPt As New struct_LonLatPt

    'declare a variable to store the result from the web service
    Dim strResult As String

    Dim dblLat As Double
    Dim dblLon As Double

    dblLat = CDbl(Worksheets("Sheet1").Range("B2").Value)
    dblLon = CDbl(Worksheets("Sheet1").Range("B3").Value)

    'assign the latitude and longitude values
    objLonLatPt.Lat = dblLat
    objLonLatPt.Lon = dblLon

    'Call the web service to return the place for that latitude
    'and longitude
    strResult = ts.wsm_ConvertLonLatPtToNearestPlace(objLonLatPt)

    'display the result in the spreadsheet cell B7
    Worksheets("Sheet1").Range("B7").Value = strResult

    Exit Sub
Handler:
    MsgBox Err.Description

End Sub
```

The previous code declares a new TerraService object and then populates the struct_LonLatPt structure with the Latitude and Longitude values that must be passed to the service. The next lines of code call the service over the Internet using SOAP and then display the results in cell B7 on Sheet1.

Let's try this out. Return to Sheet1 and turn off design mode if you are still in it. Enter search terms in cells B2 and B3, and then click the Search button. You should see results similar to those shown in Figure 9-9.

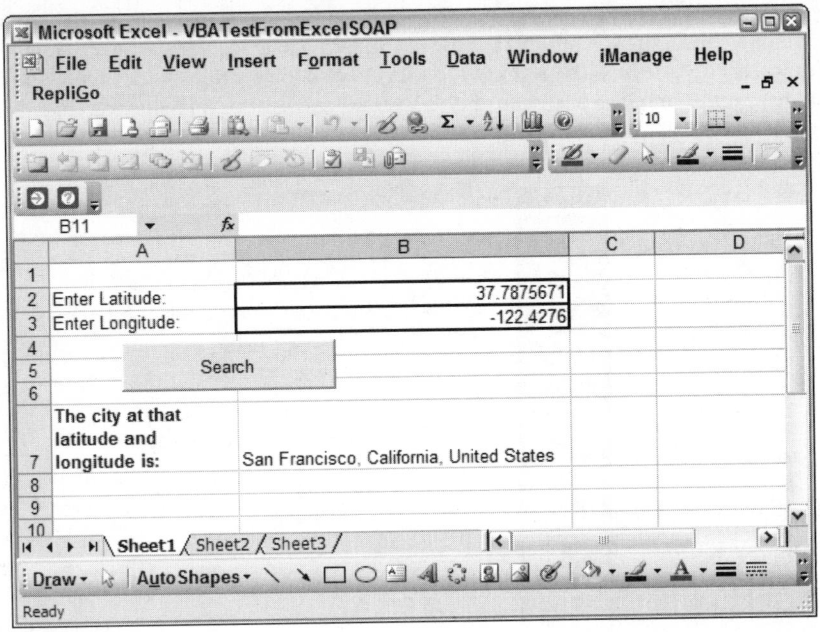

Figure 9-9

If you later go back to this spreadsheet and it stops working, you may need to refresh the reference to the wsdl. To do so, remove the classes that were imported for the service using the Project Explorer, and then re-add the Web reference again using Tools ➪ Add Web Reference.

Now that you know the basics of calling Web APIs from Microsoft Office using VBA code, let's look at how to do so using a .NET application.

Calling a Web API from Microsoft Office Using .NET

Another way you can call Web APIs from Microsoft Office is by calling a .NET program from Office. To call a .NET program from Office, you need Visual Studio .NET 2003, as well as the Visual Studio Tools for the Microsoft Office System program. Both of these are available for purchase from Microsoft, and you can find more information on Microsoft's Web site.

Visual Studio Tools for Microsoft Office basically allows you to use the Visual Studio .NET interface to create code that gets called from Microsoft Office documents. You can use the same code and familiar interface as you do with Visual Studio .NET, and you can also run those procedures from a particular document or spreadsheet. This means that you can call a Web API using SOAP or HTTP with nearly the same code as described in the earlier chapters.

Installing the Necessary Tools

To install Visual Studio .NET, launch the setup program and follow the onscreen prompts to complete the setup process. To install the Microsoft Visual Studio Tools for the Microsoft Office System program, launch the setup program. A screen similar to the one shown in Figure 9-10 is displayed.

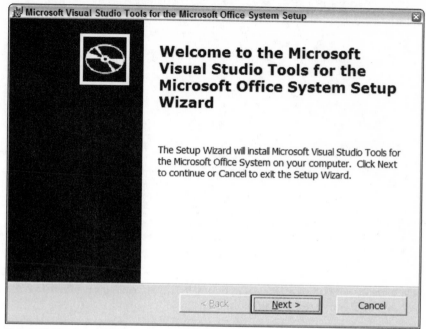

Figure 9-10

Click Next and navigate through the installation screens. If your computer already has all the prerequisites installed, a screen similar to Figure 9-11 is displayed. Otherwise, you are informed which required programs are missing.

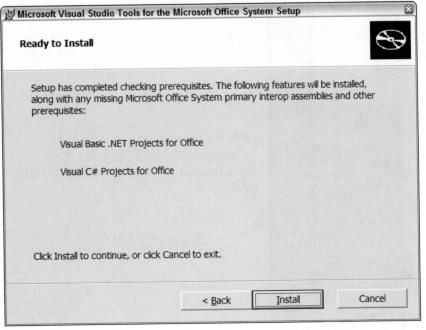

Figure 9-11

When you click the Install button as shown in Figure 9-11, you receive a confirmation screen, as shown in Figure 9-12, to indicate that setup was successful.

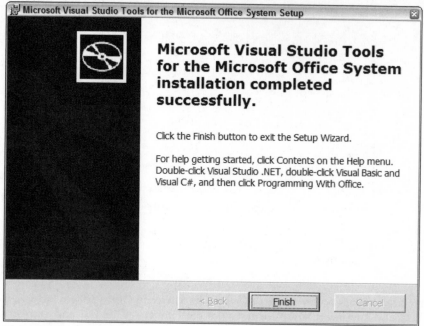

Figure 9-12

Let's now look in further detail at how the Visual Studio Tools program works.

Example — Calling Amazon.com Web Service from Word Using Visual Basic .NET and SOAP

Now, let's walk through a simple example that uses the Visual Studio Tools for Microsoft Office to call the Amazon.com Web service from Word. In this example, you write code to look up all books that are similar to a particular book. Those similar books are then displayed in a Microsoft Word document.

Open Visual Studio .NET. Select File ⇨ New ⇨ Project, and a screen similar to Figure 9-13 is displayed.

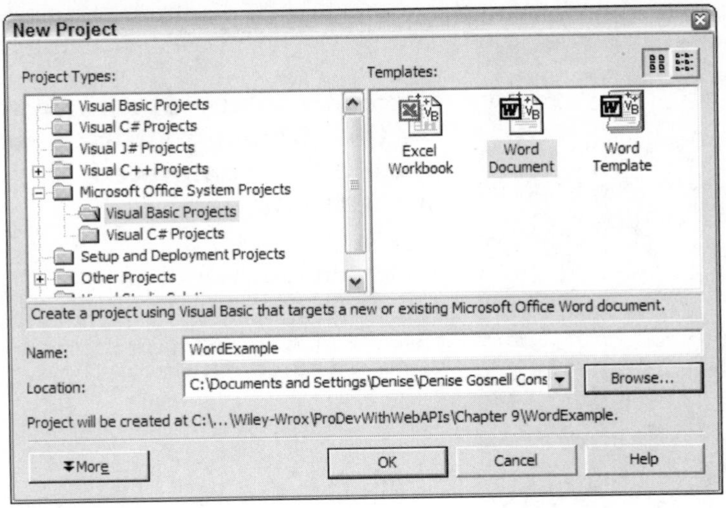

Figure 9-13

Expand the Project Types nodes so you can see all the Microsoft Office System Projects. Select Visual Basic Projects, and then select Word Document for the Template. Click OK, and a screen similar to Figure 9-14 appears.

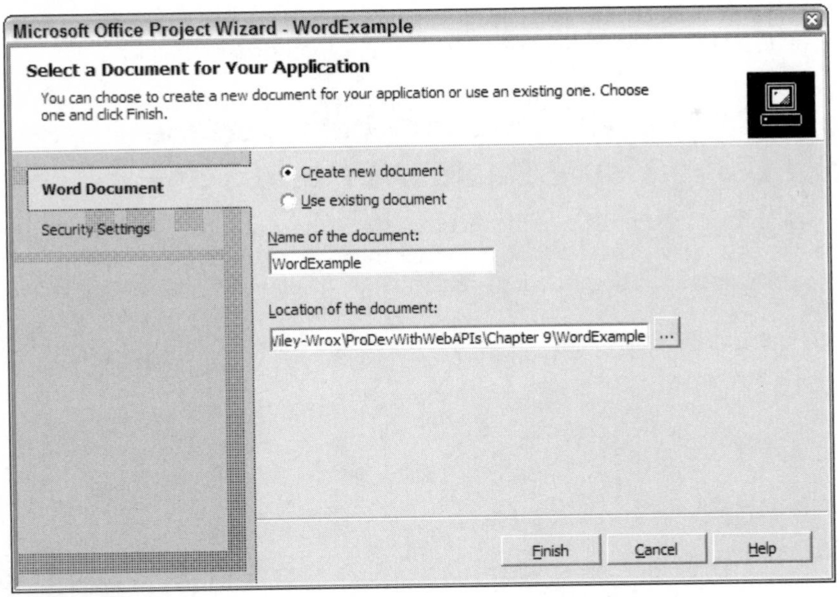

Figure 9-14

Specify the name of the document to be created (for example, WordExample) and the location where you want the file saved. Then click the Finish button. A new Visual Studio .NET project that looks like Figure 9-15 is then created.

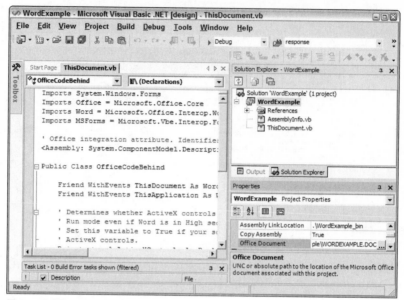

Figure 9-15

At this point, you are ready to add a reference to the Amazon API by selecting Project ⇨ Add Web Reference. For the URL field, specify the location of the WSDL file, such as `http://webservices.amazon.com/AWSECommerceService/AWSECommerceService.wsdl`.

Click the GO button so that Visual Studio can locate the Amazon Web API. Change the Web Reference Name to `Amazon` so that you can use a shorter name in your project (as shown in Figure 9-16).

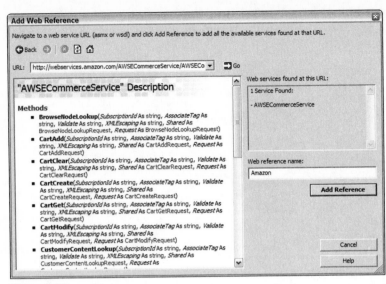

Figure 9-16

Click the Add Reference button to add the reference to your project. Visual Studio .NET uses the WSDL file to identify the methods that are available for execution from your project.

Add the following imports statement to the top of the code section of your project (`ThisDocument.vb` file), prior to all other code:

```
Imports WordExample.Amazon
```

Finally, add the following procedure to the code section of `ThisDocument.vb`, adding your Amazon.com subscription ID in the line of code where indicated:

```
Private Sub ThisDocument_Open() Handles ThisDocument.Open

        'when the document opens, update the data in the Word
        'document with the most recent information from
        'SOAP example

        On Error GoTo handle_error

        Dim AmazonProductData As New AWSECommerceService
        Dim AmazonSearch As New SimilarityLookup
        Dim AmazonResponse As New SimilarityLookupResponse
        Dim AmazonRequest(1) As SimilarityLookupRequest

        Dim strItems(1) As String

        'Specify the one or more ISBN/ASIN's to lookup
        'similar books for.
        'Add additional ones to array of strItems.
        strItems(0) = "0764556592"
```

```vbnet
        'Developer/Subscription ID
        AmazonSearch.SubscriptionId = "Insert your Subscription ID Here"

        'We are only making one request, not batching multiple requests
        'Thus element 0 of the array is all we need to assign and work with
        AmazonRequest(0) = New SimilarityLookupRequest
        AmazonRequest(0).ItemId = strItems

        'assign the search object to the request object with the assigned
        'parameters
        AmazonSearch.Request = AmazonRequest

        'run the search and populate the response
        AmazonResponse = AmazonProductData.SimilarityLookup(AmazonSearch)

        Dim item As New Item
        Dim strOutput As String

        strOutput = "Here are books that are similar to ASIN/ISBN " & _
            strItems(0) & ":" & vbCrLf & vbCrLf

        'loop through the results to build the output string
        For Each item In AmazonResponse.Items(0).Item
            strOutput = strOutput & item.ItemAttributes.Title & vbCrLf & vbCrLf
        Next

        'Output the results to the Word document
        Dim rng As Word.Range = ThisDocument.Range(Start:=0, End:=0)
        rng.Text = strOutput

        Exit Sub

handle_error:
        MsgBox("An error occurred: " & Err.Description)
        Exit Sub

    End Sub
```

The previous code declares a new Amazon.com Web service and then looks up items that are similar to a specified Item, such as an ASIN or ISBN. The results are then stored in a string, and the string value is placed into the Word document at the specified range.

When you run the previous code from Visual Basic .NET, the Word document opens, and a screen similar to Figure 9-17 is displayed.

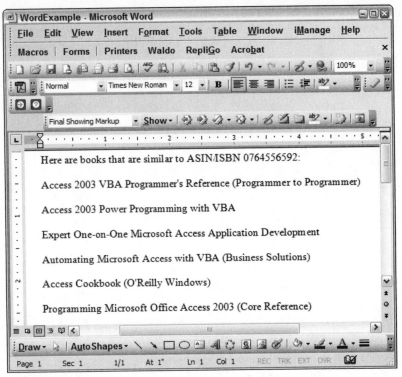

Figure 9-17

If you receive an error message stating that "The current .NET security policy does not permit WordExample to run," you can make the following change to solve the problem. Go to Control Panel and select Administrative Tools ⇨ Microsoft .NET Framework 1.1 Configuration ⇨ Runtime Search Policy and set this specific assembly to Full Trust.

At the time of this book's writing, a problem exists with the Amazon.com WSDL file that requires manual correction. If you receive an error message stating that CustomerReviews1 cannot be reflected, here is how you can work around the bug:

1. From your Visual Studio .NET Solution, double-click Web References in the Solution Explorer.

*2. Double-click the **WebReference** object and the Object Browser window will open.*

3. In the left pane of the Object Browser, double-click the object with the name WordExample.Amazon to expand the list.

*4. Double-click the **WebReference** object and this will expand to a list of objects.*

5. Double click on AWSECommerceService to open up the source code file that Visual Studio .NET generates from the WSDL.

*6. Search for **"public class CustomerReviews1"**. You should see the Public Class CustomerReviews1 declaration. Change the **TypeName** value to **CustomerReviews1**, as shown in the following.*

```
<System.Xml.Serialization.XmlTypeAttribute(TypeName:="CustomerReviews1",
[Namespace]:="http://webservices.amazon.com/AWSECommerceService/2004-11-10")>  _
Public Class CustomerReviews1
```

7. You may also need to make one other correction to keep a separate error from occurring. Search for

"public request()() as string" (Visual Basic) or "string[][] Request;" (C#).

*8. If this line is present, remove the extra parentheses or brackets. Also, remove the **GetType** parameter, so the code looks similar to the following:*

```
<System.Xml.Serialization.XmlArrayItemAttribute("BrowseNodeId", IsNullable:=false)>
_
Public Request() As String
```

9. Save this file. Rerun your application and the errors should be eliminated.

Congratulations. You have now successfully called the Amazon.com Web service using a Visual Studio .NET program from Microsoft Word.

Summary

You learned about various ways to call Web APIs from Microsoft Office, such as using VBA, the Web Services Toolkit, and Visual Studio Tools for Microsoft Office. By applying the techniques covered in this chapter, you can richly enhance your Microsoft Office applications to include functionality offered in Web APIs by various third-party vendors.

In the next chapter, you learn how you can create and capitalize on your own Web APIs.

10

Creating Your Own Web API

So far, you have learned about several XML Web APIs offered by leading companies and have seen how easy it can be to integrate these services into your own applications in creative ways. I hope, you are starting to see the potential value of offering services over the Web through a Web API. In this chapter, you explore how to create and capitalize on your own XML Web API. This chapter covers:

- ❑ Determining what features to offer in a Web API
- ❑ Determining which protocols the API will support
- ❑ Determining whether to charge for access to the Web API
- ❑ Creating and deploying a Web API
- ❑ Calling the Web API from a client computer

Designing the API

The first step in creating a Web API is to design the API on paper. You first identify a business need and then determine how to address that need with the Web API. Part of this process involves considering what features you want to make available, how your customers will access the features, and how your customers will be charged for the service. It is important to have a clear vision of what you want to accomplish before creating a Web API. Otherwise, you may end up writing a piece of software that no one will use.

What Features Should the API Offer?

You start by identifying what features to offer in the Web API. For example, does your company have some valuable data that you would like others to use? You might create an API that allows people to use your data in their own applications. Does your company have an existing software

product that you would like to make available over the Web so some of its core logic can be used in applications your customers create? Just as with any software offering, you need to brainstorm on what features you would like to offer and then finalize the list after considering the cost versus the benefit of each feature.

Which Protocols Should the API Support?

The next step is to decide what protocol your API should support. You have already learned at least three different ways to call a Web API over the Internet. You can use SOAP over HTTP, HTTP-POST, or REST (HTTP-GET). Some of the APIs discussed in earlier chapters can be called using one or more of these protocols. Amazon.com, for example, supports SOAP and REST (HTTP-GET). eBay supports SOAP and HTTP-POST.

As you learned in Chapter 1, the features offered in the Web API and the required level of security are the leading factors that determine which protocol or protocols your Web API should support. Let's look at a quick recap of some examples of when you might use REST (HTTP-GET) versus HTTP-POST versus SOAP.

REST uses a simple URL that has the service you want to call and the parameters you want to pass to it within the text of the URL. You would not want to use REST when you are transmitting sensitive data because you don't want to expose sensitive data in a text URL. Also, the URL has limits on how big it can be, so REST does not work for all Web APIs. Because REST is performing an HTTP-GET (data retrieval only) operation, it cannot typically be used to update data.

HTTP-POST allows you to post an XML document that contains the required information for calling the Web service. HTTP-POST then returns an XML document in response. HTTP-POST can be used for data retrieval as well as for updates, and for transmitting sensitive information it is a better choice than sending the information in clear text in a URL.

SOAP, unlike HTTP-GET and HTTP-POST, supports both simple and complex types. Thus, complex types such as datasets, structs, and classes can be used in SOAP communications. SOAP is the primary message format used by the .NET Framework for communicating with XML Web services. When you add a Web Reference and work with the Web API from within Visual Studio .NET, SOAP messages are created automatically for you. You can then interact in object-oriented ways with the Web API and the results it returns.

When you test and deploy your Web API, you can specify which protocols your Web API supports by modifying the configuration file used by the Web server, such as the `machine.config` or `web.config` file on the server. For example, you can include the following code in your `web.config` file to allow access to all three protocols from your Web API:

```
<system.web>
  <webServices>
    <protocols>
      <add name="HttpSoap"/>
      <add name="HttpPost"/>
      <add name="HttpGet"/>
    </protocols>
  </webServices>
</system.web>
```

If you want to disable one or more of these protocols, you simply replace the word add with the word remove.

Should the Features Be Free or for a Fee?

Another important consideration is whether to charge for access to your Web API. As you have already seen in the prior chapters, you do not have to be a software company to benefit from a Web API. Amazon.com, for example, has benefited from offering a Web API that enables users to create customized ways to search Amazon.com and to view and manage Amazon.com orders. Amazon.com currently offers the service for free, but it benefits financially in other ways by making it easier for customers to purchase its products from third-party applications.

If you decide to charge a fee for using the service, you can structure the fees in various ways. Here are some examples of how you might charge for the service:

- ❏ **Per transaction** — You charge for each call to the Web API.

- ❏ **Monthly** — You charge a monthly fee for a particular level of access.

- ❏ **One time** — You charge a one-time fee for access to the service for the entire period it is available.

The licensing fees can be structured in various ways, such as by combining one or more of the previous options. You can write your own code to keep track of the charges as customers use your Web API, or you can pay another company to keep track of charges for you. One way of keeping track of the use of your API is by issuing customers an access code or subscription ID.

You may also want to offer a free test environment and then charge fees only when the customer is ready to use your live Web service, similar to the way eBay and others handle fees.

As part of this process, you should consider how you plan to advertise your service. For example, do you need to advertise the Web API in a Web service directory and a general search engine, or do you want to restrict who is able to find out about the service. Your advertising strategy depends on how you plan to charge for the service, how you plan to restrict usage of the service, and how easily you want people to be able to find it.

Now that you have some basic ideas of what to consider in designing a Web API, let's learn how to create one.

Creating a Web API

Creating a Web API is a pretty easy process, especially using a development tool such as Visual Studio .NET. In .NET, all you have to do to create a Web service is to mark each class and method you want to make available with the WebMethod attribute and include the code in an *.asmx page*, which is the file extension for a .NET Web service. Visual Studio .NET automates most of these steps for you.

If you are interested in creating a Web API using Java, numerous resources are available on the Internet. One site you might want to visit is http://java.sun.com/webservices/jwsdp/index.jsp, which describes a Java Web Services Developer Pack.

Building an API Using Visual Studio .NET

Let's create a simple Web API using Visual Studio .NET to illustrate these concepts. This example API is a mortgage calculator that has a CalculateMonthlyPayment method. The method calculates a monthly mortgage payment from the principal, interest rate, and number of payments supplied by the user.

1. Open Visual Studio .NET and select File ⇨ New ⇨ Project.

2. Select ASP.NET Web Service for the Template. Change the Location field to http://localhost/ MortgageCalculatorSample, as shown in Figure 10-1.

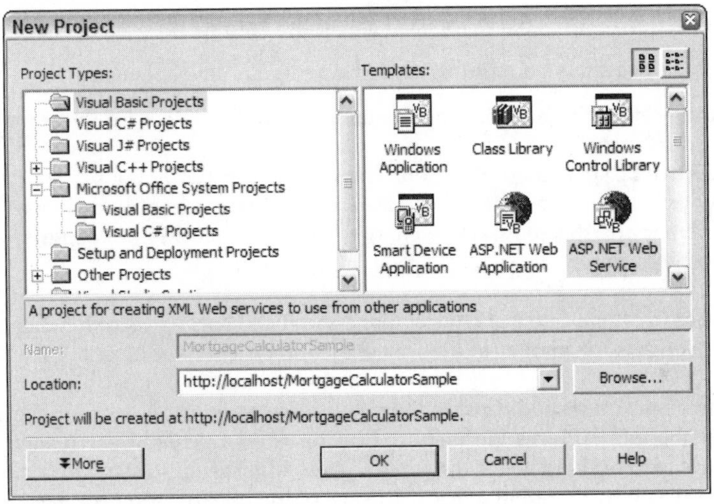

Figure 10-1

3. Click OK to have Visual Studio .NET create the new Web service project. The .asmx file of the new Web service is displayed in design view, as shown in Figure 10-2.

4. In the File Properties window, change the filename of the .asmx file from Service1 to MortgageCalculator. You should see the name of the service change in the Solution Explorer.

5. From the Solution Explorer, select MortgageCalculator.asmx, right-click, and select View Code from the shortcut menu. A screen with a code template for your new Web service is displayed, as shown in Figure 10-3.

6. Change the Public Class declaration line from Service1 to MortageCalculator.

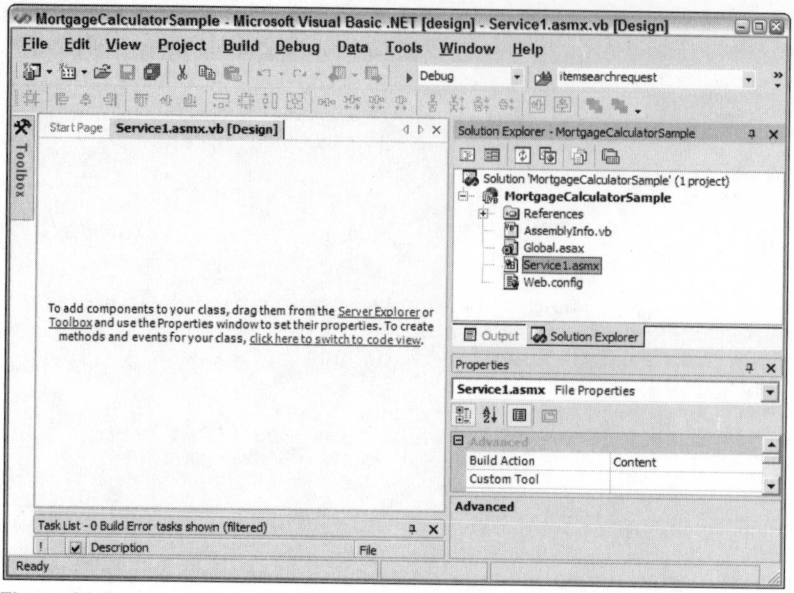

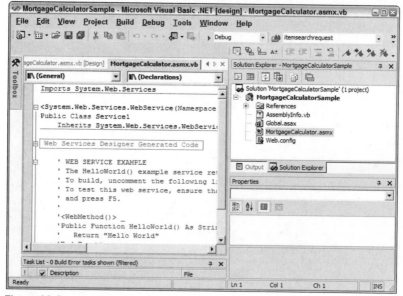

Figure 10-2

Figure 10-3

7. Add the following procedure to the code section. You can uncomment the Hello World Web service example and use it as a starting point for the following if you wish.

```vb
<WebMethod()> _
Public Function CalculateMonthlyPayment(ByVal intNumPayments _
    As Integer, ByVal dblAnnInterest As Double, ByVal _
    dblPrincipal As Double) As Double

    Dim dblTemp As Double
    Dim dblMonInt As Double

    'calculate the monthly payment from the principal, interest,
    'and number of payments values
    dblAnnInterest = dblAnnInterest / 100
    dblMonInt = dblAnnInterest / 12
    dblTemp = Math.Exp(intNumPayments * Math.Log(1 + dblMonInt))
    CalculateMonthlyPayment = (12 * dblMonInt * dblPrincipal * dblTemp) _
        / (12 * (dblTemp - 1))

End Function
```

8. At this point, your project should appear similar to the one shown in Figure 10-4.

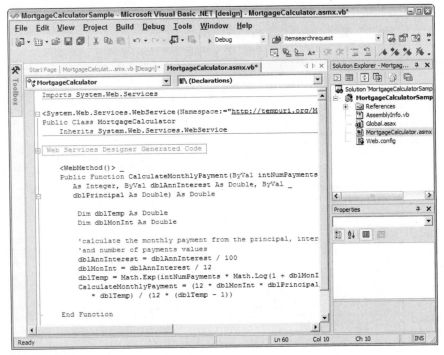

Figure 10-4

9. Save the project.

10. Test the Web service using the built-in testing utility. To do so, select Debug ⇨ Start, or press F5.

11. A screen similar to Figure 10-5 appears and displays the Web service that is available.

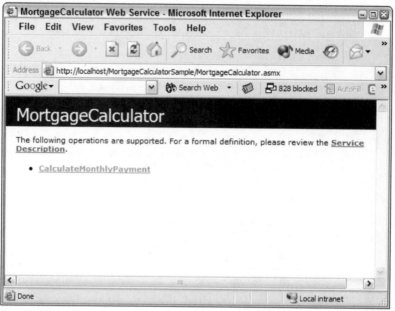

Figure 10-5

12. From this screen, you can either view the Service Description (WSDL file) for the service, or you can select a method to test.

13. If you click the Service Description link, the WSDL file that was automatically generated is displayed in the browser, as shown in Figure 10-6.

14. Select File ⇨ Save As to save this to a file called MortgageCalculator.wsdl. This WSDL file will be used by client applications to learn what methods are available and how to call the service.

When you deploy your Web API on a different computer, you must create another WSDL file because the complete path of your server is listed in the WSDL file.

15. Close the screen showing the WSDL file.

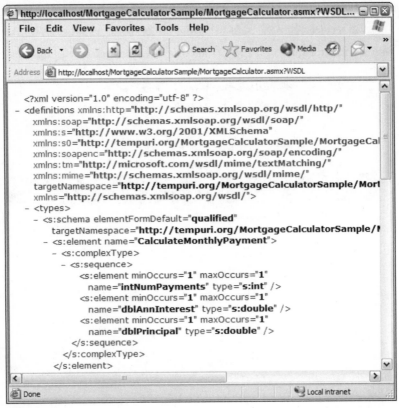

Figure 10-6

16. To test the Web API, select the `CalculateMonthlyPayment` link. A screen similar to Figure 10-7 is displayed.

17. Fill in some test values for the `intNumPayments`, `dblAnnInterest`, and `dblPrincipal` values, such as 180 (for a 15 year mortgage), 5.5, and 320,000, respectively. Select the Invoke button. A screen similar to the one shown in Figure 10-8 is then displayed with the resulting XML that was generated from running the service.

You can navigate to the .asmx file in any Web browser and this testing utility will be displayed. Any .NET Web service can be tested in this fashion, even from outside of Visual Studio .NET.

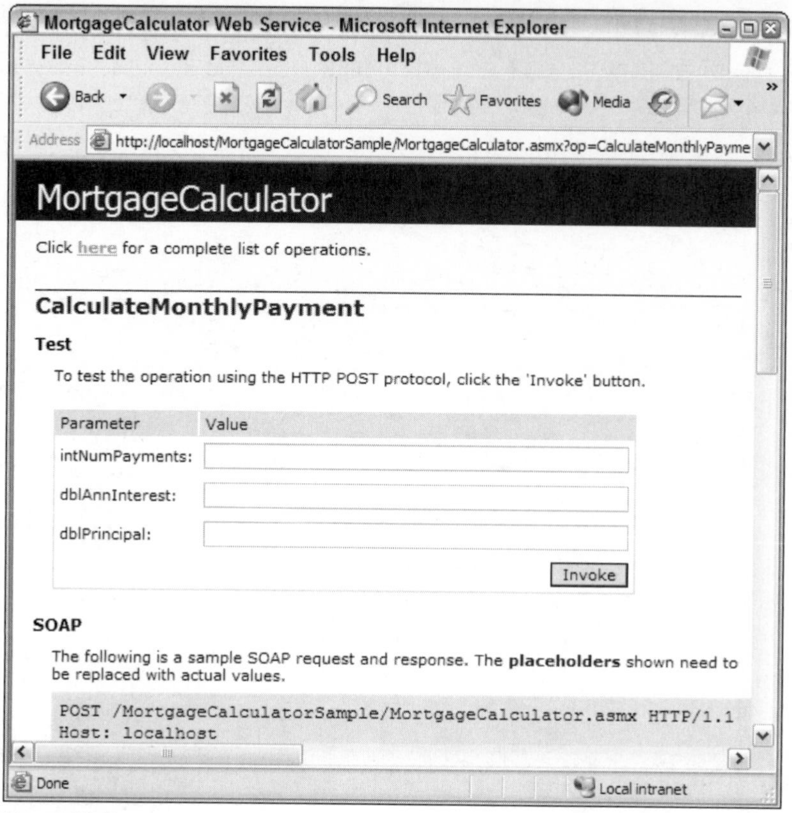

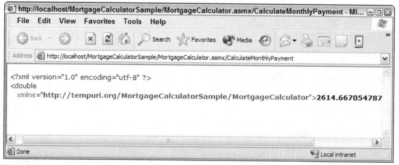

Figure 10-7

Figure 10-8

Calling the Web API from a Client Application

Before attempting to call the Web API from a client application, you should set the protocols that can be used to access the service, and you need to deploy the application to a Web server.

You can modify the web.config file of your Web service project to specify what protocols you want client applications to use to access the service. Open the Visual Studio .NET project you created in the prior section and add the webServices parameters to the web.config file as shown in Figure 10-9.

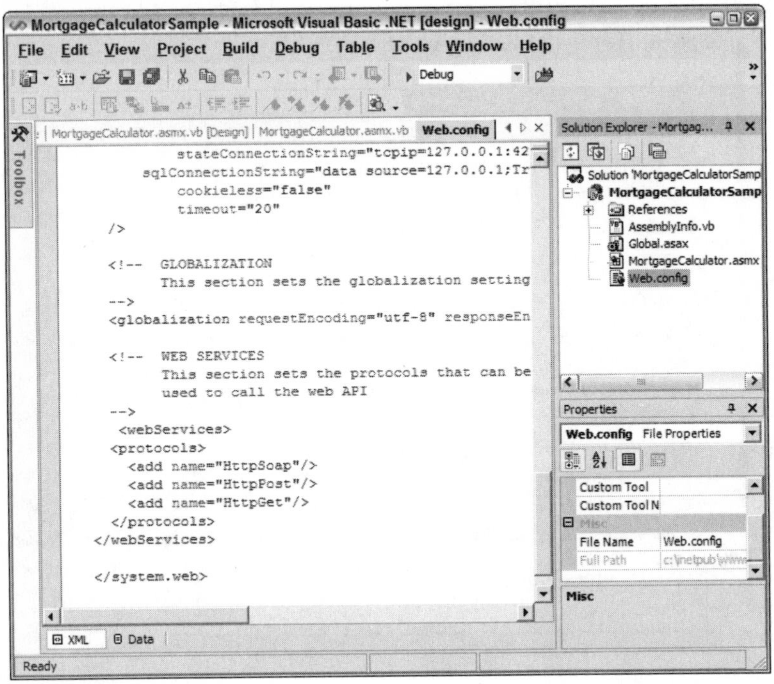

Figure 10-9

The parameters shown in Figure 10-9 grant access to the service from SOAP, HTTP-POST, and HTTP-GET protocols. If you want to deny access to the service from one or more of those protocols, simply change the add phrase to remove.

After you have specified the protocol settings, you can use the Visual Studio interface to deploy the application to the destination server. Alternatively, you can copy the project files from the respective http://inetpub/wwwroot directory to your Web server. You can make the WSDL file available on any server you like, but make sure that it points to the path of the Web server where you deployed the service.

At this point, you are ready to call the Web API from client applications. The testing tool that opens when you run the Web service from Visual Studio .NET provides sample code for how to call the Web API using SOAP, (REST) HTTP-GET, and HTTP-POST. In the prior chapters, you worked through several examples of calling Web APIs using these methods. Let's do a quick recap to refresh your memory.

To call the Web API using the SOAP protocol, perform the following steps:

1. Create a new Visual Studio .NET project (any type that you want to call the Web API from).

2. Add a Web reference to point to the WSDL file or ASMX file location of your Web API. To do so, select Project ➪ Add Web Reference and use the form that is displayed to locate the Web API and add a reference to it.

3. Declare variables in your code to reference the Web API and call its methods.

4. Use the results in your program by accessing the results in an object-oriented manner.

Please consult the prior chapters, such as Chapters 1–5 for additional examples of using SOAP to call a Web API.

To call the API using REST (HTTP-GET), perform the following steps:

1. Build a URL in your code, such as the following:

```
http://localhost/MortgageCalculatorSample/MortgageCalculator.asmx/CalculateMonthlyP
ayment?intNumPayments=180&dblAnnInterest=5.5&dblPrincipal=320000
```

2. Replace `localhost` with the name of the Web server where the service is located and replace the values for each parameter with values that were specified from the user or program.

3. Perform the HTTP-GET. For example, in .NET, you can use the `System.Net.WebRequest` object to perform the HTTP-GET.

4. Parse the XML results to use them in your program. For example, in .NET, you can use the `System.Xml.XmlTextReader` object or other XML parsing techniques to manipulate the results.

Please consult the prior chapters, such as Chapters 1 and 4 for additional examples of using HTTP-GET to call a Web API.

To call the API using HTTP-POST, perform the following steps:

1. Build the XML string in your code that can be passed to the Web API.

2. Perform the HTTP-POST and post the XML request to the Web API. For example, in .NET, you can use the `System.Net.WebClient.UploadData` method to perform an HTTP-POST operation.

3. Parse the XML results to use them in your program. For example, in .NET, you can use the `System.Text.Encoding.ASCII.GetString` object or other XML parsing techniques to manipulate the results.

Please consult the prior chapters, such as Chapters 1 and 5, for additional examples of using HTTP-POST to call a Web API.

Creating a Web API That Uses Other Programs or Services

If you already have existing software written in Visual Studio or Visual Studio .NET, it is pretty easy to wrap those existing objects as Web services. For example, you can add a reference to an existing COM object and then include calls to that COM object from your Web service. Your customer does not need to have that COM object installed on his computer. The COM object must simply be installed on the Web server.

If you have an existing .NET application, you can simply add the WebMethod attribute discussed earlier in this chapter to the methods you want to make available and place the code in an .asmx file. In either case, it is amazing how quickly you can expose your existing code to the outside world if you want to.

You can also create Web APIs that use the Web APIs of third parties, such as Amazon.com or Google. All you do is write the code from within your own Web API to call those APIs. Of course, you need to have proper licensing arrangements with those third parties before doing so.

Summary

In this chapter, you learned that creating a Web API is a lot easier than you thought. Development tools such as Visual Studio .NET make the process of creating Web APIs extremely easy. Probably the hardest part of creating a new Web API is deciding what to offer and what to charge. The sky is the limit as far as what you can offer in your own Web services, whether it be creating a new service from scratch or integrating features that you or other companies previously developed.

Let's turn to Chapter 11, where you will create a customer service application that uses various APIs discussed in this book in an integrated solution.

Case Study 1 — Customer Relations Management Application

At this point, you have explored various Web APIs and how to call those APIs from various environments, including Microsoft Office and mobile devices. These final two chapters provide two case studies that illustrate how to use multiple APIs together in your own custom solution. This chapter focuses on a Customer Relations Management (CRM) Application that uses the Google API and the Microsoft MapPoint API. More specifically, the chapter will cover:

❑ The design requirements for the CRM Application

❑ Creating the database for the CRM Application in Microsoft Access

❑ Creating the user interface for the CRM Application in Visual Studio .NET

❑ Creating the source code for the CRM Application in Visual Studio .NET

❑ Integrating features from the Google API and the Microsoft MapPoint API into the CRM Application

❑ Touring the completed CRM application

Introduction to the Customer Relations Management (CRM) Application

This chapter walks you through building a CRM Application to illustrate how easy it can be to combine features from various APIs into a single program. Let's look at the design specifications of this program in further detail.

The CRM Application is designed to allow users to track customers and potential customers. The Application stores the data in a Microsoft Access database and has the following features:

❑ It enables the user to add, update, and delete contact information for a specified contact. Contact information includes the traditional Name, Address, Phone, and E-mail fields, as well as a Notes field so the user can make notes about each conversation with him or her.

❑ It allows the user to navigate among the contact records to search for a specified contact record by last name and/or company upon request.

❑ When the user opens a particular contact record, the application uses the Google API to retrieve the first five sites that mention this customer. These results display in a Google box so the user learns more about the customer before calling him or her. If a company name is specified for the contact, the Web pages mentioning that company are also displayed. If no company name is specified, the Web pages mentioning the person are displayed. An example of the Google Box feature is illustrated in Figure 11-1.

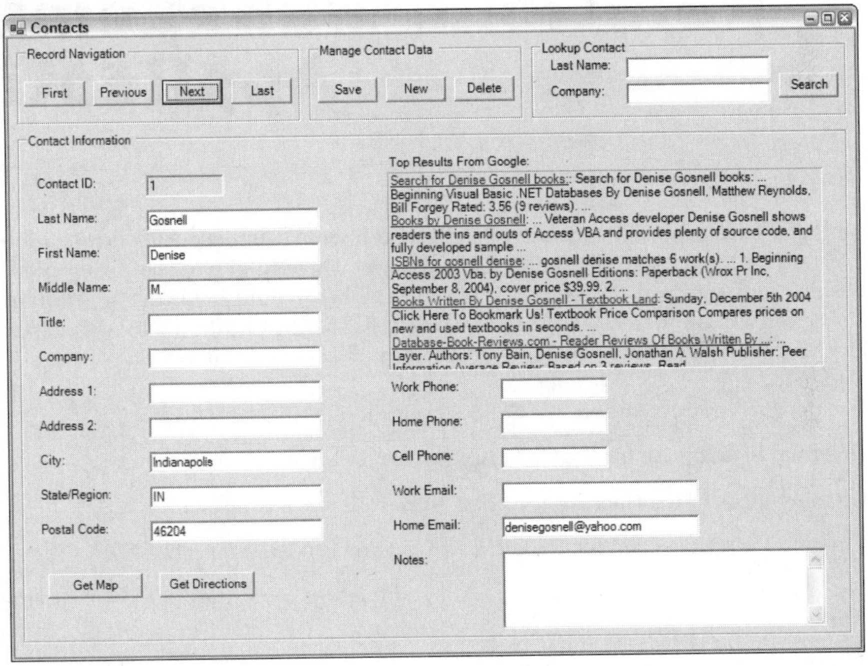

Figure 11-1

❑ Upon request of the user, the Microsoft MapPoint API retrieves a map of the contact's city and state/region. An example of the Get Map screen is shown in Figure 11-2.

❑ Upon request of the user, the Microsoft MapPoint API retrieves driving directions to the customer's location from a specified starting position that the user provides when prompted. An example of the Get Directions screen is shown in Figure 11-3.

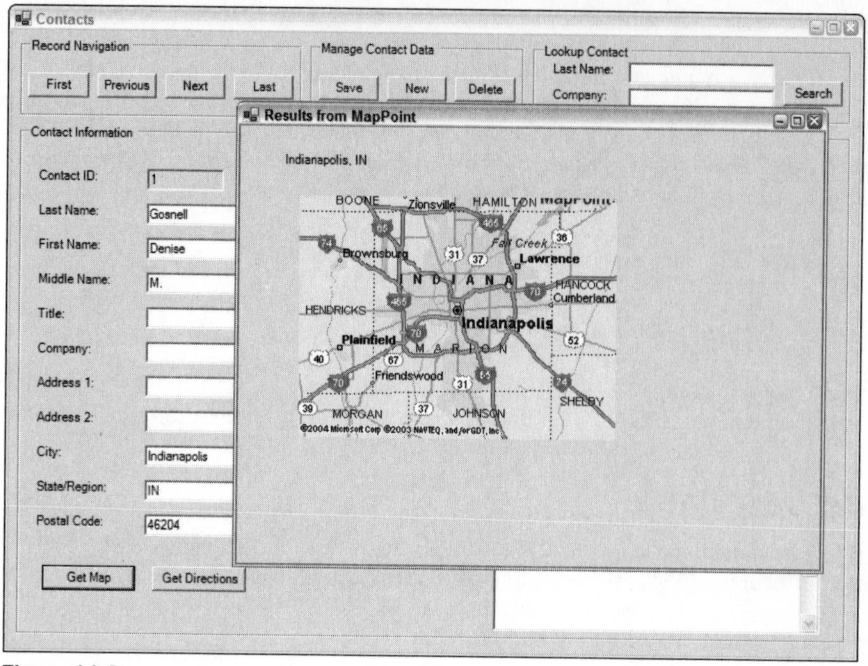

Figure 11-2

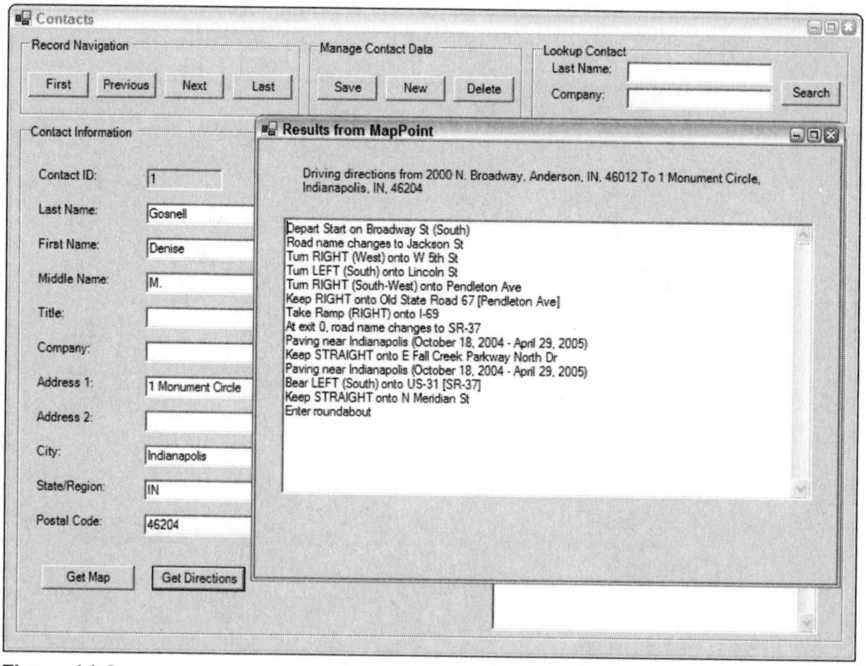

Figure 11-3

Let's jump right into building the sample application so you can try it out for yourself.

> *As with all the code examples in this chapter, you can download the entire case study in Visual Basic .NET or C# from the Wrox Web site as discussed in the Introduction. In order for the downloaded version of the case study to work, you will need to refresh the Web references to the Google API and the Microsoft MapPoint API from Visual Studio .NET by selecting the particular Web reference and choosing the refresh option. You will also need to specify your own account credentials in the source code where indicated.*

Building the Project

In this section, you build the Microsoft Access database and then use Visual Studio .NET to create the user interface and code to interact with the database. Let's start with building the database.

Build the Database

In order to create the database for the CRM case study, you need Microsoft Access. Thus, open Microsoft Access and perform the following steps to create the CRM database.

1. Select File ➪ New ➪ Blank Database.

2. Navigate to folder where you want to store the database.

3. Specify CRM for the file name.

4. Double-click "Create table in design view" as shown in Figure 11-4.

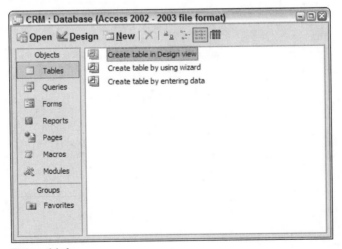

Figure 11-4

5. Create a Contacts table with the fields and data types as shown in Figure 11-5.

6. Change the Field Size property of each field to the value shown in the Description field. An example of how to change the Field Size property for the LastName field is shown in Figure 11-6.

Contacts : Table

Field Name	Data Type	Description
ContactId	AutoNumber	Set as primary key
LastName	Text	Set field size to 50
FirstName	Text	Set field size to 50
MiddleName	Text	Set field size to 50
Title	Text	Set field size to 50
Company	Text	Set field size to 50
Address1	Text	Set field size to 100
Address2	Text	Set field size to 100
City	Text	Set field size to 50
Region	Text	Set field size to 50
PostalCode	Text	Set field size to 25
WorkPhone	Text	Set field size to 15
HomePhone	Text	Set field size to 15
CellPhone	Text	Set field size to 15
WorkEmail	Text	Set field size to 50
HomeEmail	Text	Set field size to 50
Notes	Memo	

Figure 11-5

Contacts : Table

Field Name	Data Type	Description
ContactId	AutoNumber	Set as primary key
LastName	Text	Set field size to 50
FirstName	Text	Set field size to 50
MiddleName	Text	Set field size to 50
Title	Text	Set field size to 50
Company	Text	Set field size to 50
Address1	Text	Set field size to 100
Address2	Text	Set field size to 100
City	Text	Set field size to 50
Region	Text	Set field size to 50
PostalCode	Text	Set field size to 25
WorkPhone	Text	Set field size to 15
HomePhone	Text	Set field size to 15
CellPhone	Text	Set field size to 15
WorkEmail	Text	Set field size to 50
HomeEmail	Text	Set field size to 50
Notes	Memo	

Field Properties

General | Lookup

Field Size	50
Format	
Input Mask	
Caption	
Default Value	
Validation Rule	
Validation Text	
Required	No
Allow Zero Length	Yes
Indexed	No
Unicode Compression	No
IME Mode	No Control
IME Sentence Mode	None
Smart Tags	

Figure 11-6

7. Set the ContactId field as the primary key. To do so, select the ContactId field, right-click, and from the pop-up menu, select Primary Key, as shown in Figure 11-7.

8. Next, double-click on the table to open it. Add some sample data, such as shown in Figure 11-8.

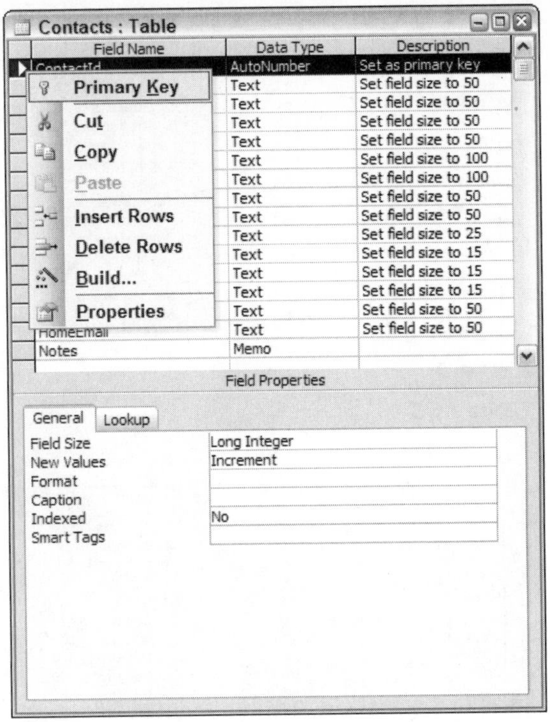

Figure 11-7

Figure 11-8

You have now completed the database. Let's move on to building the user interface and writing the source code.

Build the User Interface

In this section, we use Visual Studio .NET to design the forms for the CRM Application. Perform the following steps:

1. Open Visual Studio .NET.

2. Select File ⇨ New ⇨ Project.

3. Select Visual Basic for the Project Type and Windows Application for the Template.

4. Specify the Project Name as **CustomerRelationsManagement**.

5. Change the Location to the directory where you want to store the project. An example of how the screen should appear at this point is shown in Figure 11-9.

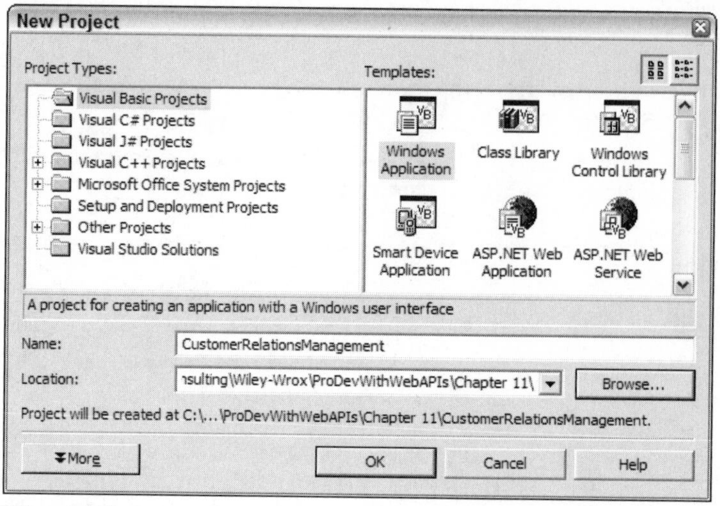

Figure 11-9

6. Change the name `Form1.vb` to `frmContacts.vb`. To do so, select `Form1.vb` from the Solution Explorer, right-click, and from the pop-up menu select Rename, as shown in Figure 11-10.

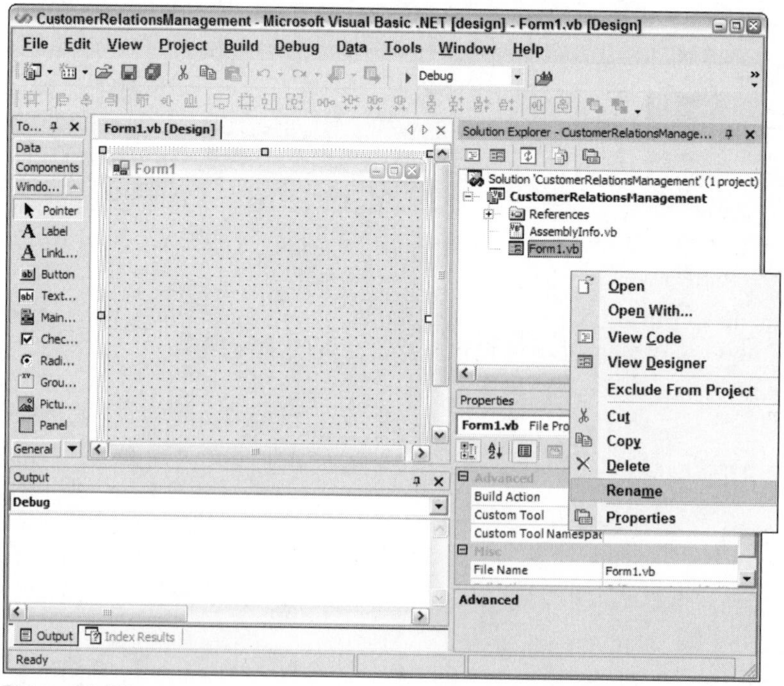

Figure 11-10

7. Type **frmContacts.vb** and press Enter to change the name.

At this point, you should save and run the project to make sure there are no errors. If you receive an error that Sub Main was not found in Form1, you will next be prompted to specify a form to use instead. Select frmContacts from the list.

8. Change the Name property of the form to frmContacts. Change the Text property of the form to Contacts. Change the Size property of the form to 800, 600.

9. Add the following controls to frmContacts: 4 group boxes, 8 buttons, 2 labels, and 2 text boxes. Arrange the controls as shown in Figure 11-11.

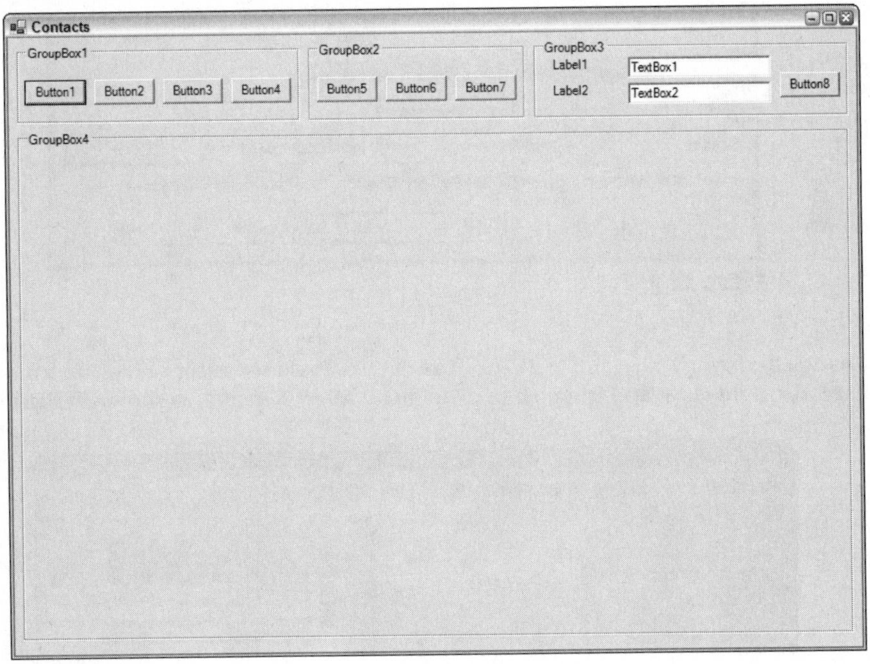

Figure 11-11

10. Within the fourth group box, add the following controls: 18 labels, 17 text boxes, 1 link label, and 2 buttons. Arrange the controls as shown in Figure 11-12.

Figure 11-12

11. Rename the Name property and the other specified Properties for each of the controls as in the following table:

Default Name (in Figure 11-12)	Name	Type of Control	Other Properties to Set from Properties Dialog
GroupBox1	grpNavigation	Group Box	Text = "Record Navigation"
GroupBox2	grpDataUpdate	Group Box	Text = "Manage Contact Data"
GroupBox3	grpSearch	Group Box	Text = "Lookup Contact"
GroupBox4	grpContact	Group Box	Text = "Contact Information"
Button1	btnMoveFirst	Button	Text = "First"
Button2	btnMovePrevious	Button	Text = "Previous"
Button3	btnMoveNext	Button	Text = "Next"
Button4	btnMoveLast	Button	Text = "Last"
Button5	btnSave	Button	Text = "Save"
Button6	btnAddNew	Button	Text = "New"
Button7	btnDelete	Button	Text = "Delete"

Table continued on following page

Default Name (in Figure 11-12)	Name	Type of Control	Other Properties to Set from Properties Dialog
Button8	btnSearch	Button	Text = "Search"
Button9	btnGetMap	Button	Text = "Get Map"
Button10	btnGetDirections	Button	Text = "Get Directions"
TextBox1	txtSearchLName	Text Box	Text = [blank] Set corresponding label text property to "Last Name:"
TextBox2	txtSearchCompany	Text Box	Text = [blank] Set corresponding label text property to "Company:"
TextBox3	txtContactId	Text Box	Text = [blank] Set read-only property to True. Set corresponding label text property to "Contact ID:"
TextBox4	txtLName	Text Box	Text = [blank] Set corresponding label text property to "Last Name:"
TextBox5	txtFName	Text Box	Text = [blank] Set corresponding label text property to "First Name:"
TextBox6	txtMName	Text Box	Text = [blank] Set corresponding label text property to "Middle Name:"
TextBox7	txtTitle	Text Box	Text = [blank] Set corresponding label text property to "Title:"
TextBox8	txtCompany	Text Box	Text = [blank] Set corresponding label text property to "Company:"
TextBox9	txtAddress1	Text Box	Text = [blank] Set corresponding label text property to "Address 1:"
TextBox10	txtAddress2	Text Box	Text = "" Set corresponding label text property to "Address 2:"
TextBox11	txtCity	Text Box	Text = [blank] Set corresponding label text property to "City:"

Default Name (in Figure 11-12)	Name	Type of Control	Other Properties to Set from Properties Dialog
TextBox12	txtRegion	Text Box	Text = [blank] Set corresponding label text property to "State/Region:"
TextBox13	txtPostalCode	Text Box	Text = [blank] Set corresponding label text property to "Postal Code:"
TextBox14	txtWorkPhone	Text Box	Text = [blank] Set corresponding label text property to "Work Phone:"
TextBox15	txtHomePhone	Text Box	Text = [blank] Set corresponding label text property to "Home Phone:"
TextBox16	txtCellPhone	Text Box	Text = [blank] Set corresponding label text property to "Cell Phone:"
TextBox17	txtWorkEmail	Text Box	Text = [blank] Set corresponding label text property to "Work Email:"
TextBox18	txtHomeEmail	Text Box	Text = [blank] Set corresponding label text property to "Home Email:"
TextBox19	txtNotes	Text Box	Text = [blank] Set multiline property to True. Set scrollbar property to Vertical. Set corresponding label text property to "Notes:"
LinkLabel1	lnklblGoogleResults	Link Label	Text = [blank] Set border style property to Fixed3D. Set corresponding label text property to "Top Results From Google:"

12. At this point, the screen should appear similar to the one shown in Figure 11-13.

13. Save your changes.

14. Add a new form. To do so, select Project ⇨ Add Windows Form. Specify Windows Form for the Template and frmMap.vb as the Name. An example is illustrated in Figure 11-14.

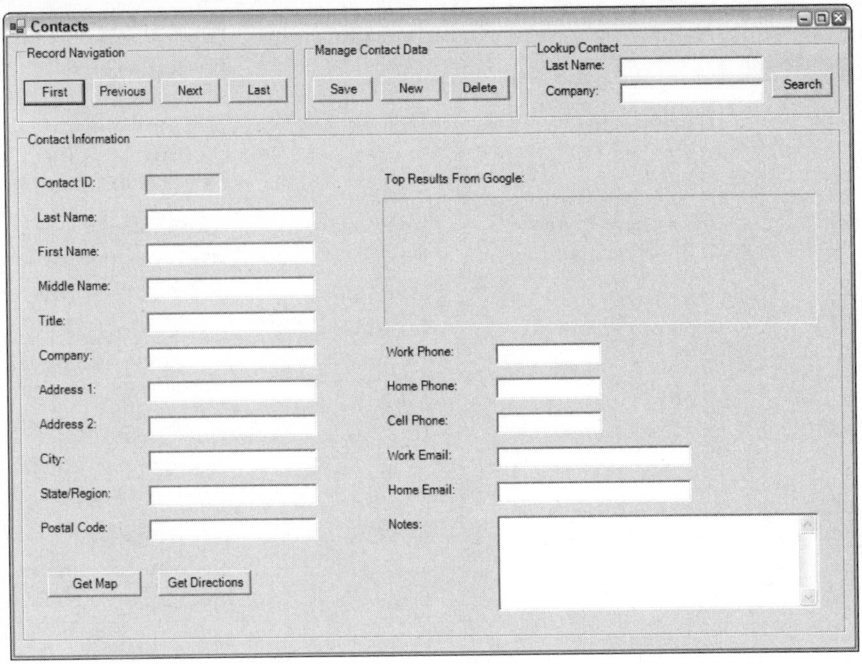

Figure 11-13

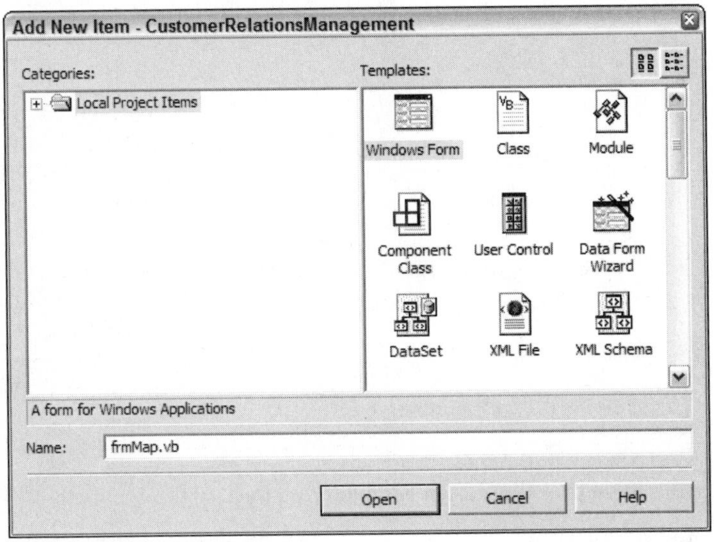

Figure 11-14

15. Add a label control, a text box control, and a picture box control to the new form as shown in Figure 11-15. It is difficult to see the picture box control on the figure because it has a transparent background.

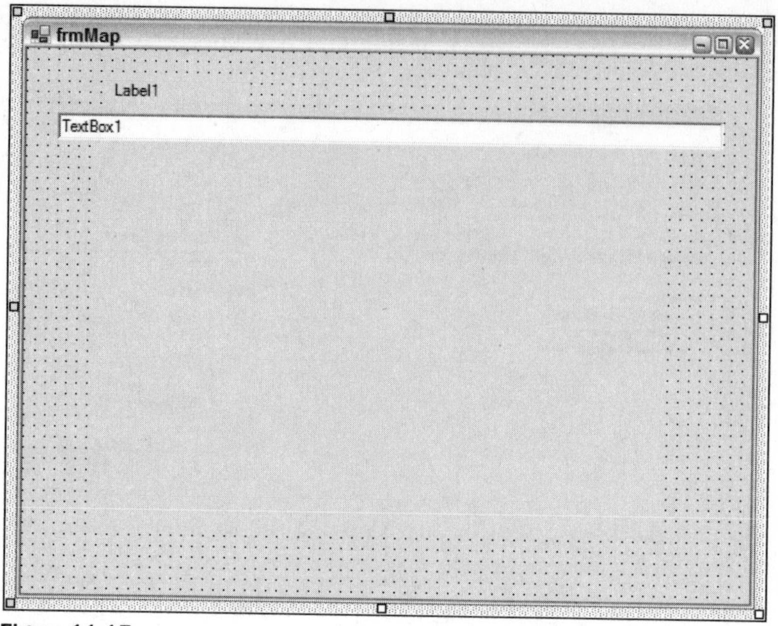

Figure 11-15

16. Rename the Name property and the other specified Properties for each of the controls as in the following table:

Default Name (in Figure 11-15)	Name	Type of Control	Other Properties to Set from Properties Dialog
frmMap	frmMap	Form	Text = "Results from Map-Point"
Label1	lblTitle	Label	Text = "Title"
TextBox1	txtDirections	Text Box	Text = [blank] Set multiline property to True. Set scrollbars to Vertical.
PictureBox1	picMap	Picture Box	

Now that you have created the user interface, let's move on to adding references to the external APIs and to coding the functionality to make the user interface work.

Build the Modules

In this section, you add the references to the Google API and the Microsoft MapPoint API and write the code to make the CRM application work. Let's jump right in.

1. Select Project ⇨ Add Web Reference. In the URL, specify the location of the Google WSDL file (http://api.google.com/GoogleSearch.wsdl) and click the GO button.

237

2. Change the Web Reference Name to `Google` so that you can use a shorter name in your project. An example of what the screen looks like at this point is shown in Figure 11-16.

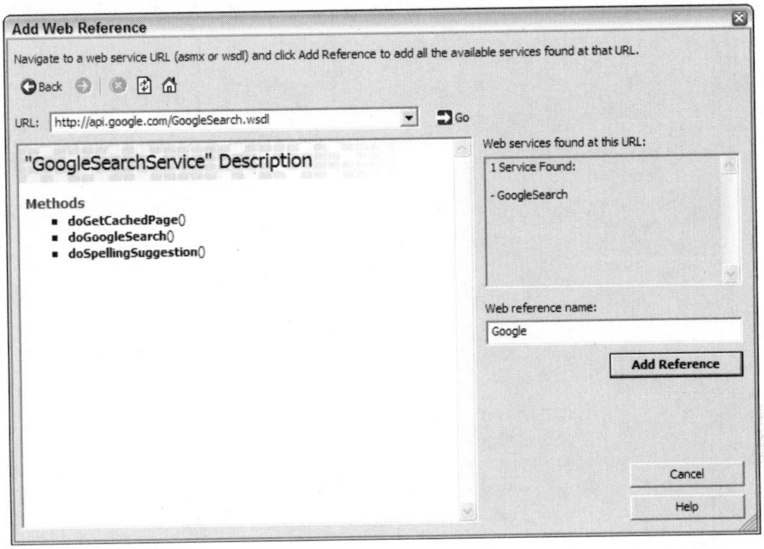

Figure 11-16

3. Click the Add Reference button to add a reference to the Google API to your project.

4. Next, let's add a reference to the Microsoft MapPoint API. (See Figure 11-17.)

5. Just as before, select Project ⇨ Add Web Reference. In the URL, specify the location of the MapPoint WSDL file (`http://staging.mappoint.net/standard-30/mappoint.wsdl`) and click the GO button.

6. Change the Web Reference Name to `MapPoint` so that you can use a shorter name in your project.

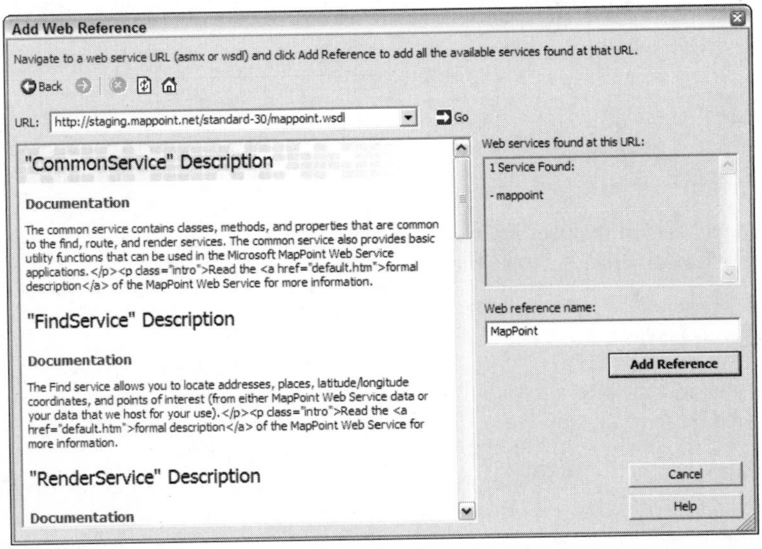

Figure 11-17

7.   Click the Add Reference button to add a reference to your project.

8.   Add the following `imports` statements to the top of the `frmContacts` code segment (before the `Public Class frmContacts` statement) so that you can refer to the various objects in the project in shorthand mode.

```
Imports System
Imports System.Data
Imports System.Data.OleDb
Imports CustomerRelationsManagement.MapPoint
```

9.   Add the following declarations beneath the `Public` Class and `Inherits` statements.

```
Public Class frmContacts
    Inherits System.Windows.Forms.Form

    'declare a database connection variable
    Dim Conn As OleDbConnection

    'declare a data adapter variable
    Dim contactDA As OleDbDataAdapter

    'declare a command builder variable

    Dim cmdbuilder As OleDbCommandBuilder

    'Declare a new dataset to hold the data locally
    Dim contactDS As DataSet = New DataSet

    'declare a counter for storing the current record
    Dim intCurRecord As Integer

    'declare a variable for tracking whether in add mode
    Dim blnAddMode As Boolean
```

10.   Add the following `frmContacts_Load` event procedure to the form, changing the path following to point to the location of the CRM Access database you created in the prior section. This event runs automatically when the form opens and loads the first contact record. It also creates a new `OleDbCommandBuilder` object called `cmdBuilder` so that SQL statements for updating the database are created automatically.

```
Private Sub frmContacts_Load(ByVal sender As System.Object, ByVal e As _
    System.EventArgs) Handles MyBase.Load

    On Error GoTo handleerror

    'Create a connection to the Access database.
    'Specify the complete path to the Access CRM database.
    conn = New _
        OleDbConnection("Provider=Microsoft.Jet.OLEDB.4.0;" & _
        "Data Source=C:\Chapter 11\CustomerRelationsManagement\CRM.mdb;")

    'Specify the SQL statement to retrieve the contacts records
    contactDA = New _
        OleDbDataAdapter("SELECT * FROM Contacts ORDER BY LastName, FirstName", _
```

```
            Conn)

        cmdbuilder = New OleDbCommandBuilder(contactDA)

        PopulateDataSet()

        'set the first record to the current record
        intCurRecord = 0

        'populate the controls on the form with the current (first)
        'contact(record)
        PopulateControlsOnForm()

        Exit Sub

handleerror:
        MsgBox("An error occurred in frmContacts_Load: " & Err.Number & " - " & _
            Err.Description)
        Exit Sub

End Sub
```

11. Add the following `PopulateDataSet` procedure to the form to populate the local dataset with values from the database when requested.

```
Sub PopulateDataSet()

        On Error GoTo handleerror

        'clear the dataset from prior values
        contactDS.Clear()

        'Open the connection to the Access database
        Conn.Open()

        'Populate the dataset with the contacts table
        contactDA.Fill(contactDS, "Contacts")

        'Close the connection to the database while we work locally with the
        'data
        Conn.Close()

        Exit Sub

handleerror:
        If Conn.State = ConnectionState.Open Then Conn.Close()

        MsgBox("An error occurred in PopulateDataSet: " & Err.Number & " - " & _
            Err.Description)
        Exit Sub

End Sub
```

12. Add the following `PopulateControlsOnForm` procedure to the form to populate the fields on the form when called.

240

```
Sub PopulateControlsOnForm()

        On Error GoTo handleerror

        'Populate the fields on the form with the current record
        'in the dataset.

        'If the value is null then set the field to an empty string
        '(otherwise an error will be raised).

        txtContactId.Text = _
            contactDS.Tables("Contacts").Rows(intCurRecord)("ContactId")

        txtLName.Text = _
        IIf(IsDBNull(contactDS.Tables("Contacts").Rows(intCurRecord)("LastName")), _
            "", contactDS.Tables("Contacts").Rows(intCurRecord)("LastName"))

        txtFName.Text = _
        IIf(IsDBNull(contactDS.Tables("Contacts").Rows(intCurRecord)("FirstName")), _
            "", contactDS.Tables("Contacts").Rows(intCurRecord)("FirstName"))

        txtMName.Text = _
        IIf(IsDBNull(contactDS.Tables("Contacts").Rows(intCurRecord)("MiddleName")), _
            "", contactDS.Tables("Contacts").Rows(intCurRecord)("MiddleName"))

        txtTitle.Text = _
        IIf(IsDBNull(contactDS.Tables("Contacts").Rows(intCurRecord)("Title")), _
            "", contactDS.Tables("Contacts").Rows(intCurRecord)("Title"))

        txtCompany.Text = _
        IIf(IsDBNull(contactDS.Tables("Contacts").Rows(intCurRecord)("Company")), _
            "", contactDS.Tables("Contacts").Rows(intCurRecord)("Company"))

        txtAddress1.Text = _
        IIf(IsDBNull(contactDS.Tables("Contacts").Rows(intCurRecord)("Address1")), _
            "", contactDS.Tables("Contacts").Rows(intCurRecord)("Address1"))

        txtAddress2.Text = _
        IIf(IsDBNull(contactDS.Tables("Contacts").Rows(intCurRecord)("Address2")), _
            "", contactDS.Tables("Contacts").Rows(intCurRecord)("Address2"))

        txtCity.Text = _
        IIf(IsDBNull(contactDS.Tables("Contacts").Rows(intCurRecord)("City")), _
            "", contactDS.Tables("Contacts").Rows(intCurRecord)("City"))

        txtRegion.Text = _
        IIf(IsDBNull(contactDS.Tables("Contacts").Rows(intCurRecord)("Region")), _
            "", contactDS.Tables("Contacts").Rows(intCurRecord)("Region"))

        txtPostalCode.Text = _
        IIf(IsDBNull(contactDS.Tables("Contacts").Rows(intCurRecord)("PostalCode")), _
            "", contactDS.Tables("Contacts").Rows(intCurRecord)("PostalCode"))

        txtWorkPhone.Text = _
        IIf(IsDBNull(contactDS.Tables("Contacts").Rows(intCurRecord)("WorkPhone")), _
```

```
                "", contactDS.Tables("Contacts").Rows(intCurRecord)("WorkPhone"))

        txtHomePhone.Text = _
    IIf(IsDBNull(contactDS.Tables("Contacts").Rows(intCurRecord)("HomePhone")), _
            "", contactDS.Tables("Contacts").Rows(intCurRecord)("HomePhone"))

        txtCellPhone.Text = _
    IIf(IsDBNull(contactDS.Tables("Contacts").Rows(intCurRecord)("CellPhone")), _
            "", contactDS.Tables("Contacts").Rows(intCurRecord)("CellPhone"))

        txtWorkEmail.Text = _
    IIf(IsDBNull(contactDS.Tables("Contacts").Rows(intCurRecord)("WorkEmail")), _
            "", contactDS.Tables("Contacts").Rows(intCurRecord)("WorkEmail"))

        txtHomeEmail.Text = _
    IIf(IsDBNull(contactDS.Tables("Contacts").Rows(intCurRecord)("HomeEmail")), _
            "", contactDS.Tables("Contacts").Rows(intCurRecord)("HomeEmail"))

        txtNotes.Text = _
    IIf(IsDBNull(contactDS.Tables("Contacts").Rows(intCurRecord)("Notes")), _
            "", contactDS.Tables("Contacts").Rows(intCurRecord)("Notes"))

        BuildGoogleBar()

        Exit Sub

handleerror:
        MsgBox("An error occured in PopulateControlsOnForm: " & Err.Number & " - " _
            & Err.Description)
        Exit Sub

    End Sub
```

13. Add the following `UpdateDataSet` procedure to the form.

```
    Sub UpdateDataSet()

        On Error GoTo handleerror

        If blnAddMode Then
            'add the new record to the dataset
            AddRecordToDataSet()
        Else
            'update the data set with any changes before
            'moving to another record
            UpdateDataSetValues()
        End If

        Exit Sub

handleerror:
        MsgBox("An error occurred in UpdateDataSet: " & Err.Number & " - " &
Err.Description)
        Exit Sub

    End Sub
```

14. Add the following btnMoveLast_Click event procedure to the form so the code will execute when the Last button is clicked.

```
Private Sub btnMoveLast_Click(ByVal sender As System.Object, ByVal e As _
    System.EventArgs) Handles btnMoveLast.Click

        On Error GoTo handleerror

        'update the current dataset record before moving to another one
        UpdateDataSet()


        'set the current record variable to point to the last record
        intCurRecord = (contactDS.Tables("Contacts").Rows.Count - 1)

        'populate the controls on the form with the last
        'contact record in the dataset
        PopulateControlsOnForm()

        Exit Sub

handleerror:
        MsgBox("An error occurred in btnMoveLast_Click: " & Err.Number & " - " &
Err.Description)
        Exit Sub

End Sub
```

15. Add the following btnMovePrevious_Click event procedure to the form so the code will execute when the Previous button is clicked.

```
Private Sub btnMovePrevious_Click(ByVal sender As System.Object, ByVal e As _
    System.EventArgs) Handles btnMovePrevious.Click

        On Error GoTo handleerror

        'set the current record variable to point to the previous record
        'after making sure not already on the firest record
        If intCurRecord >= 1 Then

        'update the current dataset record before moving to another one
        UpdateDataSet()


            intCurRecord = (intCurRecord - 1)
        Else
            MsgBox("Cannot move previous since already on first contact record.")
        End If

        'populate the controls on the form with the previous
        'contact record in the dataset
        PopulateControlsOnForm()

        Exit Sub

handleerror:
```

```
        MsgBox("An error occured in btnMovePrevious_Click: " & Err.Number & " - " & _
            Err.Description)
        Exit Sub


End Sub
```

16. Add the following `btnMoveFirst_Click` event procedure to the form so the code executes when the First button is clicked.

```
Private Sub btnMoveFirst_Click(ByVal sender As System.Object, ByVal e As _
    System.EventArgs) Handles btnMoveFirst.Click

    On Error GoTo handleerror

    'update the current dataset record before moving to another one
    UpdateDataSet()



    'set the current record variable to point to the first record
    intCurRecord = 0

    'populate the controls on the form with the first
    'contact record in the dataset
    PopulateControlsOnForm()

    Exit Sub

handleerror:
        MsgBox("An error occurred in btnMoveFirst_Click: " & Err.Number & " - " & _
            Err.Description)
        Exit Sub

End Sub
```

17. Add the following `btnMoveNext_Click` event procedure to the form so the code executes when the Next button is clicked.

```
Private Sub btnMoveNext_Click(ByVal sender As System.Object, ByVal e As _
    System.EventArgs) Handles btnMoveNext.Click

    On Error GoTo handleerror

    'set the current record variable to point to the next record
    'after making sure not already on the last record
    If intCurRecord < (contactDS.Tables("Contacts").Rows.Count - 1) Then

        'update the current dataset record before moving to another one
        UpdateDataSet()


        intCurRecord = (intCurRecord + 1)
    Else
```

```
        MsgBox("Cannot move next since already on last contact record.")
    End If

    'populate the controls on the form with the next
    'contact record in the dataset
    PopulateControlsOnForm()

    Exit Sub

handleerror:
    MsgBox("An error occurred in btnMoveNext_Click: " & Err.Number & " - " & _
        Err.Description)
    Exit Sub


End Sub
```

18. Add the following btnSave_Click event procedure to the form so the code executes when the Save button is clicked. Only when the user clicks the Save button are the changes that have been made to the local dataset saved back to the underlying Access database.

```
Private Sub btnSave_Click(ByVal sender As System.Object, ByVal e As _
    System.EventArgs) Handles btnSave.Click

    On Error GoTo handleerror

    'save the changes made to the local dataset back
    'to the database

    'update the current dataset record
    UpdateDataSet()



    'If nothing changed, do not proceed
    If Not contactDS.HasChanges(DataRowState.Added) And Not _
        contactDS.HasChanges(DataRowState.Modified) And Not _
        contactDS.HasChanges(DataRowState.Deleted) Then Exit Sub

    'update the database with the current values in the
    'dataset
    If contactDS.HasChanges(DataRowState.Modified) Then _
        UpdateDatabaseChanges()

    'update the database with the added values
    If contactDS.HasChanges(DataRowState.Added) Then _
        UpdateDatabaseAdds()

    'update the database with the deleted records
    If contactDS.HasChanges(DataRowState.Deleted) Then _
        UpdateDatabaseDeletions()

    'populate the dataset with the new values in the database
    '(in case someone else changed records too)
```

```
            PopulateDataSet()

            'populate the controls on the form with the same
            'contact record prior to the update
            PopulateControlsOnForm()

            Exit Sub

handleerror:
            MsgBox("An error occurred in btnSave_Click: " & Err.Number & " - " & _
                Err.Description)
            Exit Sub

    End Sub
```

19. Add the following `btnAddNew_Click` event procedure to the form so the code executes when the Add button is clicked. This clears the form so that a new record can be added.

```
Private Sub btnAddNew_Click(ByVal sender As System.Object, ByVal e As _
        System.EventArgs) Handles btnAddNew.Click
            On Error GoTo handleerror

            'clear the controls on the form
            ClearForm()

            'enable add mode
            blnAddMode = True

            Exit Sub

handleerror:
            MsgBox("An error occurred in btnAddNew_Click: " & Err.Number & " - " & _
                Err.Description)
            Exit Sub

    End Sub
```

20. Add the following `btnDelete_Click` event procedure to the form so the code executes when the Delete button is clicked. This procedure deletes the record from the local dataset but not from the underlying Access database. The user must also click the Save button to make the changes in the database final.

```
Private Sub btnDelete_Click(ByVal sender As System.Object, ByVal e As _
        System.EventArgs) Handles btnDelete.Click

            On Error GoTo handleerror

            Dim intResponse As Integer

            intResponse = MsgBox("Delete current record from the local dataset?", _
                MsgBoxStyle.YesNo, "Delete Record?")

            If intResponse = vbYes Then
                contactDS.Tables("Contacts").Rows(intCurRecord).Delete()
```

```
                    MsgBox("Record deleted locally, but you need to press Save to make
        changes permanent in database.")

                    'move to the first record
                    intCurRecord = 0
                    PopulateControlsOnForm()

            End If

            Exit Sub

    handleerror:
            MsgBox("An error occurred in btnDelete_Click: " & Err.Number & " - " & _
                Err.Description)
            Exit Sub

    End Sub
```

21. Add the following `btnSearch_Click` event procedure to the form so the code will execute
when the Search button is clicked. This event will navigate through the local dataset looking for
a contact record that matches the search criteria. If a match is found, that record becomes the
current record displayed on the form.

```
Private Sub btnSearch_Click(ByVal sender As System.Object, ByVal e As _
        System.EventArgs) Handles btnSearch.Click

        On Error GoTo handleerror

        Dim intRow As Integer

        'search through the dataset for a matching record
        If txtSearchLName.Text = "" And txtSearchCompany.Text <> "" Then
            'if only company was specified as search criteria
            'loop through dataset looking for matching company
            For intRow = 0 To contactDS.Tables("Contacts").Rows.Count - 1
                If contactDS.Tables("Contacts").Rows(intRow)("Company") = _
                    txtSearchCompany.Text Then
                    'a match was found so go to the record
                    intCurRecord = intRow
                    PopulateControlsOnForm()
                End If
            Next intRow

        ElseIf txtSearchLName.Text <> "" And txtSearchCompany.Text = "" Then
            'if only last name was specified as search criteria
            'loop through dataset looking for matching company
            For intRow = 0 To contactDS.Tables("Contacts").Rows.Count - 1
                If contactDS.Tables("Contacts").Rows(intRow)("LastName") = _
                    txtSearchLName.Text Then
                    'a match was found so go to the record
                    intCurRecord = intRow
                    PopulateControlsOnForm()
                End If
```

```
            Next intRow

        ElseIf txtSearchLName.Text <> "" And txtSearchCompany.Text <> "" Then
            'if both last name and company were specified as search criteria
            'loop through dataset looking for matching company
            For intRow = 0 To contactDS.Tables("Contacts").Rows.Count - 1
                If contactDS.Tables("Contacts").Rows(intRow)("Company") = _
                    txtSearchCompany.Text And _
                    contactDS.Tables("Contacts").Rows(intRow)("LastName") = _
                    txtSearchLName.Text Then

                    'a match was found so go to the record
                    intCurRecord = intRow
                    PopulateControlsOnForm()
                End If
            Next intRow

        End If

        Exit Sub

handleerror:
        MsgBox("An error occured in btnSearchClick_Click: " & Err.Number & " - " & _
            Err.Description)
        Exit Sub

End Sub
```

22. Add the following `UpdateDatabaseChanges` procedure to the form. This procedure is responsible for querying the local dataset for records that were modified and then updating the Access database with those changes.

```
Sub UpdateDatabaseChanges()

        On Error GoTo handleerror

        ' Create temporary DataSet.
        Dim tempDataSet As DataSet

        'Get the changes for each modified row.
        tempDataSet = contactDS.GetChanges(DataRowState.Modified)

        'Open the connection to the Access database
        Conn.Open()

        'Update the Access database with the DataAdapter used
        'to create the dataset
        contactDA.Update(tempDataSet, "Contacts")

        'close the connection
        Conn.Close()

        Exit Sub

handleerror:
```

```
          If Conn.State = ConnectionState.Open Then Conn.Close()

       MsgBox("An error occured in UpdateDatabaseChanges: " & Err.Number & " - " & _
          Err.Description)
          Exit Sub

   End Sub
```

23. Add the following `UpdateDatabaseAdds` procedure to the form. This procedure is responsible for querying the local dataset for records that were added and then adding those new records to the Access database.

```
Sub UpdateDatabaseAdds()

       On Error GoTo handleerror

       ' Create temporary DataSet.
       Dim tempDataSet As DataSet

       'Get the changes for each modified row.
       tempDataSet = contactDS.GetChanges(DataRowState.Added)

       'Open the connection to the Access database
       Conn.Open()

       'Update the Access database with the DataAdapter used
       'to create the dataset
       contactDA.Update(tempDataSet, "Contacts")

       'close the connection
       Conn.Close()

       Exit Sub

handleerror:
       If Conn.State = ConnectionState.Open Then Conn.Close()

       MsgBox("An error occurred in UpdateDatabaseAdds: " & Err.Number & " - " & _
          Err.Description)
          Exit Sub

   End Sub
```

24. Add the following `UpdateDatabaseDeletions` procedure to the form. This procedure is responsible for querying the local dataset to determine if any records were deleted and then deleting those records permanently from the Access database.

```
Sub UpdateDatabaseDeletions()

       On Error GoTo handleerror

       ' Create temporary DataSet.
       Dim tempDataSet As DataSet

       'Get the changes for each modified row.
```

```
        tempDataSet = contactDS.GetChanges(DataRowState.Deleted)

        'Open the connection to the Access database
        Conn.Open()

        'Update the Access database with the DataAdapter used
        'to create the dataset
        contactDA.Update(tempDataSet, "Contacts")

        'close the connection
        Conn.Close()

        Exit Sub

handleerror:
        If Conn.State = ConnectionState.Open Then Conn.Close()

        MsgBox("An error occured in UpdateDatabaseDeletions: " & Err.Number & " - " _
            & Err.Description)
        Exit Sub

End Sub
```

25. Add the following `UpdateDatasetValues` procedure to the form. This procedure is responsible for updating the local dataset with the values on the form. This procedure allows changes made by the user to be updated in the local dataset for later saving to the Access database.

```
Sub UpdateDataSetValues()

        On Error GoTo handleerror

        'update the dataset with the current values on the form

        contactDS.Tables("Contacts").Rows(intCurRecord)("LastName") = txtLName.Text
        contactDS.Tables("Contacts").Rows(intCurRecord)("FirstName") = _
            txtFName.Text
        contactDS.Tables("Contacts").Rows(intCurRecord)("MiddleName") = _
            txtMName.Text
        contactDS.Tables("Contacts").Rows(intCurRecord)("Title") = txtTitle.Text
        contactDS.Tables("Contacts").Rows(intCurRecord)("Company") = _
            txtCompany.Text
        contactDS.Tables("Contacts").Rows(intCurRecord)("Address1") = _
            txtAddress1.Text
        contactDS.Tables("Contacts").Rows(intCurRecord)("Address2") = _
            txtAddress2.Text
        contactDS.Tables("Contacts").Rows(intCurRecord)("City") = txtCity.Text
        contactDS.Tables("Contacts").Rows(intCurRecord)("Region") = txtRegion.Text
        contactDS.Tables("Contacts").Rows(intCurRecord)("PostalCode") = _
            txtPostalCode.Text
        contactDS.Tables("Contacts").Rows(intCurRecord)("WorkPhone") = _
            txtWorkPhone.Text
        contactDS.Tables("Contacts").Rows(intCurRecord)("HomePhone") = _
            txtHomePhone.Text
        contactDS.Tables("Contacts").Rows(intCurRecord)("CellPhone") = _
            txtCellPhone.Text
```

```
        contactDS.Tables("Contacts").Rows(intCurRecord)("WorkEmail") = _
            txtWorkEmail.Text
        contactDS.Tables("Contacts").Rows(intCurRecord)("HomeEmail") = _
            txtHomeEmail.Text
        contactDS.Tables("Contacts").Rows(intCurRecord)("Notes") = txtNotes.Text


    Exit Sub

handleerror:
    MsgBox("An error occurred in UpdateDataSetValues: " & Err.Number & " - " & _
        Err.Description)
    Exit Sub
End Sub
```

26. Add the following `ClearForm` procedure to the form. This procedure is responsible for clearing the controls on the form so that the user can add a new record.

```
Sub ClearForm()

    On Error GoTo handleerror

    'clear the controls on the form so can go into add mode
    txtContactId.Text = ""
    txtLName.Text = ""
    txtFName.Text = ""
    txtMName.Text = ""
    txtTitle.Text = ""
    txtCompany.Text = ""
    txtAddress1.Text = ""
    txtAddress2.Text = ""
    txtCity.Text = ""
    txtRegion.Text = ""
    txtPostalCode.Text = ""
    txtWorkPhone.Text = ""
    txtHomePhone.Text = ""
    txtCellPhone.Text = ""
    txtWorkEmail.Text = ""
    txtHomeEmail.Text = ""
    txtNotes.Text = ""
    lnklblGoogleResults.Text = ""

    blnAddMode = True

    Exit Sub

handleerror:
    MsgBox("An error occurred in ClearForm: " & Err.Number & " - " & _
        Err.Description)
    Exit Sub

End Sub
```

27. Add the following `AddRecordToDataSet` procedure to the form. This procedure is responsible for adding a new record entered by the user into the local dataset.

```
Sub AddRecordToDataSet()

        'add the new record to the local dataset

        On Error GoTo handleerror

        Dim row As DataRow

        row = contactDS.Tables("Contacts").NewRow

        row("ContactId") = 0
        row("LastName") = txtLName.Text
        row("FirstName") = txtFName.Text
        row("MiddleName") = txtMName.Text
        row("Title") = txtTitle.Text
        row("Company") = txtCompany.Text
        row("Address1") = txtAddress1.Text
        row("Address2") = txtAddress2.Text
        row("City") = txtCity.Text
        row("Region") = txtRegion.Text
        row("PostalCode") = txtPostalCode.Text
        row("WorkPhone") = txtWorkPhone.Text
        row("HomePhone") = txtHomePhone.Text
        row("CellPhone") = txtCellPhone.Text
        row("WorkEmail") = txtWorkEmail.Text
        row("HomeEmail") = txtHomeEmail.Text
        row("Notes") = txtNotes.Text

        contactDS.Tables("Contacts").Rows.Add(row)

        blnAddMode = False

        Exit Sub

handleerror:
        MsgBox("An error occurred in AddRecordToDataSet: " & Err.Number & " - " & _
            Err.Description)
        Exit Sub

End Sub
```

28. Add the following `BuildGoogleBar` procedure to the form. This procedure is responsible for communicating with the Google API to retrieve a list of five Web sites that mention the specified contact. The results are then displayed on the form to the user. You need to replace YOUR KEY GOES HERE where indicated with your Google API key.

```
Sub BuildGoogleBar()

        'retrieve the top search results about the company or
```

```
'person from Google

On Error GoTo handleerror

'Create a Google Search object
Dim Search As New Google.GoogleSearchService

Dim strLicense As String
Dim strSearchText As String
Dim intStart As Integer
Dim intMaxResults As Integer

'clear the current google bar
lnklblGoogleResults.Links.Clear()
lnklblGoogleResults.Text = ""

'set the values to pass to the Google web service
strLicense = "YOUR KEY GOES HERE"

'specify the search criteria for the google search
If txtCompany.Text <> "" Then
    'if a company is present, search on that value
    strSearchText = txtCompany.Text
Else
    'if a company is not present, search on the
    'contact name
    strSearchText = txtFName.Text & " " & txtLName.Text
End If

intStart = 0
intMaxResults = 5

'execute the doGoogleSearch method (i.e. run the Google Search)
Dim SearchResult As Google.GoogleSearchResult = _
        Search.doGoogleSearch(strLicense, strSearchText, _
        intStart, intMaxResults, False, "", False, "", "", "")

'if no results were returned then exit
If SearchResult.resultElements Is Nothing Then Exit Sub

Dim result As Google.ResultElement
intStart = 0

Dim strTitle As String
Dim strSnippet As String

'display the google results on the form
For Each result In SearchResult.resultElements
    'first, retrieve the title and snippet and strip
    'out the bold and break HTML tags
    strTitle = Replace(result.title, "<b>", "")
    strTitle = Replace(strTitle, "</b>", "")
    strTitle = Replace(strTitle, "<br>", "")
```

```
                strTitle = Replace(strTitle, "</br>", "")

                strSnippet = Replace(result.snippet, "<b>", "")
                strSnippet = Replace(strSnippet, "</b>", "")
                strSnippet = Replace(strSnippet, "<br>", "")
                strSnippet = Replace(strSnippet, "</br>", "")

                'create a string with the title and snippet
                lnklblGoogleResults.Text = lnklblGoogleResults.Text & strTitle & _
                    ": " & strSnippet & vbCrLf
                'add the hyperlink to the title
                lnklblGoogleResults.Links.Add(intStart, Len(strTitle), result.URL)
                intStart = Len(lnklblGoogleResults.Text)
        Next

        Exit Sub

handleerror:
        MsgBox("An error occurred in BuildGoogleBar: " & Err.Number & " - " & _
            Err.Description)
        Exit Sub
End Sub
```

29. Add the following `lnklblGoogleResults_LinkClicked` event procedure to the form. This procedure runs when the user clicks on a link in the Google box and opens a Web browser to display the linked page.

```
Private Sub lnklblGoogleResults_LinkClicked(ByVal sender As System.Object, _
    ByVal e As System.Windows.Forms.LinkLabelLinkClickedEventArgs) Handles _
    lnklblGoogleResults.LinkClicked

        On Error GoTo handleerror

        'Determine which link was clicked
lnklblGoogleResults.Links(lnklblGoogleResults.Links.IndexOf(e.Link)).Visited = True

        'Display the appropriate link
        Dim target As String = CType(e.Link.LinkData, String)

        'navigate to the selected URL
        System.Diagnostics.Process.Start(target)

        Exit Sub

handleerror:
        MsgBox("An error occurred in lnklblGoogleResults_LinkClicked: " & _
            Err.Number & " - " & Err.Description)
        Exit Sub

End Sub
```

30. Add the following `btnGetMap_Click` event procedure to the form. This procedure runs when the user clicks on the Get Map button to use the MapPoint API to retrieve a map for the contact's city and state/region. Replace YOUR USER ID and YOUR PASSWORD following in the two specified places with your MapPoint API account trial version credentials or purchased license credentials.

```
Private Sub btnGetMap_Click(ByVal sender As System.Object, ByVal e As _
        System.EventArgs) Handles btnGetMap.Click

    On Error GoTo handleerror

    'Purpose: Retrieve a map for a given address

    'NOTE: Make sure to include imports statement for MapPoint
    'Web service for abbreviated declarations below to work

    'Specify the credentials for the find service
    'Use the customer id and password you were provided
    Dim findService As New FindServiceSoap
    findService.Credentials = New _
        System.Net.NetworkCredential("YOUR USER ID", "YOUR PASSWORD")
    findService.PreAuthenticate = True

    'Get a map of a specified address
    Dim findSpec As New FindSpecification
    'specify the data source - change as desired - North America below
    findSpec.DataSourceName = "MapPoint.NA"

    'retrieve the City and State/Region of the current company
    findSpec.InputPlace = txtCity.Text & ", " & txtRegion.Text

    Dim foundResults As FindResults
    foundResults = findService.Find(findSpec)

    Dim Views(0) As ViewByHeightWidth
    Views(0) = foundResults.Results(0).FoundLocation.BestMapView.ByHeightWidth

    'Specify the credentials for the render service
    'Use the customer id and password you were provided
    Dim renderService As New RenderServiceSoap
    renderService.Credentials = New _
        System.Net.NetworkCredential("YOUR USER ID", "YOUR PASSWORD")
    renderService.PreAuthenticate = True

    Dim mapSpec As New MapSpecification
    mapSpec.DataSourceName = "MapPoint.NA"
    mapSpec.Views = Views

    'get the map from MapPoint
    Dim mapImages() As MapImage
    mapImages = renderService.GetMap(mapSpec)

    'read the map into a stream for display
```

```
                'as a bitmap on the form
                Dim streamImage As System.IO.Stream
                streamImage = New System.IO.MemoryStream(mapImages(0).MimeData.Bits)
                Dim bitmapImage As Bitmap
                bitmapImage = New Bitmap(streamImage)

                Dim frmResults As New frmMap

                'show the map in a different form
                frmResults.picMap.Image = bitmapImage
                frmResults.txtDirections.Visible = False
                frmResults.lblTitle.Text = txtCity.Text & ", " & txtRegion.Text
                frmResults.Show()
                frmResults.TopMost = True

                Exit Sub

        handleerror:
                MsgBox("An error occurred in btnGetMap_Click: " & Err.Number & " - " & _
                    Err.Description)
                Exit Sub

        End Sub
```

31. Add the following `btnDirections_Click` event procedure to the form. This procedure runs when the user clicks on the Get Directions button and uses the MapPoint API to retrieve point-to-point directions to the contact's location from a location specified by the user when prompted.

```
Private Sub btnGetDirections_Click(ByVal sender As System.Object, ByVal e As _
        System.EventArgs) Handles btnGetDirections.Click

        'NOTE: Make sure to include imports statement for MapPoint
        'Web service for abbreviated declarations below to work

        'Purpose: perform a Geocode lookup to lookup latitude and
        'longitude based on a specified address, and then get
        'point to point directions based on those coordinates

        Dim dblLatitudeStart As Double
        Dim dblLongitudeStart As Double
        Dim dblLatitudeEnd As Double
        Dim dblLongitudeEnd As Double

        Dim strAddress As String
        Dim strCity As String
        Dim strRegion As String
        Dim strPostalCode As String

        'prompt the user to specify a starting address
        strAddress = InputBox("Please enter starting street address, if known (ex:
1 Monument Circle)")
        strCity = InputBox("Please enter starting city (ex: Indianapolis)")
        strRegion = InputBox("Please enter starting region (ex: IN)")
```

```
        strPostalCode = InputBox("Please enter postal code, if known (ex: 46204)")

        'retrieve the coordinates for the starting and ending addresses
        GetCoordinates(dblLatitudeStart, dblLatitudeEnd, dblLongitudeStart, _
            dblLongitudeEnd, strAddress, strCity, strRegion, strPostalCode)

        Dim strOutput As String
        strOutput = GetDrivingDirections(dblLatitudeStart, dblLatitudeEnd, _
            dblLongitudeStart, dblLongitudeEnd)

        Dim frmresults As New frmMap

        'display driving directions on other form
        frmresults.lblTitle.Text = "Driving directions from " & strAddress & ", " _
            & strCity & ", " & strRegion & ", " & strPostalCode & " To " & _
            txtAddress1.Text & ", " & txtCity.Text & ", " & txtRegion.Text & _
            ", " & txtPostalCode.Text
        'show directions in text box
        frmresults.txtDirections.Text = strOutput
        'make sure directions not selected
        frmresults.txtDirections.Select(0, 0)
        frmresults.picMap.Visible = False
        'show the form
        frmresults.Show()
        frmresults.TopMost = True

        Exit Sub

handleerror:
        MsgBox("An error occured in btnGetDirections_Click: " & Err.Number & " - " _
            & Err.Description)
        Exit Sub

End Sub
```

32. Add the following `GetCoordinates` procedure to the form. This procedure uses the MapPoint API to retrieve the coordinates of the starting and ending addresses to be used in the point-to-point directions. Again, replace YOUR USER ID and YOUR PASSWORD where indicated with those for your MapPoint account.

```
Sub GetCoordinates(ByRef dblLatitudeStart As Double, ByRef dblLatitudeEnd _
    As Double, ByRef dblLongitudeStart As Double, ByRef dblLongitudeEnd _
    As Double, ByVal strAddress As String, ByVal strCity As String, ByVal _
    strRegion As String, ByVal strPostalCode As String)

        On Error GoTo handleerror

        'Specify the credentials for the find service
        'Use the customer id and password you were provided
        Dim findService As New FindServiceSoap
        findService.Credentials = New _
            System.Net.NetworkCredential("YOUR USER ID", "YOUR PASSWORD")
        findService.PreAuthenticate = True

        'set up the destination Address
```

```
        Dim Address As New Address
        Address.AddressLine = txtAddress1.Text
        Address.PrimaryCity = txtCity.Text
        Address.Subdivision = txtRegion.Text
        Address.PostalCode = txtPostalCode.Text

        'set up the FindAddressSpecification
        Dim findAddressSpec As New FindAddressSpecification
        findAddressSpec.InputAddress = Address
        findAddressSpec.DataSourceName = "MapPoint.NA"

        'call the FindAddress method to look up the address
        Dim foundResults As FindResults
        foundResults = findService.FindAddress(findAddressSpec)

        'set the values for the destination address
        If (foundResults.NumberFound = 1) Then
            dblLatitudeEnd = foundResults.Results(0).FoundLocation.LatLong.Latitude
            dblLongitudeEnd = _
                foundResults.Results(0).FoundLocation.LatLong.Longitude
        Else
            dblLatitudeEnd = 0
            dblLongitudeEnd = 0
        End If

        '***NOW, FOR STARTING ADDRESS COORDINATES****

        'now, set up the starting Address
        Address.AddressLine = strAddress
        Address.PrimaryCity = strCity
        Address.Subdivision = strRegion
        Address.PostalCode = strPostalCode

        'call the FindAddress method to look up the address
        foundResults = findService.FindAddress(findAddressSpec)

        'set the values for the starting address
        If (foundResults.NumberFound = 1) Then
            dblLatitudeStart = _
                foundResults.Results(0).FoundLocation.LatLong.Latitude
            dblLongitudeStart = _
                foundResults.Results(0).FoundLocation.LatLong.Longitude
        Else
            dblLatitudeStart = 0
            dblLongitudeStart = 0
        End If

        Exit Sub

handleerror:
        MsgBox("An error occurred in GetCoordinates: " & Err.Number & " - " & _
            Err.Description)
        Exit Sub

End Sub
```

33. Add the following GetDrivingDirections procedure to the form. This procedure uses the MapPoint API to retrieve driving directions for the starting and ending coordinates. Again, replace YOUR USER ID and YOUR PASSWORD where indicated with those for your MapPoint account.

```
Function GetDrivingDirections(ByVal dblLatitudeStart As Double, ByVal _
    dblLatitudeEnd As Double, ByVal dblLongitudeStart As Double, ByVal _
    dblLongitudeEnd As Double) As String

        On Error GoTo handleerror

        'Calculate driving directions between two latitude and longitude
        'coordinates
        Dim latLongs(1) As LatLong
        latLongs(0) = New LatLong
        latLongs(0).Latitude = dblLatitudeStart
        latLongs(0).Longitude = dblLongitudeStart
        latLongs(1) = New LatLong
        latLongs(1).Latitude = dblLatitudeEnd
        latLongs(1).Longitude = dblLongitudeEnd

        Dim routeService As New RouteServiceSoap
        routeService.Credentials = New _
          System.Net.NetworkCredential("YOUR USER ID", "YOUR PASSWORD")
        routeService.PreAuthenticate = True

        Dim findRoute As Route
        findRoute = routeService.CalculateSimpleRoute(latLongs, _
            "MapPoint.NA", SegmentPreference.Quickest)

        Dim intCounter As Integer
        Dim strDirections As String

        'output the directions into a string
        For intCounter = 0 To findRoute.Itinerary.Segments(0).Directions.Length - 1
            strDirections = strDirections & _
        findRoute.Itinerary.Segments(0).Directions(intCounter).Instruction & vbCrLf
        Next intCounter

        GetDrivingDirections = strDirections

        Exit Function

handleerror:
        MsgBox("An error occured in GetDrivingDirections: " & Err.Number & " - " & _
            Err.Description)
        Exit Function

End Function
```

Congratulations! You've now added all the code needed to make the CRM Application work. At this point, if you have not been doing so periodically anyway, you should save your changes to the project. You should also compile the program and make sure there are no compiler errors.

Touring the Completed Application

At this point, you're ready to take a tour of the application. When you run the program, as you can by pressing F5, the screen opens and displays the first contact in the database. The records are sorted alphabetically by Last Name and First Name. The Contact ID is shown for display purposes, but gets automatically assigned by the database. An example of the starting screen is shown in Figure 11-18.

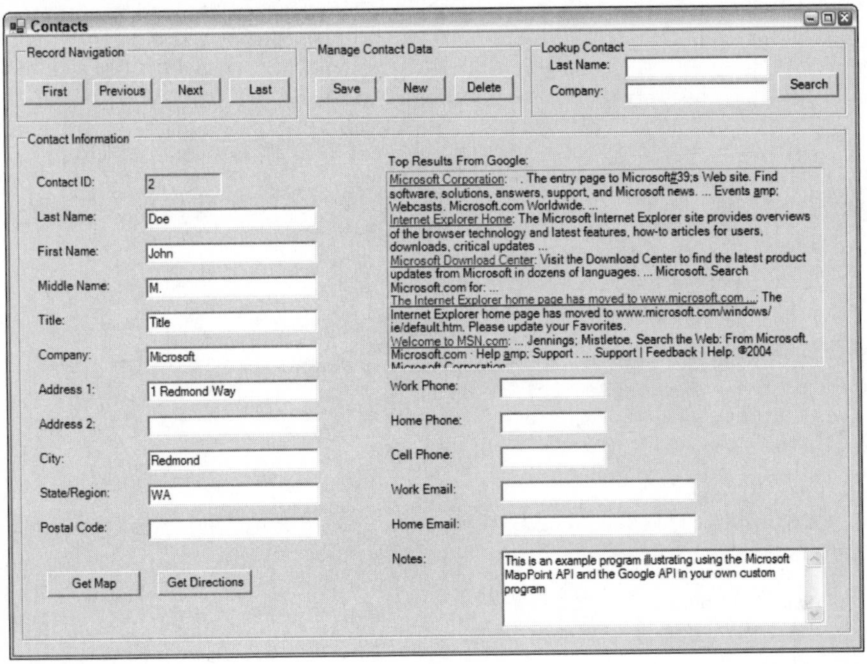

Figure 11-18

Notice how the Google box has been populated with records mentioning Microsoft, which is the company that the fictitious John Doe works for. These records were retrieved using the Google API. You can click on any of the hyperlinks in the Google box to review the actual Web site in more detail. When you do so, a separate browser window is opened.

The idea behind having this Google box is to provide your user with quick information about his customer or contact before he gives that contact a call. For example, the user might see that the customer has recently been in the news, or he might just want to look at the Web site of that company for more information. In either case, it is possible that one of the top-five ranking results from Google will have useful information about the customer.

Next, if you want to test out the MapPoint features, click the Get Map button on the form. The Microsoft MapPoint API is then called and a map of the city and state/region of the contact is displayed. This is illustrated in Figure 11-19.

The user also can obtain driving directions to this customer's location. When the user clicks the Get Directions button on the form, he or she is prompted to specify a street address, city, state/region, and

postal code of the starting location for the directions. An example of one of the prompts a user sees is shown in Figure 11-20.

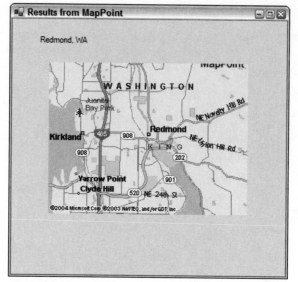

Figure 11-19

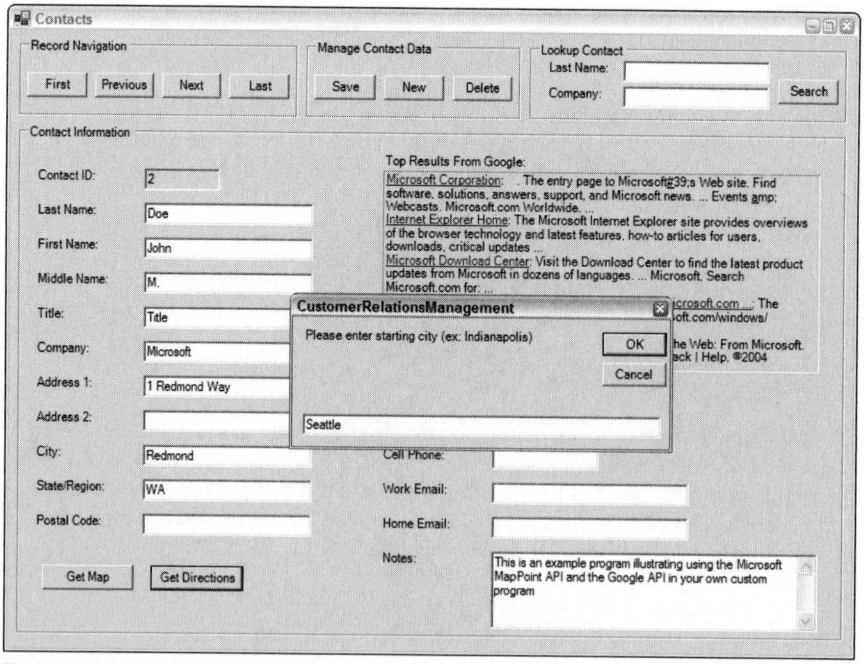

Figure 11-20

After the user specifies the starting address, the MapPoint API is then called to retrieve the exact coordinates of the starting and ending addresses as well as driving directions using those exact coordinates. A form displaying the driving directions from the starting location to the address of the contact is then shown, as you can see in Figure 11-21.

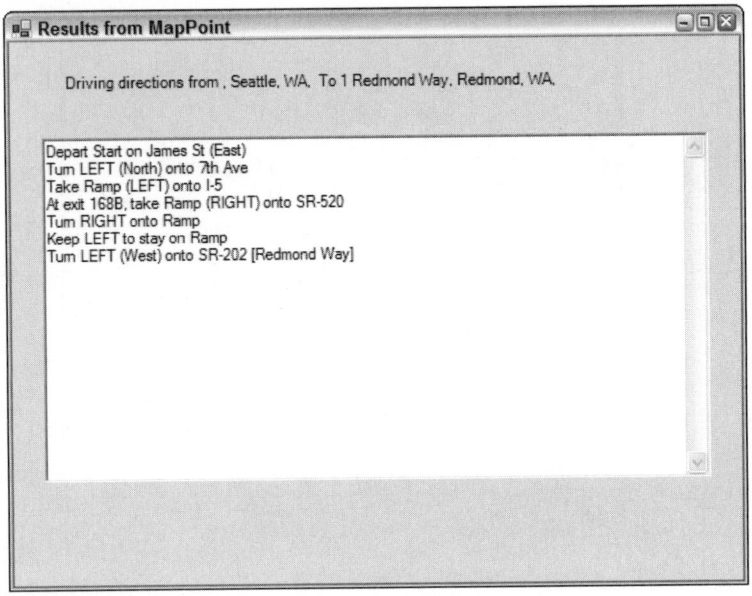

Figure 11-21

To navigate among the Contact records, the user clicks a button from the navigation pane, as shown in Figure 11-22. For example, he can navigate to the first contact record, the previous one, the next one, and the last one. If he attempts to navigate too far, a message displays to let him know.

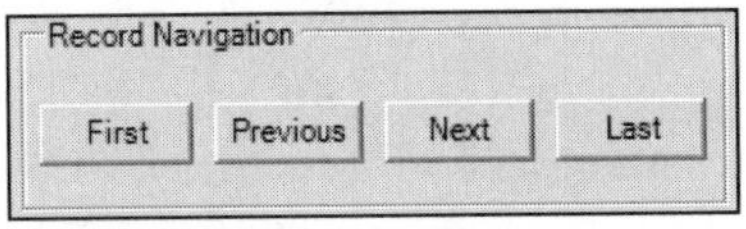

Figure 11-22

The user can manage changes to the Contact records by using the Save, Add, and Delete buttons, as shown in Figure 11-23. When the user navigates around the records, his changes are made to the local dataset. However, as mentioned before, these changes are not saved in the underlying database until the user clicks the Save button. Clicking New clears the field so a new record can be added. Clicking Delete enables the user to remove the record from the local dataset.

Figure 11-23

Finally, the user can specify a search criteria of a Last Name and/or a Company Name to go directly to a particular contact record, as shown in Figure 11-24. In order for a match to be found, the value must match the value in the database exactly, including case (that means that Company and company are not the same). This is just a simple example, but in a more sophisticated application you might allow partial matching. Either the Last Name or the Company can be specified, or both. If a match is found, the matching record becomes the current record and is displayed on the form.

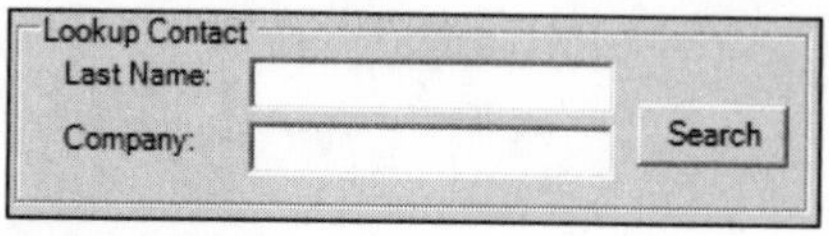

Figure 11-24

You have now completed a tour of the CRM Application. Take some time to play around with the features and poke around in the code to see exactly what is going on behind the scenes.

Summary

In this chapter, you created a sample CRM Application that illustrates ways to use the Google API and the Microsoft MapPoint API in a custom program. Although the application may not be fancy or sophisticated, it certainly does illustrate just how easy it can be to integrate third-party APIs into your custom solutions in creative ways.

Let's move on to the second case study, which provides another example by integrating the Amazon.com, Google, and eBay APIs together into an application.

Case Study 2 — Executive Dashboard Application

In this chapter, you work through a case study that is referred to as the Executive Dashboard Application. The application is very simple in function, but it illustrates how easy it can be to combine multiple APIs together in a single program. This chapter discusses:

❑ The design requirements for the dashboard application

❑ Creating the user interface for the dashboard application in Visual Studio .NET

❑ Creating the source code for the dashboard application in Visual Studio .NET

❑ Integrating features from the Google API, the Amazon.com API, and the eBay API into the dashboard application

❑ Touring the completed dashboard application

Introduction to the Executive Dashboard Application

This chapter walks you through building a browser-based application referred to as the Executive Dashboard Application. The name of the application is not important, and it could also be appropriately named Product Information Dashboard, or any other such name. What is important about the dashboard application is that it illustrates how to combine results from Amazon.com, Google, and eBay API calls into your own custom program.

Let's look at the basic requirements of the application and a sample screen to give you an idea of how it works:

❑ The dashboard application is designed to allow users, such as business executives, to easily retrieve product information and reviews from multiple sources. Business executives may want to use the program to quickly review information about products they sell, as well as products sold by competitors. Other individuals, who are shopping for information about a product before making a purchase, can also benefit from the application.

❑ A user is able to fill in a search criteria and click a Search option on the screen.

❑ The Amazon.com API is called to retrieve the first result in the electronics department that contains the specified search criteria. The URL corresponding to the page is then retrieved so the physical Amazon.com page can be loaded into the browser for display.

❑ The Google API is called to retrieve the first result on the epinions.com domain that contains the specified search criteria. By limiting the Google search to the epinions.com domain, the first result is likely to be an exact or close match to the actual search criteria. After the URL is identified by Google, the contents of the physical Epinions page can be loaded into the browser for display.

❑ The eBay API is called to retrieve a list of auctions that match the specified search criteria. The application uses the eBay Sandbox test API, although the exact code would also work with the live eBay site.

❑ The results from the Amazon.com, Google, and eBay APIs are displayed in a single browser window so the user can simply scroll down to view the search results. An example of the dashboard application showing a search based upon "microsoft natural keyboard" is shown in Figure 12-1.

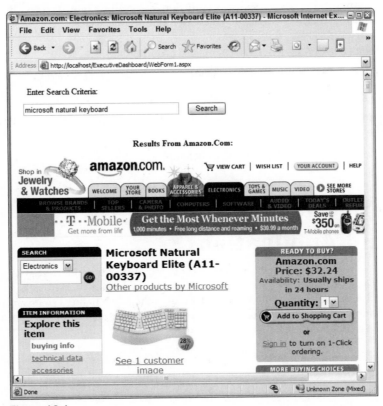

Figure 12-1

As the user scrolls down the browser window, results from Epinions (retrieved from Google) and from eBay are also displayed. Examples of these screens are illustrated at the end of this chapter.

At this point, you're ready to begin building the dashboard application.

You can download the entire case study in Visual Basic .NET or C# from the Wrox Web site. In order for the downloaded version of the case study to work, you first copy the project to your Web server, such as c:\inetpub\wwwroot. You then need to refresh the Web references to the Google API, the Amazon.com API, and the eBay API from Visual Studio .NET by selecting the particular Web reference and choosing the Refresh option. Finally, you need to specify your own account credentials in the source code where indicated.

Building the User Interface

The dashboard application is a simple example that does not require any database. You first create the user interface and write the code to make the interface work. Let's get started with the user interface. You use Visual Studio .NET to design the forms for the dashboard application.

Creating the New Project

The first step in building the user interface for the dashboard application is to set up the new project. To do so, perform the following steps:

1. Open Visual Studio .NET.

2. Select File ⇨ New ⇨ Project.

3. Select Visual Basic for the Project Type, and ASP.NET Web Application for the Template.

4. Specify the Project Name as ExecutiveDashboard or another suitable name. An example of how the screen should appear at this point is shown in Figure 12-2.

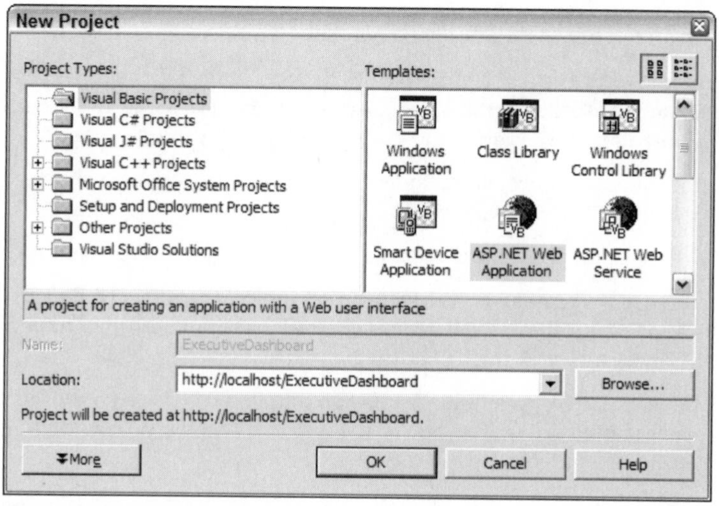

Figure 12-2

267

Adding References to the Web APIs

The next stage in building the dashboard application is to add Web references to the Google, Amazon.com, and eBay APIs. Perform the following steps to add these references.

1. Select Project ➪ Add Web Reference. In the URL, specify the location of the Google WSDL file (`http://api.google.com/GoogleSearch.wsdl`) and click the GO button.

2. Change the Web Reference Name to `Google` so that you can use a shorter name in your project. An example of what the screen looks like at this point is shown in Figure 12-3.

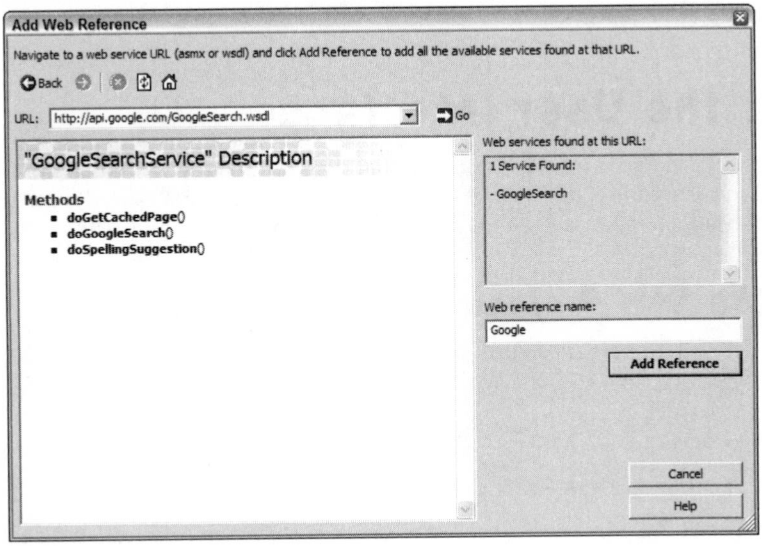

Figure 12-3

3. Click the Add Reference button to add a reference to the Google API to your project.

4. Next, add a reference to the Amazon.com API.

5. Just as before, select Project ➪ Add Web Reference. In the URL, specify the location of the Amazon.com WSDL file (`http://webservices.amazon.com/AWSECommerceService/AWSECommerceService.wsdl`) and click the GO button.

6. Change the Web Reference Name to `Amazon` so that you can use a shorter name in your project. An example of this screen is shown in Figure 12-4.

7. Click the Add Reference button to add a reference to the Amazon.com API to your program.

8. Add a reference to the eBay API. Again, select Project ➪ Add Web Reference. In the URL, specify the location of the eBay WSDL file (`http://developer.ebay.com/webservices/latest/eBaySvc.wsdl`) and click the GO button.

9. Change the Web Reference Name to `eBay` so that you can use a shorter name in your project. This screen is shown in Figure 12-5.

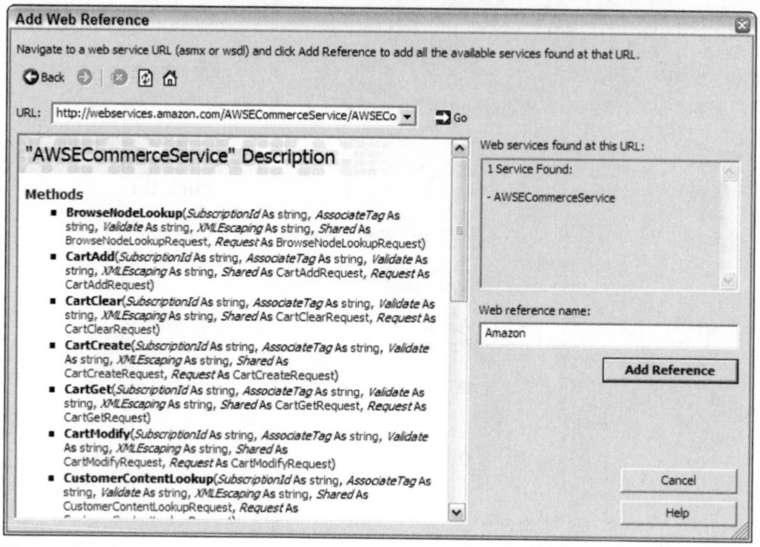

Figure 12-4

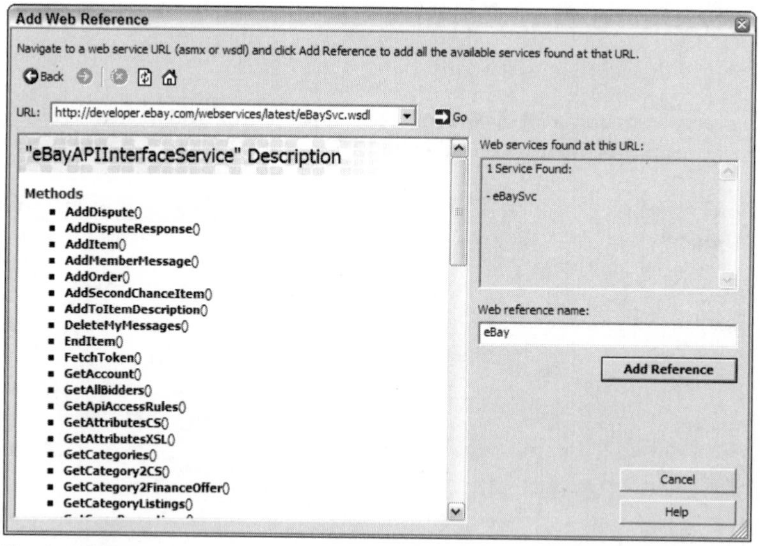

Figure 12-5

10. Click the Add Reference button to add a reference to the eBay API in your project.

11. At this point, the project should appear similar to what is shown in Figure 12-6.

Figure 12-6

Adding Controls to the Form

Now, it's time to add the controls to the form.

1. Use the toolbox to add a label control, a text box control, and a button control to webform1.aspx, as illustrated in Figure 12-7.

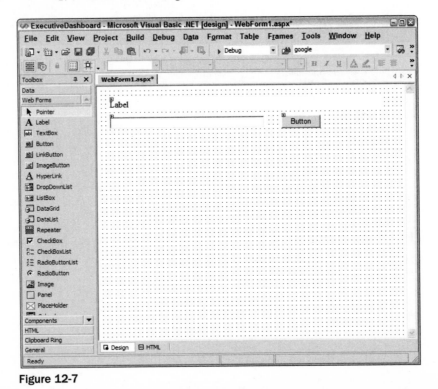

Figure 12-7

2. Rename the ID property and the other specified properties for each of the controls as in the following table:

Default Name (in Figure 12-7)	Name	Type of Control	Other Properties to Set from Properties Dialog
Label1	lblSearch	Label	Text = "Enter Search Criteria:"
TextBox1	txtSearch	Text Box	
Button1	btnSearch	Button	Text = "Search"

3. To rename properties for controls, use the Properties window as shown in Figure 12-8.

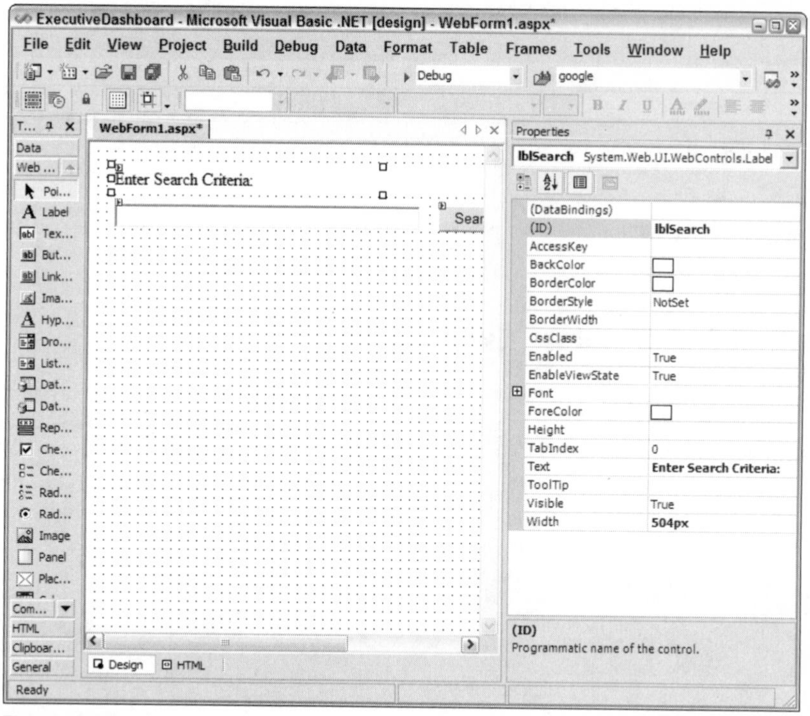

Figure 12-8

4. After you make the changes shown in the table, the form should look similar to the one shown in Figure 12-9.

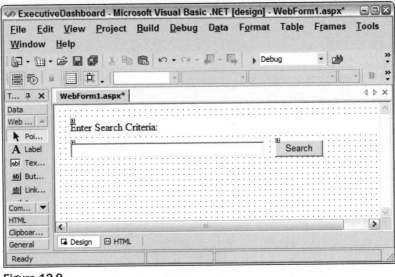

Figure 12-9

At this point, you're done with the user interface and can move on to writing the code.

Building the Code Modules

In this section, you write some routines to implement the functionality of the dashboard application.

1. Add the following imports statements to the top of the WebForm1 code segment (before the Public Class WebForm1 statement) so that you can import the namespaces for the various objects you will be using in the code. This allows you to refer to those objects in an abbreviated fashion.

```
Imports System.Net
Imports System.IO
Imports ExecutiveDashboard.Amazon
Imports ExecutiveDashboard.eBay
```

2. Add the btnSearch_Click event to WebForm1. This event is called when the user fills in the search criteria and clicks the Search button.

```
Private Sub btnSearch_Click(ByVal sender As System.Object, ByVal e As _
        System.EventArgs) Handles btnSearch.Click

        'This procedure will perform the search against Google,
        'Amazon.com, and eBay and display the results in the
        'browser

        'insert some blank lines in the browser
```

```
                Response.Write("<BR><BR><BR><BR><BR><BR>")

                SearchAmazon()

                SearchGoogle()

                SearchEbay()

        End Sub
```

3. Add the `SearchAmazon` procedure to the code section:

```
Sub SearchAmazon()

            'This procedure searches Amazon.com for the specified
            'criteria and then displays the first Amazon.com page
            'that corresponds to the particular item.

            Response.Write("<center><b>Results From Amazon.Com:</b></center><br><br>")

            Dim AmazonProductData As New AWSECommerceService
            Dim AmazonSearch As New ItemSearch
            Dim AmazonResponse As New ItemSearchResponse
            Dim AmazonRequest(1) As ItemSearchRequest

            'Developer/Subscription Code
            AmazonSearch.SubscriptionId = "YOUR AMAZON SUBSCRIPTION ID HERE"

            'We are only making one request, not batching multiple requests
            'Thus element 0 of the array is all we need to assign and work with
            AmazonRequest(0) = New ItemSearchRequest
            AmazonRequest(0).SearchIndex = "Electronics"
            AmazonRequest(0).Keywords = txtSearch.Text

            'assign the search object to the request object with the assigned
            'parameters
            AmazonSearch.Request = AmazonRequest

            'run the search and populate the response
            AmazonResponse = AmazonProductData.ItemSearch(AmazonSearch)

            If AmazonResponse.Items(0).Item Is Nothing Then Exit Sub

            Dim item As New Item

            'loop through the results
            For Each item In AmazonResponse.Items(0).Item
                'display the amazon.com page in the browser
                WritePageContentsToBrowser(item.DetailPageURL)
                Exit For
            Next


End Sub
```

4. Add the `SearchGoogle` procedure to the code section:

```
Sub SearchGoogle()

        'This procedure will retrieve and display the first page from
        'google that is contained on epinions.com with the specified
        'search criteria. Epinions.com is a consumer review web site.

        Response.Write("----------------------------------------------<br>")
        Response.Write("<b>Epinions Page Found Using Google:</b><br><br>")

        'Create a Google Search object
        Dim Search As New Google.GoogleSearchService

        Dim strLicense As String
        Dim strSearchText As String
        Dim intStart As Integer
        Dim intMaxResults As Integer

        'set the values to pass to the Google web service

        'set your developer license key
        strLicense = "YOUR GOOGLE LICENSE KEY"

        'Set the search criteria to search the epinions
        'site for the value the user entered in the search text box.
        strSearchText = "site:www.epinions.com " & txtSearch.Text
        intStart = 0
        intMaxResults = 1

        'execute the doGoogleSearch method
        'to retrieve the epinions page for the particular
        'product matching the search criteria
        Dim SearchResult As Google.GoogleSearchResult = _
                Search.doGoogleSearch(strLicense, strSearchText, _
                intStart, intMaxResults, False, "", False, "", "", "")

        'if no results were returned then exit
        If SearchResult.resultElements Is Nothing Then Exit Sub

        'work with the results to retrieve the URL
        'of the epinions page that was returned in
        'the search
        Dim result As Google.ResultElement
        Dim strURL As String

        For Each result In SearchResult.resultElements
            'write the page to the browser
            WritePageContentsToBrowser(result.URL)
            Exit For
        Next

End Sub
```

5. Add the `SearchEbay` procedure to the code section:

```
Sub SearchEbay()

        'This procedure searches eBay for the specified
        'criteria and then displays a list of auctions that
        'contain the criteria


        Dim strToken As String
        Dim strDevId As String
        Dim strAppId As String
        Dim strCertId As String

        Response.Write("------------------------------------------------<br>")
        Response.Write _
            ("<b>Results From eBay (Sandbox test environment):</b><br><br>")

        'specify credentials required to access API
        strToken = "YOUR EBAY TOKEN"
        strDevId = "YOUR EBAY DEV ID"
        strAppId = "YOUR EBAY APP ID"
        strCertId = "YOUR EBAY CERT ID"

        Dim SOAPService As New eBay.eBayAPIInterfaceService
        SOAPService.Url = "https://api.sandbox.ebay.com/wsapi" & _
                        "?callname=GetSearchResults&siteid=0&appid=" & _
                        strAppId & "version=383"

        SOAPService.RequesterCredentials = New eBay.CustomSecurityHeaderType
        SOAPService.RequesterCredentials.eBayAuthToken = strToken
        SOAPService.RequesterCredentials.Credentials = New eBay.UserIdPasswordType
        SOAPService.RequesterCredentials.Credentials.AppId = strAppId
        SOAPService.RequesterCredentials.Credentials.DevId = strDevId
        SOAPService.RequesterCredentials.Credentials.AuthCert = strCertId


        Dim Request As New eBay.GetSearchResultsRequestType
        Dim Resp As New eBay.GetSearchResultsResponseType

        'specify the search criteria and version
        Request.Query = txtSearch.Text
        Request.Version = "383"

        'call the GetSearchResults method to run the search
        Resp = SOAPService.GetSearchResults(Request)

        Dim items As eBay.SearchResultItemType
        Dim strOutput As String

        If Resp.SearchResultItemArray Is Nothing Then Exit Sub

        'loop through the results and display the results
        For Each items In Resp.SearchResultItemArray
            strOutput = strOutput & "Title: " & items.Item.Title & "<br>"
            strOutput = strOutput & "Item Id: " & items.Item.ItemID & "<br>"
            strOutput = strOutput & "Item URL: <a href=" & _
                    items.Item.ListingDetails.ViewItemURL & ">" & _
```

```
                        items.Item.ListingDetails.ViewItemURL & "</a><br>"
              strOutput = strOutput & "Listing Duration: " & _
                        items.Item.ListingDuration & vbCrLf
              strOutput = strOutput & "Time Left: " & items.Item.TimeLeft & _
                        "<br><br>"

          Next

          Response.Write(strOutput)

    End Sub
```

6.   Add the `WritePageContentsToBrowser` procedure to the code section:

```
Sub WritePageContentsToBrowser(ByVal strURL As String)

        'retrieve the page at the specified URL into
        'a response stream
        Dim wrq As WebRequest = WebRequest.Create(strURL)
        Dim wrp As WebResponse = wrq.GetResponse()
        Dim sr As StreamReader = New StreamReader(wrp.GetResponseStream())

        'read the entire stream containing the specified page and
        'display it in the browser
        Response.Write(sr.ReadToEnd)

        'write some blank lines to the browser
        Response.Write("<BR><BR>")

    End Sub
```

Nice work—you are now finished writing the code for the dashboard application. Make sure to save your changes to the project and to compile and resolve any compiler errors.

At the time of this book's writing, there is a problem with the Amazon.com WSDL file that requires manual correction. If you receive an error message stating that CustomerReviews1 cannot be reflected or a similar error regarding CustomerReviews1, then please consult Chapter 4 for a detailed description of how to resolve the error.

Touring the Completed Application

As you tour the dashboard application, you can see for yourself that it really is a simple example that could be enhanced in many ways. I purposely kept the example simple to illustrate how much you can do with third-party APIs and just a little code. Go ahead and run the program by pressing F5. You should see an opening screen similar to the one shown in Figure 12-10.

Enter some search criteria for some electronic equipment of interest and click the Search button. The code currently filters the Amazon.com results by the electronic category, but you can revise the category to books or something else by changing the property in the code section.

Suppose that you specified criteria for `ipod`, to search for reviews and availability of Apple iPod devices. When you click the Search button, you should see a screen similar to the one shown in Figure 12-11.

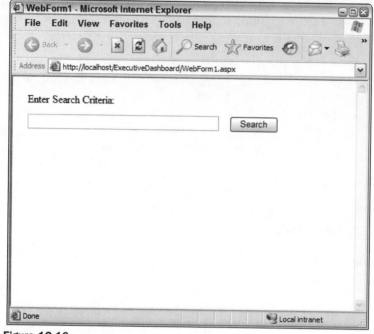

Figure 12-10

Figure 12-11

On first glance, this screen looks like nothing more than the Amazon.com page that corresponds to the iPod device. However, if you scroll down in the browser window, you also see information displayed from the Epinions.com Web site that contains reviews of the iPod. An example of this is illustrated in Figure 12-12.

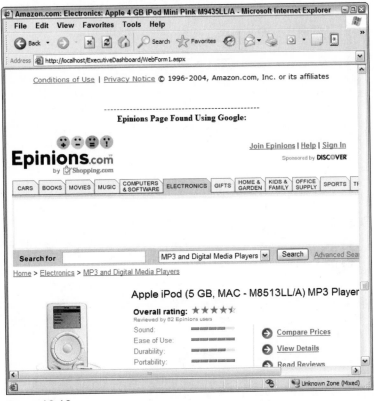

Figure 12-12

If you think about what was done here, it is really pretty cool. You used Google to retrieve a link to an Epinions Web page containing a review of the product specified in the search. You then retrieved the actual page from the Epinions Web page and programmatically displayed it in the same browser window with the rest of the results.

Scrolling down even farther leads you to a section of the browser page where the eBay search results are shown. Figure 12-13 provides an example of what this screen might look like.

In the eBay section, some basic information is provided about the item along with a hyperlink to the auction listing.

The calls to Amazon.com and Google are hitting the live sites, whereas the call to eBay is hitting the Sandbox test environment. The same code would also work against the live eBay site.

That's it. See, it really is simple to integrate data from multiple APIs into your programs.

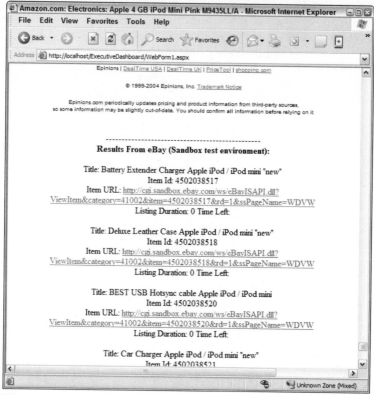

Figure 12-13

Summary

In this chapter, you created a simple dashboard application that uses the Google, Amazon.com, and eBay APIs to retrieve data that is used in interesting ways in the browser. You have successfully completed all the chapters in this book. You should now have a basic ability to interact with the Web APIs covered herein and also feel comfortable learning about new APIs on your own. This book just scratches the surface on the wonderful opportunities that are available to you today with some existing Web APIs and a little bit of your imagination.

Index

Index

InterFax API
  developer account for, 164–165
  features of, 163–164
  sending test fax, 165–168
intext: **option, Google, 18**
intitle: **option, Google, 18**
inurl: **option, Google, 18**
InvoiceId **property,** TransactionSearch **method, 159**
ItemLookup **operation, ECS, 97**
ItemSearch **operation, ECS, 98, 109, 110**

J

Java Web Services Developer Pack, 216

L

latitude, finding, with MapPoint API, 77–80
LeaveFeedback **method, eBay API, 126**
link: **option, Google, 19**
links
  descriptive text of, searching in Google, 18
  related to URL, listing with Google, 19
  to URL, listing with Google, 19
list queries, ECS, 99, 110–111
listing an item for sale, eBay, 133–136
ListLookup **operation, ECS, 99, 110–111**
ListMyQueues **operation, Simple Queue Service, 104**
ListSearch **operation, ECS, 99, 110–111**
lnklblGoogleResults_LinkClicked **event, CRM application, 254**
longitude, finding, with MapPoint API, 77–80

M

MapPoint API
  driving directions, obtaining, 72–74, 184–189
  errors from
    methods not recognized, 58
    operation not authorized, 58, 64
  evaluation account for, obtaining, 52–56
  fees for, 52

geocode lookups, 77–80
maps
  querying, 60–63
  retrieving, 75–77
nearby places, finding, 80–82
object model for, viewing, 59–60
points of interest, finding, 82–84
production environment, 63
protocols supported, 51
query
  executing from Pocket PC, 184–189
  executing using .NET Framework, 68–71
  executing using Visual Studio .NET, 64–67
  services for, 59–63
  specifying credentials for, 63–64
SDK
  configuring, 58–59
  downloading, 56–58
test environment, 63
third-party extensions for, 85
used in Customer Relations Management (CRM) application, 226, 238, 255–259, 260–262
uses of, 84–85
MapPoint (Microsoft), features of, 50–51
MapPoint Web service Web site, 52
maps
  querying with MapPoint API, 60–63
  retrieving with MapPoint API, 75–77
mass payments, with PayPal API, 149, 159
MassPay **method, PayPal API, 149, 159**
Memo **property,** RefundTransaction **method, 158**
meter number, FedEx APIs, 174
Microsoft Access, used in Customer Relations Management (CRM) application, 228–230
Microsoft eMbedded Visual Tools, 183
Microsoft MapPoint API
  driving directions, obtaining, 72–74, 184–189
  errors from
    methods not recognized, 58
    operation not authorized, 58, 64
  evaluation account for, obtaining, 52–56
  geocode lookups, 77–80

Professional Web APIs: Google®, eBay®, Amazon.com®, MapPoint®, FedEx®